No: 1.

STONEHENGE

As above, so below
Flying is easy—
just do it!

Thank you for
Listening!

UNVEILING THE SPIRIT PATH
ON SALISBURY PLAIN

PAUL D. BURLEY

AUTHOR OF *THE SACRED SPHERE*

 New Generation Publishing

Published by New Generation Publishing in 2014

Copyright © Paul Burley 2014

First Edition

Hardback ISBN 13: 978-1-910162-77-4
Paperback ISBN 13: 978-1-910162-76-7

www.newgeneration-publishing.com

 New Generation Publishing

For Elin and Elizabeth

Contents

Acknowledgements

NEVER LOOK BACK
FACE THE WIND
HEAD UP
MOVE FORWARD

As always my first debt of gratitude is to you, the reader. The journey is long. It is not easy. Thank you for walking with me. The road is not so difficult when we walk together.

Courage, Generosity, Fortitude, Wisdom. Acquiring these four things is like grasping at straws. I cannot make the wind stop so I can take the straws easily. However, if I pay attention, and listen, I may be prepared when the wind blows the straws toward me. The wind is powerful whenever I visit Pine Ridge and Rosebud Reservations. For some reason I am fortunate to catch some straw each time before I leave for home. The wind is very powerful.

I am grateful for good friends at Pine Ridge and Rosebud—Becky Chief Eagle, Dallas Chief Eagle, Mel Lone Hill, Jhon Goes In Center, Victor Douville, Duane Hollow Horn Bear, Stanley Red Bird Jr, Javier Livas, Andrew James Campbell, Mushin, and others who have entered my life. I will always be indebted to Everett Poor Thunder. I began to experience real courage, generosity, fortitude and wisdom the first day we met. Everett and everyone else have shown me perhaps the most important thing a man can have, something to be kept close to the heart at all times. It is the straw of humility. *Wopila heca yelo.*

I'm grateful for everyone at New Generation Publishing who has been more than willing to take this stone, dress it, and set it in place. There are many stones out there. Thank you for helping me with this one. Once again James Monroe Design prepared the cover and interior design. Thank you Jay, for capturing the vision and putting it in place. Thank you Gary Evans at Infinite Connections. It's an honor working with you. Thank you Jon and Phil for your love and support. Elin and Elizabeth, you are the world to me. I was blessed when you entered my life. Thank you for your love. Thank you Dad, you are my hero. With head up, I move forward.

Mitakuye oyasin.

All my relatives

Paul Burley
February 2014

Introduction

Stonehenge has been the focus of study by historians, antiquarians and archaeologists for well over 300 years, a rather short period compared to the length of time since the monument's first architectural elements were built, perhaps more than 5000 years ago. Recent theories suggest the stone monument was the center of a landscape where burial of the dead included various rituals and ceremonies. The architecture of various monuments such as Woodhenge and Stonehenge was designed to take advantage of solar and lunar alignments. The architecture in tandem with burials of human and animal remains indicates a cultural understanding of relationship between the end of life and events observed in the cosmos.

We know very little of the people who designed, built and made use of this greatest of European megalithic (Latin *mega*:large, *lith*:stone) monuments. Archaeologists have conducted site investigations across the British Isles, sites ranging from domestic to ritual, celebratory to industrial, and sometimes of enigmatic purpose. They continue to discover, date and describe many thousands of artefacts made and used by people thousands of years ago. We know more about the *things* those people had, than we know of the people themselves.

We have no record of why observations of the Sun and Moon were important to the populace of the time, and how the culture related those astronomical observations with human mortality. We don't know the manner in which Stonehenge was used, or if the architect and builders of the monument gave it a name. Most probably they did give it a name, but I doubt it was as prosaic as 'Stonehenge', or equivalent name from the pre-Indo-European substrate language used at the time. The name, like the monument itself, must have been most grand.

My purpose for studying the Neolithic (Latin *neo*:new, *lith*:stone) Stonehenge Landscape was to understand the relationship between the landscape's early stages of development and the people who conceived, designed and built it. Between 3500 BC and 2900 BC more than 50,000 tons of soil and chalk were excavated, transported, placed and compacted to build henges, long barrows and cursus located within a 3 km (2 mi) radius of Stonehenge. Excavation and mound building continued. Over 2500 tons of megaliths were quarried, transported, shaped and installed at Stonehenge by 2400 BC.

Many hundreds of structures including cursus, long barrows, round barrows, henges, housing and community structures were built across Salisbury Plain during the Neolithic and Bronze Ages.[1] We can safely assume great numbers of people were extremely motivated to plan, design, and execute construction of what archaeologists call the Stonehenge Ritual Landscape. However the work did not stop. The structures needed maintenance over the centuries. Ditches and banks needed repair. Many megaliths were used, reused, and transported between construction locations.

Scholars and non-scholars alike have developed theories explaining various astronomical alignments of Stonehenge's megaliths.[2] Yet none of the suggested alignments accurately define the orientation of Sun, Moon, planets or stars with respect to specific astronomical events from the center of the monument or any other location inside the henge. Some of the proposed alignments turn out to be less accurate when the stones were installed 4500 years ago than they are now. If Stonehenge was built as an observatory, the as-built structure was not constructed to ensure accuracy of alignment when viewing astronomical events.

People who built Stonehenge were as intelligent as human's today. They had the will, ability and means to transport and install megaliths in ways that remain enigmas today. Could the builders have been uncaring, installing stones such that alignments were less accurate than the design called? After working many years to bring together, shape and install thousands of tons of stone to create specified astronomical alignments, would the community have accepted anything less than precision? We should have every reason to believe the stones could be placed as precisely as needed for whatever purpose the alignments were intended.

Contrary to popular belief there is no evidence that Stonehenge and other monuments in the area were used as astronomical observatories. It is possible that certain features of the architecture assisted people to determine the time of a solar or lunar eclipse, or confirming solstice and equinox events. Those are astronomical events we know were concerns for contemporary religious beliefs and agricultural activities. The idea does have merit given the various solar and lunar alignments that have been proposed during the last 300 years or so. However it would be quite unreasonable to transport stones weighing forty tons or more across central southern England, and many additional megaliths from quarries in Wales, and install them in ways that create *possible* astronomical alignments which *might* have some cultural value. It is far more likely that such alignments were already known before construction took place. Stonehenge would have been constructed in accordance with an architectural plan demonstrating both the designer's awareness of those alignments and affirming their cultural value.

Why weren't the stones set to create alignments that were more accurate? I suggest giving credit where credit is due. Precise placement of megaliths was not required during their installation. The alignments were as accurate as needed. Increased precision was unnecessary.

It is probable that the stones provided qualified alignments—within a range of sight that was readily observable but without need for accuracy. The alignments do not reflect their purpose for scientific study. They were created for something far more important.

Numerous ancient structures such as long barrows, round barrows, cursus and henges across the Stonehenge Landscape were constructed between about 4000 BC and 1500 BC, some before and some after. An untold number of other structures appear only as crop marks on the ground surface or buried and awaiting discovery beneath the surface. The Greater Cursus (also known as the Stonehenge or Amesbury Cursus) is located 800 m (2600 ft) north of Stonehenge. It is nearly 3 km (1.7 mi) long and covers about 35 hectares (1.35 sq mi) of pasture. Although its great size makes it a prominent feature on the landscape, no one knows whether or not its purpose was for ritual or ceremony, or how it may relate to the purpose and functioning of other monuments on Salisbury Plain.

Is it possible to make sense of the myriad monuments placed in such apparently chaotic fashion across the landscape over the course of the last 6000 years or more? The Greater Cursus, long barrows, and henges were constructed sometime between 3500 BC and 2500 BC. What were the reasons for concentrating such a wealth of archaeological wonders in central south England, particularly during the mid-to late Neolithic Age? What of Stonehenge itself? If Stonehenge is not a Neolithic astronomical observatory built for scientific purpose, then what is it? Why was it constructed in the midst of numerous contemporary burial structures, an area that archaeologists believe was a 'place of healing' and 'Domain of the Ancestors'?[3,4] Is there anything about its structure that can help us better understand the purpose of this world renowned yet most enigmatic of prehistoric monuments?

No doubt the truths about the originally intended purpose of Stonehenge, methods of its construction, and ways in which prehistoric people interacted with the henge and great stones are complicated. We are fascinated to know that truth. However people who designed, built and used the Stonehenge ritual landscape left us no written record of themselves, their cultures, their thoughts. We might not ever fully understand the story of Stonehenge and its unique landscape. A theory tying together the many threads of information gathered from archaeological investigations, presenting a truthful, detailed account of the prehistory of the area might never be told.

We are not at loss for trying. Although without written records, we have means of sifting through the evidence, separating the wheat from the chaff, to identify some part of the unwritten story making sense of the apparently random placement of Stonehenge and its landscape. With objective study of the evidence, employing perspectives rarely applied to archaeological investigations, it is possible to achieve new understanding of what the ancient ones achieved on Salisbury Plain.

This book addresses implications of spatial relationships between a number of mid-Neolithic elements of the landscape, and how those elements related to the broader context of people and landscape interacting with Earth below and sky above. We look at the readily apparent type, shape, size, orientation and location of such features as long barrows, henges, cursus, lone megaliths, natural topography, and Stonehenge itself. Geometrical aspects of those features are considered through space and time. The complex of elements is evaluated for evidence of intent which gave the Neolithic landscape a unity of purpose.

Recent scientific investigations have provided a wealth of information concerning the parameters of space and time as they relate to elements of the Stonehenge Landscape. Archaeologists have uncovered important information helping us understand how peripheral sites such as Durrington Walls, Woodhenge, the recently discovered Bluestonehenge, and even the River Avon itself are integral parts of the landscape.

During the 12th century Cleric Geoffrey of Monmouth suggested megaliths at Stonehenge exhibited curative properties and the structure was built in association with burials in the area. Stonehenge is indeed the site of numerous burials of human bones and cremated remains, as well as bones of animals and numerous artefacts. Modern investigations of the burial sites yielded indications of trauma to the head and other bones of some of the deceased. Human deformities are also encountered. Some burials include remains of individuals from other areas of Britain, the European continent or Mediterranean region.[5]

Several significant investigations of Stonehenge and the surrounding area were conducted during the last thirty years. The landscape was the subject of a detailed study during the Stonehenge Environs project led by

Julian Richards in the early 1980s. Analyses conducted for that work provided dates for the Lesser Cursus (about 3500 BC), Coneybury Henge (2900 BC or earlier) located on Coneybury Hill about 1.5 km east of Stonehenge, and additional elements of the landscape. By the early 1990s Dr.Terence Meaden had discovered geometrical relationships between long barrows and the Greater Cursus. In 1995 English Heritage published 'Stonehenge in its landscape', the result of research performed over two years to obtain and collate historical archaeological information about the monument.[6]

Mike Parker Pearson of Sheffield University proffers a theory that the area surrounding Stonehenge is a ritual landscape in which the monument and other notable sites were interconnected by preferred land and surface water transportation routes.[7,8] The theory proposes Durrington Walls, located near the west bank of the River Avon about 3 km (2 mi) northeast of Stonehenge, was the site of contemporaneous facilities and activities including residential and ceremonial structures, feasting, and a pathway leading to the riverbank nearby. The deceased were transported downstream before being carried overland to Stonehenge where additional ritual and ceremony occurred. More than one thousand people might have lived at Durrington Walls. Parker Pearson proposes about 8 sq km (5 sq mi) south of the Greater Cursus, centered at Stonehenge were the 'Domain of the Dead' while the surrounding area including Durrington Walls was the 'Domain of the Living'. Some archaeologists suggest the landscape is evidence of ancestor worship.[9]

Where did the many people helping construct Stonehenge and other great monuments on Salisbury Plain come from? They arrived from across Britain according to another theory proposed by Parker Pearson in 2012.[10] The idea is that people from across England and Wales traveled to Stonehenge to assist construction of the henge and megalithic structure between 3000 and 2500 BC. Presumably a tremendous number of bodies were needed to quarry, move and dress the stones, excavate soil and chalk bedrock, then place the stones into position, including the thirty-five megaliths installed along the top of the great sarsen circle and trilithon structures. The theory proposes the work required organization and cooperation amongst everyone involved in the construction, and this instilled a sense of island-wide unity and peaceful conditions during the late Neolithic. Additional investigation will be needed to determine whether or not Stonehenge was the source of peace and unity across Britain. Nonetheless it is certain many people with various skills were needed.

The 'Stonehenge Riverside Project' was conducted between 2003 and 2009. The project included archeological excavations most of which were located beyond the Stonehenge monument. The sites included the Greater Cursus, Lesser Cursus, Woodhenge, Durrington Walls, banks of the River Avon, long barrows and locations of individual megalithic stones. Results of the project are significant. Analysis of organic material from a posthole at Stonehenge provided evidence of Mesolithic activity within the area of the henge as early as 7300 BC to 7000 BC. Neolithic activity associated with Stonehenge dated as early as about 3000 BC. The primary period of development at Durrington Walls was found to have occurred between 2500 BC and 2450 BC. The Avenue extending from Stonehenge to the River Avon was found to terminate at the site of four megaliths on the west bank of the river. Also a henge with a blue-stone circle was discovered near the bank. Based on results of the archaeological investigation the site was named Bluestonehenge.

Since the 1980s large areas that include burial structures such as passage graves, long barrows and round barrows have been referred to by archaeologists as 'ritual landscapes'.[11] The concept of ritual landscape is applied to land believed to have been devoted to events such as rituals and ceremonies associated with the dead. It is most often applied to landscapes dated to the Neolithic and early Bronze Age, from about 3500 BC to 1800 BC. Artefacts bearing indications of non-utilitarian purpose and communal structures such as Stonehenge, which is interpreted as a temple in this context, are commonly found in those areas.

Social structure and a culture's sense of identity and territoriality of a landscape can emerge as they relate to ritual space.[12] This can be seen by analysis of constructions ranging from lithic monuments to simple arrangements of stones, topographical relationships, and locations of artworks, cemeteries or settlements within which a ritualized landscape may be defined. Many such landscapes have been developed by cultures in which archaeologists can identify an archetypal package of Neolithic technologies. Examples are found in pre-dynastic Egypt, Brittany ca. 3800 BC, and the pre-Columbian Americas.

The term *ritual landscape* implies that a landscape is associated with performance of established, formal ceremonies typically perceived to have been performed within the context of religious practice, in other words rites. The rites concern activities within sequestered space, separated from the profane. Temples, churches, henges, even a simple circle, are examples of such spaces that when considered within a prescribed area help define the meaning and purpose of a ritual landscape. In many instances the landscape will contain *sacred* symbolism. Often sacred symbolism is unrecognized during archaeological investigations.

The origin of the word 'sacred' goes back to the Proto-Indo-European (PIE) language, the ancestral language of the majority of European and Indian languages. The language developed in the Pontic-Caspian steppe of Eastern Europe and Central Asia between the 5th and 4th millennia BCE, possibly thousands of years earlier. The PIE word *sak- meant to sacrifice, suffer or sanctify, to make pure or holy; Latin *sanus* (sane, sound, whole). The Indo-European:*ros* (Slavic:*rosa*, Greek: *fluō'*, Latin:*fluo*) means flow as in a flowing liquid. Therefore, the intent of the Indo-European word *sakrós* (*sak*:to giving or making pure, *rós*:flowing) is communication or flowing of information. The receiver is thus made whole, complete, sanctified with knowledge and understanding.

Many ancient and indigenous cultures expressed understanding of sacred relationships between human beings, Earth, the cosmos and Creator. They 'knew' relationships with god(s), cosmologies, and creation of life, were by invocation from a mysterious life force. The cosmology of biblical Genesis involves the first flow of information in which "In the beginning was the Word, and the Word was with God, and the Word was God." Each act of creation begins with the words "Let there be . . . ." In fact the etymology of the word 'god' may be the reconstructed Proto-Indo-European form * ǵhu-tó-m based on the root * ǵhau(ə)-, which means either "to call" or "to invoke."[13]

For ancient and indigenous cultures creation—and re-creation, reincarnation, resurrection—of life was actuated by a mysterious life force, the sum of all universal energy (Sanskrit *prana*: the breath, life force; *prana vayu*:wind, air; Lakotan *Wakan Tanka*:Great Mystery, Tákuškanškan:that which causes everything to move, *ni*:breath of life). The mysterious force, power or energy was the source of all creation and life throughout the universe. This was not the power *over* other life, but the power *of* life. Human understanding of this power was aided by giving it human form, intelligence, emotions and environment. Cosmology and mythology were means through which people could understand this anthropomorphic power of life and its sacred relationships with humans, Earth and the cosmos. Those understandings were communicated to succeeding generations.

This book presents findings that support conclusions made by the archaeological community concerning an evolution of the Stonehenge Landscape, an area that in truth was and remains a *Sacred Landscape*. Some of the findings and conclusions challenge current understanding of the intent of the Stonehenge designers, builders and general population, and the purpose of the many other prehistoric sites found across Salisbury Plain, and indeed the UK. We pay particular attention to spatial and temporal development of the landscape during the mid-to late Neolithic Age between about 3600 BC and 2400 BC, from the time when long barrows were constructed as burial chambers and the Stonehenge Greater Cursus was built, to installation of the monumental sarsen and bluestone megaliths we see today.

Research conducted for this book included gathering archaeological information from numerous sources. The majority of information is found in peer reviewed scientific papers and articles. It is supplemented by data provided in publications written by well-respected scientists and engineers, many of them associated with university departments and laboratories located across the UK and Ireland. Those resources were applied in tandem with results of new research, field study and analysis by the author. The research entailed almost three years of gathering and reviewing archaeological records, test methods, results, findings and conclusions about Stonehenge and the prehistory of Salisbury Plain. Numerous Neolithic artefacts from sites across the British Isles were studied. Stonehenge and other archaeological sites dating from the mid-to late-Neolithic were visited, observations made and recorded, and photographs taken.

The emphasis is on information readily available from investigations and analyses conducted in accordance with modern scientific methods and procedures, and the knowledge of many reputable scientists and engineers. The works include 1) study of the skeletal framework of Stonehenge and other mid-Neolithic structures nearby which are essentially devoid of cultural context, and 2) observations and testable evidence derived from scientific investigations most of which were conducted within the last 100 years or so.

The content of this book is arranged so as to benefit 1) the general interest of many readers having a curious or vested interest in Stonehenge who desire a basic level of understanding about the purpose of Stonehenge and the 'Grand Plan' constructed across the Stonehenge Landscape, and 2) those who are curious to know more detail of the purpose and methods by which the Grand Plan was constructed, and the original purpose of the Stonehenge monument as it relates to the four Station Stones. The more general information is provided in the main text. Further details are included in appendices.

Early in 2012 I gave myself the task of finding any other available sources of pertinent information about the Stonehenge Landscape. As it turned out, the sources were hidden in broad daylight, not difficult at all to discover, waiting for their secrets to be revealed. The sources provide readily available information useful for helping explain why Stonehenge and its environment developed as they did. They also provide evidence for the purpose of Stonehenge and surrounding mid-to late Neolithic structures. As we shall see, the information may even indicate the intent of persons who designed, constructed and used Stonehenge and other monuments located across the landscape. These sources of information are underutilized far more than any other. Specifically, they are the spatial relationships between numerous structures—long barrows, the Greater Cursus, Stonehenge, even the natural topography. Those relationships provide context within which the various elements of the landscape were constructed over time.

This book focuses on two aspects of the Stonehenge landscape that are more than curious. One is the alignment of certain long barrows pointed toward one end or the other the Greater Cursus. The other is the rectangle of four megaliths at Stonehenge—the Station Stones. Of the former, Terence Meaden wrote of his discovery in the early 1990s of geometrical relationships between nine long barrows and the Greater Cursus.

"With the exception of the east-west barrow Figheldean 27 (Knighton Barrow), all long barrows within sight of one or other end of the Stonehenge Cursus were aligned on one of the cursus terminals . . . This is an amazing and far-reaching discovery, which has been checked and confirmed by others in the last few years"[14].

Since then there have been numerous attempts to identify the purpose of the long barrow-cursus alignments, including studies of potential alignments with certain stars at their rising or setting during the time the cursus and barrows were constructed. However none of those studies proved fruitful. Some long barrows do not align through either end of the cursus or point to any star of consequence. The mystery remained unresolved. There was a reason for this to be the case.

It was the geometrical relationship between the long barrows and the Greater Cursus that turned the tide for understanding what the Stonehenge Landscape—a sacred landscape—was all about. With over thirty years of experience as a professional civil engineer, geotechnical engineer and environmental geologist, I analyzed the built landscape from the perspective of a land surveyor involved in a very large construction project, applying fundamental surveying techniques that are known to have been used during the Neolithic. The results are astounding and conclusive. For the first time spatial relationships between monuments are deciphered, relationships intended for structures built almost 5500 years ago, a thousand years older that the Great Pyramid in Egypt. The purpose for the long barrow-cursus alignments is described for the first time. The findings greatly improve our understanding of the people who devoted their lives to constructing one of the most outstanding prehistoric monuments we are privileged to see and experience today. A *Grand Plan* was envisioned and constructed across the Stonehenge Sacred Landscape.

The inability to resolve Stonehenge's enigmatic purpose may be a case of not seeing the wood for the trees. The great circle of sarsen stones and trilithons are pawns in a great scheme displayed openly within the henge. The details are in plain view yet overshadowed by the megaliths. Megaliths of sarsen and bluestone capture everyone's attention when viewing the monument. Few people take notice of the two Station Stones that remain at the site, the other two having been broken and carried off an unknown time ago. The Station Stones formed a rectangle seemingly out of place, situated outside the rings of stones but inside the circular bank and ditch. It is as if they were discarded after the process of megalithic construction, pushed to the side and left to stare at the monumental configuration of sarsens and bluestones which remains the focus of our own attention.

The two remaining Station Stones have a secret to tell. It is a secret that is visible to everyone visiting Stonehenge, but it has remained unrecognized. There is a reason why the four stones were configured as no other stones at the monument, a quadrilateral amongst curves. It does not concern the Sun or Moon, but the stars. It represents a map which justifies the presence of the monument in its entirety. It is a secret that can now be revealed.

If we listen, if we pay attention, the designers of Stonehenge and its landscape are communicating the purpose of these many monuments to generation after generation. The message continues to be communicated today. You are about to receive the key that will unlock the mystery of Stonehenge.

Chapter 1
THE PEOPLE—6000 TO 3000 BC

Sea level rose around the world as glaciers retreated at the end of the most recent glaciation, about 12,000 years ago. Within 2000 years (by 10,000 BC) Ireland was an island while Britain remained a peninsula connected to the European continent.[1] The population of Britain increased as the climate rapidly warmed until about 6000 BC when the rate of population growth began to decline. For unknown reasons Britain and Ireland were sparsely populated between about 6000 and 4100 BC. Ireland's population might have never exceeded several thousand throughout the Mesolithic (*meso*:middle, *lithic*:of stone) Age.

In about 6100 BC a huge underwater landslide occurred off the coast of Norway (the Storegga Slide).[2] The 70 foot tsunami caused by the slide struck the northeast coast of Scotland. Lowlands of the Orkneys, recently appearing above sea level for the first time in many thousands of years, may have been inundated. Doggerland, located between Britain and the Netherlands, was all but gone. Britain was an island by 6000 BC. Yet the populations of Britain and Ireland did not become entirely isolated. An estimated 2700 to 5500 people occupied Britain in about 5700 BC.[3] The population stabilized by 5000 BC.

The term *Neolithic* is defined by "technological, economic, social and ideological aspects [of a culture] as a whole," including but not limited to farming.[4] For cultures in the Middle East the Neolithic occurred by the middle of the 10th millennium BC. In contrast, some indigenous peoples of pre-Columbian tribes in North America lived within Neolithic cultures until the early 20th Century AD. Between those extremes, the entire 'package' of Neolithic culture reached the British Isles by the beginning of the 4th millennium BC.

However indigenous populations of the British Isles were increasingly aware of certain elements of Neolithic culture and technology well before 4000 BC. Transition from Mesolithic to Neolithic is indicated by the presence (albeit somewhat limited) of domesticated animals such as cattle brought from the continent by the late Mesolithic, sometime between about 5500 and 4000 BC. By 4000 BC Great Britain's population was approaching 100,000 whilst an estimated 40,000 people thrived in Ireland.

Britain continued to experience a rapidly increasing population during the early Neolithic (Refer to Figure 1). Most of the growth is attributed to two migrations from areas of northwest France, where Neolithic culture was more established.[5,6] The most intensive emigration occurred in southwest England, but the central area of Scotland experienced significant population growth as well. Most of the first migration into Scotland occurred between 3800 and 3700 BC. The first migration into southwest England occurred later, between about 3700 and 3600 BC when people crossed the Strait of Dover from the region of Lower Normandy and the Nord-Pas-de-Calais.

Between 3600 and 3500 BC the number of people crossing the Strait of Dover was on the increase again. This second migration originated from Brittany and reached shores as far away as Wales and Scotland. The agrarian culture of northwest France was relatively homogeneous and in all likelihood the emigrants brought their cosmology and technology for megalithic architecture with them. Their skills working with stone may have derived from Portugal and west Spain where the early Neolithic had developed by about 5000 BC, when Britain and Ireland were only beginning their transition from the Mesolithic.[7]

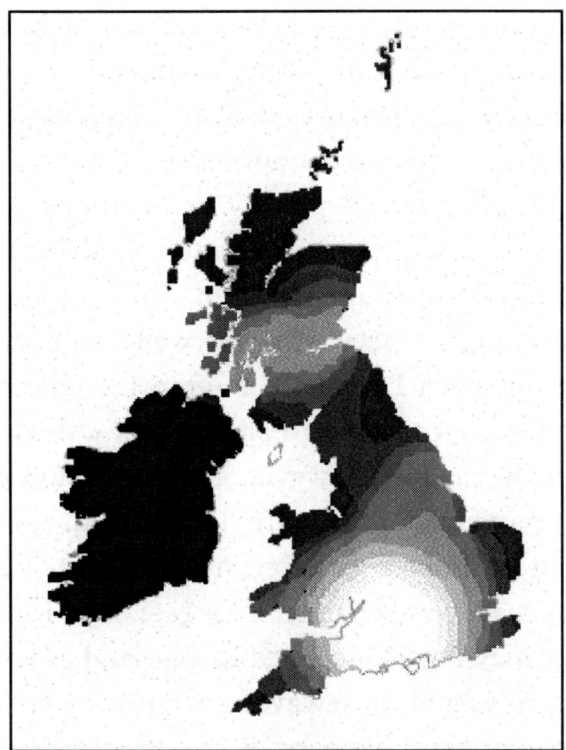

Figure 1: Areas of increasing population density ca. 3600-3500BC. During the first half of the 4th millennium BC Britain's most intensive increase in population density occurred in southwest England, centered on Salisbury Plain (Figure based on Collard etal 2010).

The population of the British Isles increased quickly as food production shifted to an agrarian system between 4000 and 3500 BC. Domesticated animals, cereals, lithic monuments and housing types innovative for the time were being established in England, Wales and Scotland, and introduced to Ireland. The architecture of passage graves was evolving in Ireland. However there were spatial and temporal variations in the introduction of agriculture across Britain and Ireland. Cultural values were not uniform after 3400 BC.

The two waves of migration between 3800 and 3500 BC would forever impact the indigenous hunter-gatherers, and nominal, diverse base of agricultural cultures that had been developing over the previous 500 to 600 years. Change to, and adoption of Neolithic culture occurred rapidly if not uniformly. There is little evidence of Mesolithic culture remaining in Britain by the mid-4th millennium.

For some areas of the British Isles the transition from late Mesolithic to early Neolithic was a metamorphosis centuries in the making.[8] Most of the indigenous either adapted over time to the new technologies and economies surrounding them, or adopted Neolithic cultures as their own in the early 4th millennium. Undoubtedly infrastructure-transportation and communication networks-was well established prior to the migrations from northern France. It is often the case that indigenous people are quick to adopt new technologies that enhance food supplies and protection of the people. However, acceptance and participation in new sets of cultural values are usually not so rapid. A complete transition from Mesolithic hunter-gatherer subsistence to formation of an agrarian economy may have occurred more rapidly in Ireland than across Britain.[9] The pace may have quickened in Scotland as well. By the mid-Neolithic long barrows and causewayed enclosures were in use.

Stone circles, dolmens and passage graves date as early as 4500 BC at such places as Carrowmore, Co. Sligo, in the northwest of Ireland. With sizable migrations occurring between 3800 and 3500 BC and rapid progression of Neolithic culture across the landscape, it is surprising that the population of the British Isles was decreasing by 3500 BC. The cause is unknown, although environmental impacts are very real possibilities. If the decrease was associated with rising mortality rates it is probable this would increase the need to care for the dead, including preparing and burying or cremating the body, and deepening of relationships with religious cosmologies. The number of chambered cairn-type passage graves appears to have been increasing at Carrowkeel, Co. Sligo, Loughcrew, Co. Meath and others between about 3500 and 3300 BC.

There are numerous prehistoric sites throughout the UK and Ireland that are associated with astronomical alignments. They include Stonehenge, Avebury, Maeshowe, Newgrange, and many other passage tombs, long barrows, round barrows, henges, stone circles, and so on. Through the work of archaeologists and archaeoastronomers we know that a number of those structures are associated with burial of the dead and observations of certain solar, lunar or planetary phenomenon. People observed astronomical events and related them in some way with burial structures and remains of the dead. Some of those burial sites were of importance during the mid-Neolithic or earlier. Several passage graves at Loughcrew were aligned with sunrise on the vernal and autumnal equinoxes, and other astronomical alignments are known at many other contemporary Irish structures.

Archaeological evidence suggests ceremonies and rituals took place at burial sites. Polished stone axe heads, pottery, disarticulated bones and other items were placed in burials, and there appears to have been greater emphasis on alignment with the solstices in British passage graves. By about 3000 BC construction of causewayed enclosures had evolved to building henges that included alignments with solar and lunar events.

Together the various Neolithic structures across the UK and Ireland are indicative of several important spatial and temporal relationships.

- In general, construction of monumental architecture in the British Isles began with arrival of Neolithic technology from mainland Europe, including farming and domestication of animals, and working megalithic stone.

- There was an evolution in location of monumental architecture across the British Isles throughout the Neolithic, early to mid-Neolithic structures often found on hill tops, with increasing use of plains and lowlands over time.

- Many of the burial structures were located in the vicinity of, or within sight of water bodies.

- Many of the structures were circular or sub-circular, including cairns, mounded soil and henges.

- The complexity of monumental landscapes increased through time, beginning with construction of individual structures and progressing to development of large landscapes such as

Stonehenge, Maeshowe and Newgrange where structures of different types became components of a larger framework.

- Long barrow construction began by about 4000 BC with many of the structures located in the south and east of England.

- Cursus appear in Scotland by about 3800 BC and construction of the ditch and bank structures spreads southward to southern England within two to three centuries; most cursus are located in England (more than 100) and Scotland (50); only a few are in Wales and Ireland (12).

- Henge construction began by about 3000 BC.

- As design of monuments increased in complexity over time so did the complexity of monumental landscapes, as type, size and location of individual monuments within the larger environmental context became part of the design process.

The ways in which these relationships are demonstrated today on the natural physiography of Salisbury Plain is the topic of the next chapter, and for that matter, the remainder of the book.

Chapter 2
THE ENVIRONMENT

Salisbury Plain is located in the south portion of County Wiltshire and adjoining County Hampshire in central south of England (Figures 2, 3, and 4). The plain extends about 25 miles east-west and 15 miles north-south. For purpose of describing Salisbury Plain with respect to the Stonehenge Landscape the following discussion addresses a rather rectangular shaped area extending from Bulford Camp in the east to Maddington on the River Till in the west, and from Figheldean on the River Avon in the north to Berwick St. James in the south (Figure 2 and Figure 3).

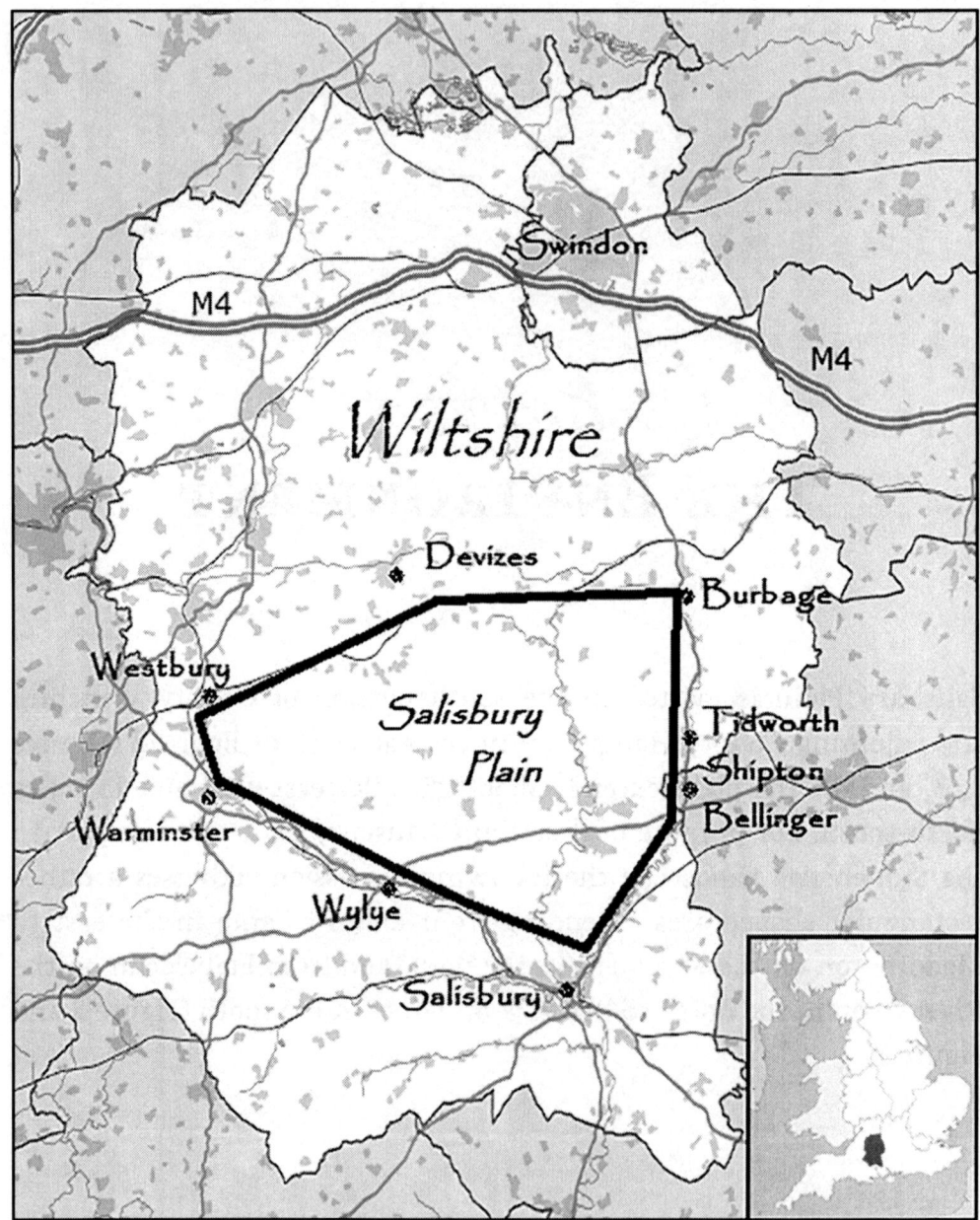

Figure 2: Location of Salisbury Plain. Stonehenge is located in the south portion of the plane, about half way between Wylye and Shipton Bellinger. (Contains Ordnance Survey data copyright Crown copyright and database right)

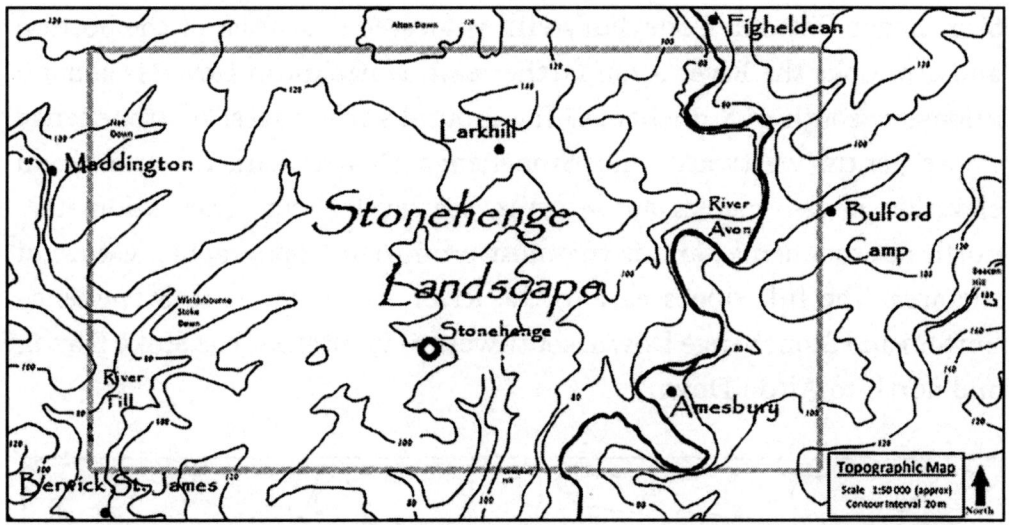

Figure 3: Area of Stonehenge Landscape discussed in this book

Figure 4: Aerial photograph of the Stonehenge Landscape (base photo copyright 2014 Infoterra Ltd & Bluesky, copyright 2013 Google)

The Stonehenge monument is located in the north-central portion of Salisbury Plain. It sits on a rather level ground surface (elevation 102 m, 335 ft) of a less than prominent ridge (Figure 5). The ground surface dips gently east, toward a five hundred meter wide swale named

Stonehenge Bottom. Coneybury Hill is located southeast of the bottom and overlooks the River Avon farther east. Normanton Down is about a kilometer south of Stonehenge. The ground surface west of Stonehenge slopes gently westward into Stonehenge Down. Larkhill attains an elevation of 147 meters above mean sea level about three kilometers north of Stonehenge, and is the most prominent topographic feature of the area. The hill slopes east to the River Avon, south to Stonehenge Bottom and Stonehenge Down, southwest to Winterbourne Stoke Down, and north to Alton Down.

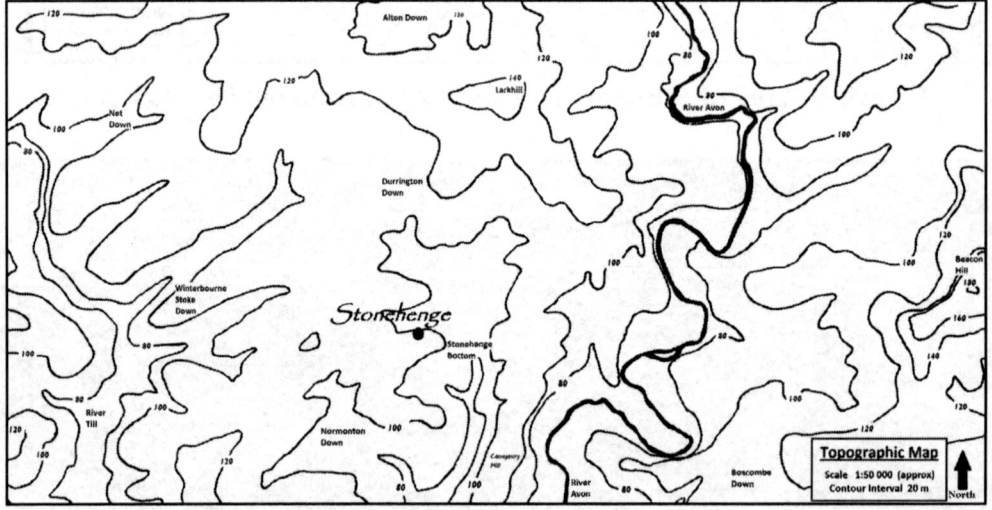

Figure 5: Topographic map of the Stonehenge Landscape, scale 1:50 000 approx. (Courtesy Ordnance Survey, Southampton, United Kingdom)

Much of the landscape south and west of Stonehenge is used for agricultural purposes or as grassland conservation area. The village of West Amesbury is about two kilometers east of the henge. The town of Amesbury lies just beyond, across the River Avon. Villages of Larkhill (military), Bulford and Durrington are situated within several kilometers to the north and northeast. Motorways in the immediate vicinity include the M303 and M344, which until mid-2013 intersected less than a kilometer to the east of Stonehenge.

Hills and swales direct rainfall and melt water runoff toward all directions of the compass. Widespread agricultural activity over the last five to six thousand years affected soil stratigraphy and erosion, and a broad range of soil types developed across the plain. The soils are generally calcareous—containing calcium carbonate derived from weathering and erosion of underlying chalk bedrock often found within inches to a few feet of the ground surface.

The underlying bedrock of Salisbury Plain consists of a chalk plateau that has been dissected by various surface waters mentioned below. The rolling chalkland directs runoff rapidly off the hills and into the streams and rivers. This results in rather dry soil conditions.

Britain experienced several periods of glaciation during the last 500,000 years and earlier. Southern England was not covered by ice during the most recent glacial event ending about 10,000 years ago. Salisbury Plain features gently rolling countryside with little apparent evidence of glaciation. The topography is indicative of water and wind erosion of the plain's ground surface over many thousands of years.

Numerous broad swales course across the Plain, and generally direct runoff east to the River Avon or west to the River Winterbourne (Refer to Figure 4). The dry valleys are referred to as *bournes*. Bourne is a term denoting a stream valley through which surface water flows only intermittently or on an ephemeral basis, such as times of spring melt or significant rainfall.

The River Avon meanders across the east portion of the plain, flowing south to the English Channel. There are several rivers with the name 'Avon' in Great Britain, *avon* being a Celtic (Proto-Brythonic) word meaning 'river'. Therefore the river bounding the east side of Plain is also called Salisbury Avon or Hampshire Avon to distinguish it from the others. The river enters the Hampshire Basin south of Salisbury, a city located about 11 km (7 mi) southeast of Stonehenge monument. Four rivers empty into the River Avon at or near Salisbury.

Navigable waters such as the Salisbury Avon were favored routes for transportation prior to introduction of the horse and carriageways. This would have been the situation during the Neolithic Age when Stonehenge was constructed. The River Avon is the nearest surface water feature to Stonehenge, and the largest water body in this portion of Salisbury Plain (Refer to Figure 4). It is navigable between the English Channel and the river banks at Amesbury and Durrington. The river was likely a major north-south line of transportation across the east portion of Salisbury Plain for many thousands of years.

Almost half of Britain's unimproved chalk downland is located on Salisbury Plain. Ninety-five percent of the plain is dry grassland, some of which is used for grazing (Refer to Figure 3). Numerous grass species are common and a breadth of wildflowers can be seen. About half of the grassland is cultivated. Woodlands and areas of scrub vegetation make up only three percent of vegetated land dotting the countryside and extending along bottoms of river valleys. Botanical Society of the British Isles guidelines concerning Salisbury Plain state there are more than a dozen 'Rare and Scarce Plant Species' such as orchid, bedstraw, worts, thistle, tyme and sedges.

During the 4th millennium BC Salisbury Plain was grassland with little if any woody vegetation. The numerous copses, and extensive lines of woods (some of them planted) now seen on the slopes of Larkhill and other areas did not exist during the mid-to late Neolithic when a number of significant henges, burial features and other structures were built.

The plain is home for many vertebrates and invertebrates. Juniper on heaths and calcareous grasslands provide excellent habitat in addition to the semi-natural dry grasslands and scrublands. Fox, badger, vole, squirrel, hare and red deer are common. Otter populations are returning along the waterways.

Urban and rural developments, grasslands in conservation, and military facilities at Larkhill are situated within a three kilometer radius of Stonehenge. There is also widespread evidence of numerous Meso-lithic, Neolithic and Bronze Age community buildings, houses, henges, cursus, long barrows, round barrows, refuse pits and other structures across the landscape. However, only a minority remain readily apparent aboveground. Figure 6 shows locations of many elements of archaeo-logical importance located across the Stonehenge Landscape. To date only a fraction of the area's subsurface has been investigated in detail for evidence of prehistoric activity.

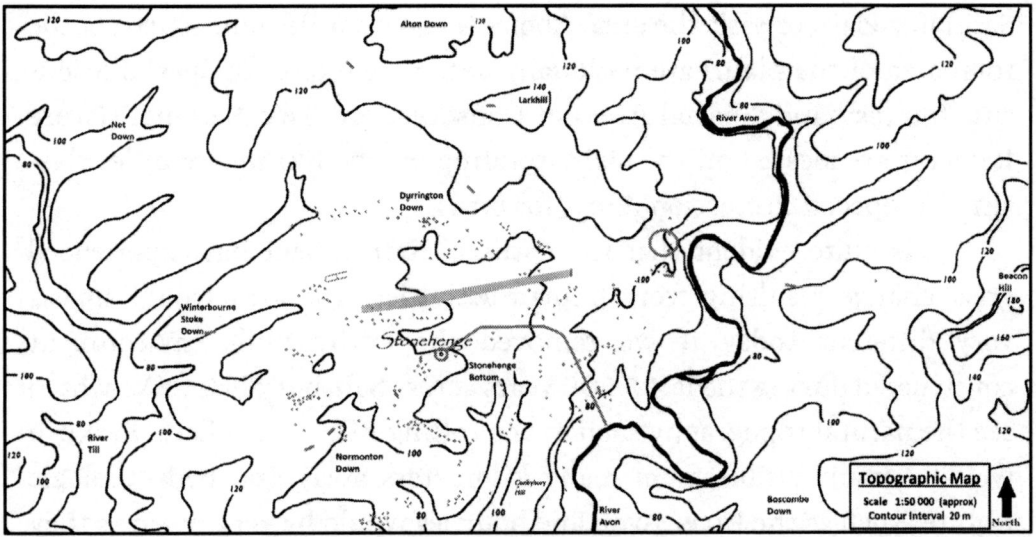

Figure 6: Map showing many of the known archaeological sites of importance on the Stonehenge Landscape.

The most readily apparent impacts of human activity on the natural landscape of Salisbury Plain are very recent. The urban areas have grown significantly over the last 250 years. With the growth came a progression of improvements to transportation, communications, housing, agriculture, commerce, military affairs and so forth, all very evident today.

Not so apparent is evidence of prehistoric human activity on Salisbury Plain prior to about 5500 years ago. Mesolithic Age effects to the environment did not include development of roadways, villages, agriculture, land division, and so forth in Wiltshire, let alone all of Britain. The full extent of Mesolithic through Iron Age impacts to land and habitat remains unknown, and likely will remain so. However there is evidence of mounded soil, excavating, hunting, agriculture and animal husbandry, residential and community buildings, byways, waste disposal in pits, and many other activities associated with people living as hunter gatherers or farmers long ago.

A critical component of archaeological work at Stonehenge and its surrounding environment is ensuring that land is protected for its value as habitat, agricultural use, and livelihood of people who either live on

Salisbury Plain or visit the area. About 77 square miles (one fourth of the total area of the plain) are nationally designated 'Sites of Special Scientific Interest' and 'Special Areas of Conservation'. Two National Nature Reserves are located on the plain, totaling nearly 300 square miles classified as Special Protection Areas for birds.

It is quite evident that the natural environment has experienced great change resulting from human activities. The area would appear very different today if we removed the entire built environment constructed during the last 5,500 years across Salisbury Plain. We would see the natural topography such as the rolling hills and valleys. Larkhill would remain visible from many kilometers away and hydrogeologic features such as the River Avon and bournes would be very much as they appear today. Vegetation patterns would adjust and animal populations would change accordingly. Nature would provide the only source of sound. Figure 7 illustrates topography and surface hydrologic features on Salisbury Plain without evidence of human activity.

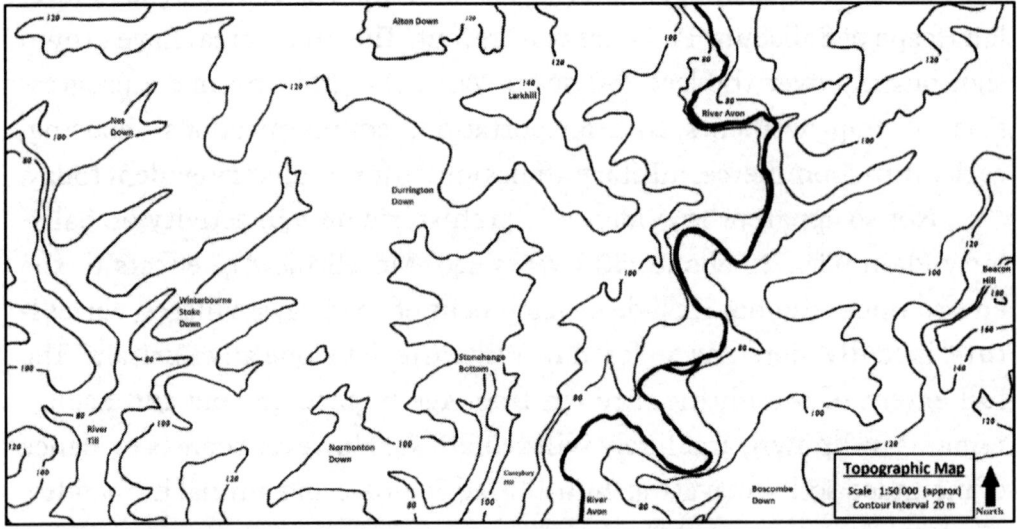

Figure 7: Topographic map of Salisbury Plain ca. 3500 BC

In 2500 BC we would find Stonehenge to be in a very special place in a very remote location. In stark contrast to its natural setting, the monument would be one of few human creations to be found, or seemingly so. Although with a much smaller population during the late Neolithic, the cultural significance of Salisbury Plain was perhaps greater than we consider it to be today. The architecture of Stonehenge's massive structure is organic in form, rude, circular, spherical, sacred.

By the end of the Neolithic Age, about 2400 BC, people had impacted the environment on Salisbury Plain for thousands of years. Natural resources—animal, vegetable and mineral-were used as building materials, furniture, firewood, tools, house ware, utensils, clothing and food. Domesticated animals such as pigs, sheep, cattle and dogs were common, although horses had not yet arrived from the European continent. Land was cleared, crops raised, soil productivity changed, soil erosion increased, and manmade fire might have accidently or intentionally ravaged some areas. All of those events would affect the ecology and physiography of Salisbury Plain during the Neolithic Age.

Nature has been unable to reclaim the land and return to pristine wilderness ever since. The human population continued to increase over the many centuries. Indeed, the megaliths of Stonehenge will not weather to sand and clay for many, many thousands of years. It is quite reasonable to believe this was an intention of the monument's designer.

Stonehenge is a World Heritage Site. Much of the Stonehenge Landscape is property of The National Trust and is in the process of being restored to chalk grassland for use as pasture and public open access. Almost 400 monuments dating from the Neolithic to Iron Age are located on land owned by the Trust. The monuments include Stonehenge, the Avenue between Stonehenge and the River Avon, the Greater Cursus, Woodhenge, Durrington Walls, Neolithic long barrows and round barrows from the Bronze age and later. Previously named Stonehenge Historic Landscape, it now includes about 2,100 acres (850 ha) maintained and administered by English Heritage. Grassland surrounding the monument and other open areas are included in the Chalk Grassland Reversion Project.

Chapter 3
CONTEXT

In the realm of archaeology context is everything. If a superbly polished stone axe head from the Neolithic was discovered in an area without other evidence of the presence of human activity, then beyond speculation little can be said as to the reason the artefact was left at that location. However if the axe head is found in addition to other items beside remains of a person buried in a round barrow dated to 2300 BC, and located one mile south of Stonehenge, then archaeology can help us understand why the axe might have been found within that context.

Further, the context can be broadened to include any number of archaeological sites and artefacts. That may be done for the purpose of understanding not only specific cultural affiliations with those artefacts and sites, but human use of an entire landscape at a specific time of occupation. At the outset this appears to be a daunting task. Yet with a necessary and sufficient base of archaeological evidence and knowledge of human behavior, it is possible to discover the intended purpose behind a landscape worked by human hands long ago. The evidence may also indicate how each element relates to others, the process by which the landscape was developed, and how people interacted with the built environment they created.

A universal trait of humans is concern and care for bodies of the dead. There is a great amount of evidence demonstrating that the loss of loved ones in Neolithic Britain was of great concern. Just as today, people during the Neolithic arranged appropriate means for burying the body, and conceived ways in which the spirit would continue living. Death is a natural and necessary part of human existence, indeed of all life. Prehistoric hunter gatherers, farmers, and indigenous tribes recognized this reality. They knew death is not the end of life, but part of the cycle of birth, life, death and re-birth.

For over two hundred years antiquarians and archaeologists have encountered a wealth of evidence concerning deposition of human remains and bones of domesticated animals in and around Stonehenge. They've found complete human skeletons, disarticulated bones, cattle bones, pig bones, cremated bones, broken bones, bones with cuts, ashes, and a network of river and overland routes to transport bodies of the dead to Stonehenge. Scholars generally agree that the purpose of Stonehenge was directly related to the dead, at times possibly including human and animal sacrifice.

Most theories about the purpose of Stonehenge spotlight Neolithic ritual and ceremonial concern for improving health or addressing death and the dead. Local feasting was related to the recently departed. The living at Durrington Walls and Woodhenge floated the deceased ceremoniously down the River Avon, arriving at Bluestonehenge to begin processing along the Avenue to Stonehenge where the dead would be honored before burial in a pit or under a barrow. Before the Avenue was constructed as a pathway for bringing the dead from Bluestonehenge to Stonehenge, the Greater Cursus offered ample space to process nearly 3 km (1.7 mi) end to end while ceremoniously and ritually transporting the dead to unknown locations, possibly Stonehenge. However the cursus has yielded no evidence of its original purpose or use, including procession.

For some very curious reason death of the body forms the basis upon which ideas of ritual and ceremony are proposed to explain why the Stonehenge Landscape was built and how it was intended to be used.

With emphasis on Neolithic through Iron Age, and Stonehenge being an important place to honor and bury the dead, we may lose sight of the larger picture. Certainly a more accurate representation will develop regarding the likely prehistoric purpose and use of the Stonehenge Landscape, prior to the Roman invasion.

Architectural and archaeological evidence suggests that the Stonehenge Landscape expresses prehistoric concern for the dead. But that is only part of the story. Current theories about Stonehenge conclude that ancient ritual and ceremony pertained to death of the body. However they do not address an issue that has been, and remains a central concern in all cultures-the continued life of the spirit. All religions everywhere, throughout time, expressed belief in an afterlife. Is it possible that no one at anytime, anywhere, celebrated death except at Stonehenge? Is there any evidence at all supporting the theory that everyone everywhere, throughout time, mourned the dead while also celebrating the departed's life, except at Stonehenge? Yet this seems to be the case presented in many modern theories concerning the Stonehenge Landscape.

There is much to be said about fundamental geometrical symbolism and its application to art and architecture. This includes symbols relating the concept of death as part of the natural and universal cycle of life. Plainly all evidence points to ancient and indigenous cultures understanding death of the body does not mean death of the spirit. There is a wealth of readily available information on this topic, and it is not the intent here to provide details. However, worldwide symbols associated with the cycle of birth, life, death and re-birth are found across the Stonehenge Landscape. Its relevance is presented in brief.

Space and time are factors of vital importance here, just as they are with complex engineering and construction activities in general. This is so for works of art and architecture as well. If for no other reason, the mere fact that the architecture of Stonehenge includes circles of stones of megalithic proportions should alert us that recognizing and understanding context—space and time—is important to solving the riddle of what Stonehenge meant to the people who built it.

Numerous Native American tribes (such as the Dakota, Kiowa, Pawnee, Cheyenne, Blackfoot, Crow, and others) in what is now the north central United States were living a North American version of the Neolithic until about 1840 AD. In many ways the cultures of those tribes appear to parallel what we know of the culture in central south England circa 3500 to 2500 BC. An important symbol indicative of similarities between Neolithic cultures in Britain and North America is the circle.

Native Americans such as the Lakota living on the Northern Great Plains observed that circles are found everywhere in nature. They are observed in the perimeter of a daisy flower, the trunk of a tree, ripples extending outward when a stone is dropped into a pond, the Sun, Moon, and Earth itself. Indigenous tribes knew the Moon orbits Earth, and Earth orbits our Sun. They also knew the Sun, Moon and Earth were spherical.

The sphere was of primary importance in indigenous, traditional understanding of life and relationships between all things. The symbol used by the Lakota, like many Neolithic and indigenous people, to express the power and sacredness of those relationships is the circle. The circle separates interior space from exterior space, and is perceived as separating the inner and outer spaces of spirit. The equivalent distance between the center of a circle and each point on the circle, and sphere, provides the geometric, symbolic importance of equality.

Gregory Cajete describes radii of the circle as bridges between the inner and outer realities.[1] Black Elk, a wičháša wakȟáŋ (man of power, holy man) of the Oglala Lakota during the latter 19th and early 20th centuries made this clear when he described the making of a sacred place simply by drawing lines on the ground:

"A pinch of the purified earth was offered above and to the ground and was then placed at the center of the sacred place. Another pinch of earth was . . . placed at the west of the circle . . . earth was placed at the other three directions, and then spread evenly around within the circle . . . He first took up a stick, pointed it to the six directions, and then, bringing it down, he made a small circle at the center; and this we understand to be the home of Wakan Tanka [great mystery,

Tákuškanškan:that which causes everything to move, *ni*:breath of life]. Again, after pointing the stick to the six directions, . . . made a mark starting from the west and leading to the edge of the circle. In the same manner he drew a line from the east to the edge of the circle, from the north to the circle, and from the south to the circle . . . everything leads into, or returns to, the center."[2]

The focus of the circle is its center from which all else radiates. "In this manner the alter was made, and, as I have said before, it is very sacred, for we have here established the center of the Earth, and this center, which in reality is everywhere, is the home, the dwelling place of Wakan Tanka."[3]

For these reasons the symbol of a circle with a dot at its center is called the *sun circle*. This symbol has ancient origins. It is the Egyptian hieroglyphic symbol for the Sun and therefore of Re, and the ancient Chinese symbol for the Sun, or the 'day' sign. Similarly, the circle has symbolized Earth, world, universe and self.

A circle represents all circles, any circle, centered at any location. It may be the center of the Milky Way, or the center of the Solar System. It may be the center of Earth or centered in ourselves—our hearts. As such the center is defined. The radius of the circle, however, is undefined. In geometry shape is not a function of size. A circle may have any size radius. The indigenous understood that using free will we may apply any size radius to our own circle, but that circle must be appropriately centered if we are to benefit in a spiritual manner.

The modern scientific method has difficulty studying unobservable or immeasurable relationships between source, place and time. This is not a slight on modern science. Science requires testable data and demonstrable predictability. When dealing with religion and spirituality, however, source, place and time are not quantifiable. We cannot test to find out if spirits exist, where it exists, and for how long. There are no tests to determine if the universe was created with intent, or if miracles really are miracles. Rather, those events involve qualified relationships addressed by religious studies in general, and spirituality in particular.

From the perspective of ancient and indigenous cultures the very act of creation—from gods creating the universe to separation of spirit from mortality—is sacred. It is power. Creation with intent is untestable, but that does not mean it is not possible, probable, or true. We are simply not aware of any scientific means for testing the presence of such events. The matter becomes one of either believing they are true, or believing they are not true.

This was the case for prehistoric shamans and indigenous artists reaching into the recesses of conscious being to discover dimensions of reality that modern science views as illusory. The shaman and artist expressed those unseen dimensions as sacred truths. By viewing cultures of Neolithic Britain as not only prehistoric but indigenous, comparable with that of pre-Columbian North America, ancient Egypt and others, the intent of the designer and purpose of monuments located across the Stonehenge Landscape become more identifiable and better understood. The design and construction of Stonehenge may be likened to the untold number of artworks and decorative artefacts associated with many ancient and indigenous Neolithic cultures. Gregory Cajete, Assistant Professor of Education at the University of New Mexico describes the purpose behind those artworks and decorations.

"This is primarily a conscious effort to simplify, to become aware, to sharpen the senses, to concentrate, to revitalize the whole being. The idea here is to develop the ability to imbue an artefact with pure and simple vitality and to have the clarity of mind and stamina required to undertake a very difficult and sometimes dangerous task, such as the initiatory paintings of the caves of Lascaux and Les trios Frères, France. There is a guiding spirit, or "consistent adherence to original intent," the notion of applying one's will to concentrate one's whole being into a task, a creation, a song, a dance, a painting, an event, a ceremony, a ritual."[5]

Cajete identifies a general pattern in the creation of indigenous ceremonial art. The first step in this pattern is the artist's preparation (purification) for the journey. This is followed by attention toward sources, an adherence to patterns of form, time and place. These steps in indigenous artistry are abundantly evident across the Stonehenge

Landscape. They appear to have been integral with the Neolithic pattern of life.

Professor Arnold De Loof of Katholieke Universiteit Leuven, Belgium proposes a definition of 'life' in which the concept of life is not a thing (noun), but an action (verb). He suggests life is "nothing else than the total sum of all acts of communication/problem-solving executed by a given sender-receiver compartment, at all levels of compartmental organization at any moment."[6] In other words, life is a function of sender-receiver relationship in time. It is defined as the sum of all communications. De Loof concludes, "it can be used in both biology and the humanities . . . . it also makes it possible to seamlessly unite organic- and cultural evolution as being two key aspects of evolution based on the very same principles of communication . . ."[7]

An inherent and vital aspect of communication is *intent* to transmit information from sender to receiver. This is so throughout the animal kingdom, and might be found in plants as well. Therefore a revised definition of life would read: Life is communication/problem-solving with intent.[8]

De Loof's definition of life requires a 'compartment', a portion or division of space. For example, a compartment may take the form of the human body, a room, or the complex nature of a landscape. However, a compartment can also be a particular aspect or function of something. This allows sender-receiver compartments to be associated with animate or inanimate, physical life forms or metaphysical entities such as the soul or spirit. Native Americans living traditional sacred ways (pre-Columbian Neolithic cultures) believe that all existence, animate and inanimate, contains spirit capable of communicating with people with intent.[9] Every stone—from a microscopic clay particle to Earth itself-is known to have spirit, life. Earth is compartmentalized (inner core, outer core, mantle, crust, water bodies, air) and communicates via energy and mass transfer (plate tectonics, lava, heat, winds and waves). If it has a spirit, then it too is life. This is the Earth Goddess of Neolithic Europe and the Middle East, as well as the Celts. It is Gaia, Earth personified in Greek Mythology, and Grandmother as expressed by Native Americans.

Similarly the Sun, the cosmological Sky King, and black hole at the center of our galaxy are 'Life'.

Whether or not you or I believe life can be animate or inanimate is not the issue. Rather, it is important to recognize that ancient and indigenous knowledge of the universe included belief that life is everywhere and in all things. For the archaeologist it is important to realize and accept that many ancient and indigenous cultures knew this was true, that this is how the universe operates. This *knowing* provides a basis for recognizing that everything in the world is related to everything else. The Lakota expression 'Mitakuye Oyasin', meaning all my relations or we are all related, is an acknowledgement of this knowing. Of course, aspects of this *knowing* were, and remain, important in major religions across the world.

Knowing each human being is part of everything, and everything is part of the human being, provided inspiration for Lakota to 'experience' life, interact with nature, listen and pay attention to the world—the universe—because experience is all about communication and relationships. This knowing is apparent in the mythology and cosmology of the Lakota, Maya, Celts, Egyptians, Aborigines, and other cultures—prehistoric and indigenous. Many of those cultures were essentially 'Neolithic' when they developed their mythologies and cosmologies. However, while it is certain that they engaged in ritual and ceremony, and experiencing sacred relationships, prehistoric cultures left us no documentation. Material evidence helping us identify prehistoric connections to Earth and sky is often found not in artefacts, but the wider landscape that human beings integrated into their belief systems—their knowing-about the cycles of all things.

The late Vine Deloria was a professor of history at the University of Arizona and the University of Colorado, Boulder. He was a leading scholar who researched, wrote and taught extensively about indigenous history, law, religion and political science. Deloria defined 'religion' from the world-wide indigenous perspective.

"Religion is not conceived as a personal relationship between the deity and each individual. It is rather a covenant between a particular god and a community. The people of this community are the primary residue of the religion's legends, practice, and beliefs. Ceremonies of a community scope are the chief characteristic feature of religious activity. . . . Stories, songs, games and art were used to instill respect [for the sacred]. Life, as a whole, was tied to spirit."[10]

In his book *Native Science: Natural Laws of Interdependence*, Gregory Cajete defines 'science', as in Native science, "in terms of the most inclusive of its meanings, that is, as a story of the world and a practiced way of living it."[11] This certainly is not applying the modern scientific method, nor is it religion. For indigenous people life is not lived without direct contact with, and immersion in nature. Life cannot be understood by reading books. It is not found in science laboratories. Cajete writes, "In native languages there is no word for "science," or for "philosophy," psychology," or any other foundational way of coming to know and understand the nature of life and our relationship therein . . . For native people, *seeking life* was the all-encompassing task."[12]

This search for life and recognition of sacred relationships between all things, at all times, requires attention in all aspects of human interaction with the environment. A *sacred lifeway* is lifelong experience with the environment, knowing that everything in the universe is sacred. This knowledge and experience leads to greater understanding of *life* made manifest in all that is sensed and communicated. As Gregory Cajete explains, a sacred lifeway encompasses all aspects of indigenous human experience through Native science.

"Native science is a metaphor for a wide range of tribal processes of perceiving, thinking, acting, and "coming to know" that have evolved through human experience with the natural world. Native science is born of a lived and storied participation with the natural landscape. To gain a sense of Native science one must participate with the natural world. To understand the foundations of native science one must become open to the roles of sensation, perception, imagination, emotion, symbols, and spirit as well as that of concept, logic, and rational empiricism . . . Much of the essence of Native science is beyond literal description . . . (It) may be seen as an exemplification of "biophilia", or the innate instinct that all life forms share for affiliation with each other . . . Native science is a broad term that can include metaphysics and philosophy; art and architecture; practical technologies and agriculture; and ritual and ceremony practiced by Indigenous peoples both past and present. More specifically, Native science encompasses such areas as astronomy, farming, plant domestication, plant medicine, animal husbandry, hunting, fishing, metallurgy, and geology-in brief, studies related to plants, animals, and natural phenomena. Yet, Native science extends to include spirituality, community, creativity, and technologies that sustain environments and support essential aspects of human life. It may even include exploration of questions such as the nature of language, thought, and perception; the movement of time and space; the nature of human knowing and feeling; the nature of human relationship to the cosmos; and all questions related to natural reality . . . All the basic components of scientific thought and application are metaphorically represented in most Native stories of creation and origin. Indeed, both native science and modern science have elements of the primal human story in common."[13]

With the process of 'coming to know' encompassing so much of the life experience of people living in indigenous, 'virtually Neolithic' cultures around the world, the possibility that a sacred lifeway was a vital part of human experience of Neolithic Britain becomes a very real possibility. Evidence is lacking to demonstrate that this was indeed the case, but there is no evidence providing greater support for any other possibility.

The implications are profound. The possibility of a sacred lifeway as the norm during the mid-to late Neolithic alters our perspective concerning many facets of life including development of the Stonehenge Landscape. It provides reasons why specific developments such as Woodhenge, Stonehenge, and Greater Cursus are where they are, and the spatial relationship each site has with the others, including the overall scheme of development. It also brings to light the possibility that the people who quarried, transported, shaped and installed the monument's megaliths did not need exterior motivation to do so, such as demands of a tribal chieftain.

This scenario accords with the fact that construction of the Greater Cursus, Stonehenge, Woodhenge, Durrington Walls, Avebury, Ring of Brodgar, Brú na Bóinne, and many other important sites across the British Isles required not only organization and cooperation amongst everyone involved in those works, but courage, fortitude, generosity and wisdom to accomplish each task at hand. The motivation would come from the physical, intellectual, emotional and spiritual nature of each individual contributing to the cause. It was a cause we can see the effects of even today. It is a message formed with soil and sculpted in stone, built to be communicated for millennia. All we need do is see the symbols and read the signs. As we shall see, the results are greater than we had imagined.

Throughout history people have not been as concerned with death as they were about continuation of life. Universal sacred symbolism reflects the idea of the eternal cyclicity of all things.[14] One life is not as important as the whole. Each person strives to contribute for the benefit of all, and upon passing we honor him or her, we pay tribute through funerary ceremony and ritual, and remember and celebrate life.

Honoring and celebrating the lives of the departed is a global phenomenon. It is evidence of human intent and action, gaining knowledge by observing and experiencing life in its broadest array of form, recognizing, appreciating and honoring the eternal cycle of life. And for many ancient and indigenous cultures this related to all things animate and inanimate. For as people understood that an acorn becomes an oak tree producing more acorns, and then dies and becomes the matter from which new life is created, so clay becomes stone until it weathers and erodes, becoming clay once again. Although no longer stone the clay remains present and contributing to the universal cycle of life in the world.

This process directly concerns many facets of ritual, ceremony and celebration associated with the Celtic festival of Lughnasadh (Galic: Lúnasa, the month of August) when the Earth goddess was thanked for her fertility and the corn god died at harvest to become the god of the

Underworld. The corn god was sacrificed, and his body was stored until it was needed so that people might live through the coming year. Lugh (lugos: oath), the son born from the marriage of the sky king and earth goddess, took his place as the new king of fertility.

As a wake for this scenario of death and anointment of a new king, Lughnasadh included games of strength, drinking and feasting. Bulls, and at times humans, were considered suitable sacrifices for the good of the people. But this is certainly not a festival of death. It celebrates life by way of the community engaging in activities emphasizing the cycle of birth, life, death and rebirth. Life and death are not rent asunder, but celebrated together as vital parts of the cycle of life.

There is another aspect of the yearly cycle of birth and death that does not receive as much attention. Death of the old king of fertility, the father, is death of the body, but not death of the spirit. Once sacrificed, the king's body—grain—remains with the people as food for survival through the coming winter, while the stalk is returned to Earth. However the spirit of the old king would return from whence it came, to the stars. Lugh, the son, the new king replaces his father to bring forth life next spring. He is the new Sky King, and the miraculous mating of Lugh and the earth Goddess brings forth life in the year following. Who is Lugh, the sky king, earth goddess and power which fertilizes the seed of life?

"The God of Light appears in Gaul and in Ireland as Lugh, or Lugus, who has left his traces in many place-names such as Lug-dunum (Leyden), Lyons, &c. Lugh appears in Irish legend with distinctly solar attributes. When he meets his army before the great conflict with the Fomorians, they feel, says the saga, as if they beheld the rising of the sun. Yet he is also . . . a god of the Underworld, belonging on the side of his mother Ethlinn, daughter of Balor, to the Powers of Darkness. The fact is that the Celtic conception of the realm of death . . . resembled that of Egyptian religion. The Other-world was not a place of gloom and suffering, but of light and liberation."[15]

Lugh is the Celtic god Lugus (Proto-Indo-European root *leuk-, "flashing light," shine, fiery; Proto-Celtic *k change to-gh-and-ch-in

Brythonic Breton and Cornish). Note also Proto-Indo European *Leuk- (English:'light'; Sanskrit:'rócate'; Greek:'leukós'; Latin:lūx; Lithuanian: 'laŭkas'). Lugh is the god of Light, the Bringer of Light.

In Irish mythology Lugh is skilled in the use of the sword, spear and sling. His sling rod is the Milky Way. He can throw lightning bolts. His dog is Failinis. He is *Lámhfhada* ("long arm" or "long hand"), *Ildánach* ("skilled in many arts"), *Samhildánach* ("Equally skilled in many arts"), *Lonnbeimnech* ("fierce striker") and and *Macnia* ("boy hero"). The Welsh call him Nudd or Lleu Llaw Gyffes, "The Bright One with the Strong Hand." The same characteristics and attributes of Lugh are seen in Nuada ('silver hand'), Dagda (Proto-Indo-European*Dhagho-deiwos*:shining divinity).

Thor, Týr, Apollo, Jupiter, Mercury, Osiris, Shiva, as well as many other gods are also associated with bringing life, destroying, and light. This is not to say that all of those gods have direct correspondence as Lugh. However all of them and many other deities represent various aspects of the masculine human being.

From perspectives of mythology and cosmology in many Indo-European cultures, the astronomical representation of Lugh and his various derivatives is the constellation Orion—his right arm reaching up into the Milky Way, his hand at the ecliptic, his weapons the spear, sword and sling. As he rises above the east horizon during the summer, he carries the orb of the sun in his right hand. He is the Bringer of Light. He is the Sky King. The form of the Orion constellation represents numerous male and female deities.

The triad of Old King, New King and Earth Goddess has a very direct parallel with Osiris (father), Horus (son) and Isis (mother) in Old Kingdom Egypt ca. 2600 BC, and likely as far back as predynastic cults c. 6000 to 3100 BC. Osiris was god of the underworld (afterworld, otherworld), vegetation, the dead and the afterlife. A new Pharaoh adopted the name of Horus upon taking the throne. Upon death his body was prepared and entombed, while his ahk (the intellect) was free to return to the stars to become the next Osiris. We see a very similar transition of the New King—king of life and vegetation—transitioning through the year to become the next Old King, summarily sacrificed during Lughnasadh, and returning to the stars.

The Celts did not arrive in Britain and Ireland until the end of the 2nd millennium BC. However there are surprising correspondences between ancient Celtic sacred beliefs and deities in the British Isles, and those of late Predynastic Egypt ca. 3300 BC. While there is little evidence to support a common ancestry for religions associated with those two temporally and spatially disconnected cultures, the same concept of the astronomical location of Otherworld in the region of Orion is more than notable.

Chapter 4
A Grand Plan on Salisbury Plain

"Interpretation is still obviously the central and most difficult problem. In principle, we can always bring up the question of the validity of a hermeneutics. Through cross-references, clear assertions (texts, rites, representative monuments) and half-veiled allusions, we can demonstrate precisely what such and such symbol 'means.' But we can also state the problem in another manner: do those who utilize symbols realize all their theoretical implications? For instance, when studying the symbolism of the 'Cosmic Tree,' we say that this tree is located in the 'Centre of the World'. Are all individuals belonging to societies that know of such Cosmic Trees equally conscious of the integral symbolism of the 'Centre'? But the validity of the symbol as a form of knowledge does not depend on the degree of understanding of such and such an individual. Texts and representative monuments prove extensively that, at least to certain individuals of an archaic society, the symbolism of the 'Centre' was transparent in its totality; the rest of society was satisfied with the act of 'participating' in symbolism. Moreover, it is hard to state precisely the limits of such participation; it varies according to an indeterminate number of factors. All we can say is that the *actualization of a symbol is not mechanical; it is related to the tensions and alternations of social life and ultimately with cosmic rhythms* (emphasis added)."

—*M. Eliade*[1]

In pursuit of understanding the purpose, meaning, and spatial relationships of the hundreds of monuments located on the Stonehenge Landscape, this chapter identifies three types of prominent, sacred, mid-to late Neolithic structures-cursus, long barrow, and henge.

Cursus

In 1723 William Stukeley was observing the Stonehenge countryside about one kilometer north of the monument when he noticed a shallow ditch oriented almost due east-west. A low bank adjoined the outside slope of the ditch. Upon further observation he discovered the ditch and bank system was about 2.7 kilometers (1.71 miles) long. A similar ditch of equal length and approximate cross section paralleled the first, the two separated by a distance of about 100 to 150 meters. The west ends of the ditches were connected by another ditch oriented north-south. The east ends of the ditches were similarly connected. A long barrow oriented north-south extended along the east end of the cursus.

Stukeley thought the unusually lengthy ditch and bank structure might be some sort of ancient race course, rather similar to a hippodrome—an ancient, oblong course and stadium constructed for horse racing and chariot racing. He referred to it as a *cursus* (plural *cursus* or *cursuses*), a Latin word meaning 'course'.

The structure Stukeley discovered is the Greater (Stonehenge, Amesbury) Cursus (Figure 8). A much smaller cursus—the Lesser Cursus (Winterbourne Stoke Cursus)—is located about 500 meters north of the west end of the Greater Cursus. Centuries of ploughing rendered the Lesser Cursus little more than a crop mark. No relationship between the two cursus is known other than both date to between 3600 and 3300 BC. They are the only cursus in the Stonehenge Landscape.

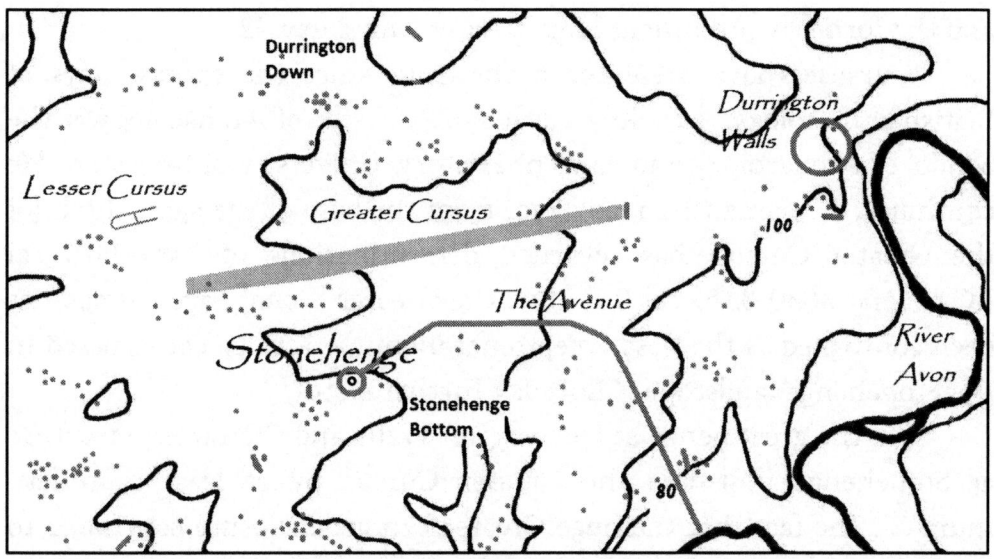

Figure 8: Locations of the Stonehenge Greater Cursus and Lesser Cursus

More than fifty cursus are known in Britain, all dating to the Neolithic. Each appears unique in length, width, orientation of the long axis, and configuration of the peripheral ditch and bank system. The largest is the Dorset Cursus located about 21 kilometers (13 miles) southwest of Stonehenge. The Dorset Cursus courses its way snake-like across the rolling countryside for about 10 km (6 mi), crossing two rivers in the process. A long barrow is located at each of its ends and additional long barrows are found along its north and south sides.

Cursus are no longer believed to be race courses. The ditch and bank structures predate arrival of the horse in Britain by one thousand years. However their functions have remained mysteries. In general they date to the mid-to late 4th millennium BC, similar to the two cursus on the Stonehenge Landscape. To date the Greater Cursus yields no indication of significant wear from use, although the ditches have partially filled and the banks are low. A Bronze Age round barrow remains near the west end (terminus) of the cursus. The west third and east third of the cursus can be seen from Stonehenge but the middle third cannot. That area is hidden as the cursus drops into the upper reach of Stonehenge Bottom before rising to the east end of the cursus and the formerly prominent long barrow Amesbury 42.

"Cursuses have presented a challenge since the earliest days of British archaeology," says Roy Loveday , Professor of Archaeology at the School of Archaeology and Ancient History, University of Leicester.[2] He continues, ". . . an antler recovered, from the base of the same ditch [of the Greater Cursus] has returned determinations of 3632-3375 cal BC . . . and 3630-3370 cal BC. Thus the Greater Stonehenge Cursus has been confirmed as the first exceptional monument to be constructed in the Stonehenge landscape."[3] Loveday further states,

". . . the great henge at Durrington Walls and the sarsen structure at Stonehenge post-date the Greater Cursus by at least a millennium . . . The fact that the huge Greater Cursus enclosure continued to be respected as much as 2000 years after its construction when 'Wessex' style round barrows were aligned alongside it . . . confirms its pivotal role in the development of the ritual focus."[4]

Figure 9 illustrates the prominent size and location of the Greater Cursus on the Stonehenge Landscape. Admittedly the Greater Cursus is a tremendously large feature somehow related with nearby barrows as much as two millennia younger. However we must be careful in drawing conclusions that might tie the original purpose and use of the cursus, to any purpose or use thereafter. There is no evidence that the cursus was built for the purpose of ancient ritual or ceremony. The idea appears reasonable enough, but it is little more than educated speculation. The cursus size and context within a landscape built for the ancestors does not necessarily mean it is a relic of ritual, most commonly interpreted to be a religious procession moving from one end to the other.

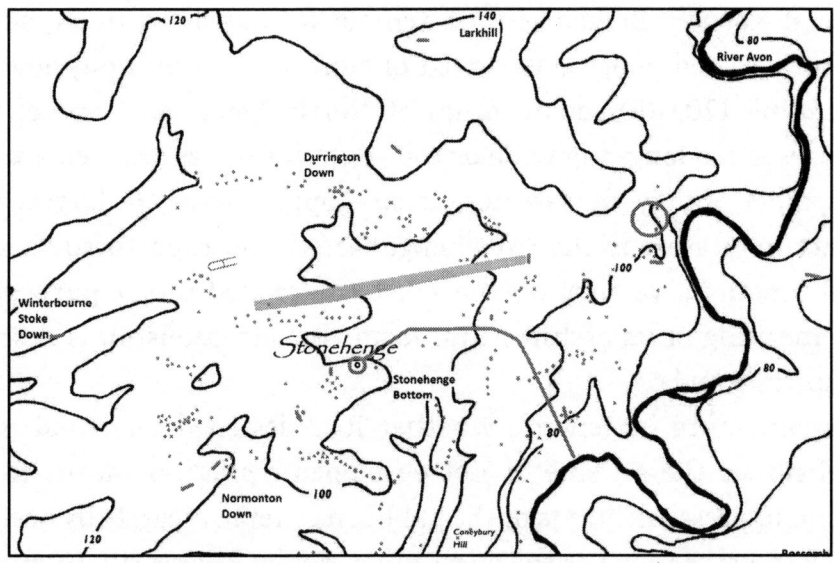

Figure 9: Note size and central location of the Greater Cursus in the Stonehenge Landscape.

However, size and context of the cursus indicates its construction was important to the people on Salisbury Plain 5500 years ago. Participation in its construction might very well have been a rite in and of itself during that time. The structure was soon related to certain long barrows located about it. Loveday continues,

"But what was its purpose, and that of the many other such sites constructed between c. 3600 and 3000 cal BC (Barclay & Bayliss 1999; Loveday 2006a; Thomas et al. 2009)? Size and layout preclude mundane explanations yet these structures are quite simply too long, too wide, and too slight to have fulfilled the obvious monumental functions of ritual architecture—to lead, focus, and impress celebrants."[5]

He is right. The great size and form of the cursus must be related to the sacred, yet the structure does not conform to archaeological understanding of what constitutes Neolithic ritual architecture in Britain. That can only mean that our current understanding of what constitutes ritual architecture in Britain is not compatible with what the people who built the cursus understood to be ritual architecture. In other words our understanding is wrong. Witness the great pyramids at Giza, the

Temple at Karnak, Brihadeshwara temple at Thanjavur, India, and the prehistoric sacred hoop constructed of stone and natural physiography, surrounding 120,000 square miles of North America.[6] None of those structures is too long, too wide or too slight for use as a sacred architectural symbol. Simply, the Greater Cursus happens to be the largest single architectural feature in the Stonehenge sacred landscape. As to its monumental function, we should expect it to be related to the purpose and sacred meaning of its architectural form. That relationship is described in Chapters 5 and 6.

Architecture in general, whether it is designed for ritual, sacred symbolism, or the profane, is not developed *a priori* as means to lead, focus and impress celebrants or the public in general. A carefully designed, complex structure such as the cursus may not be necessarily intended to direct a person's attention or movement, or require admiration or respect of the builder or the structure itself. Architecture is creation of symbolism. It communicates information from sender to receiver.

The most common archaeological explanation for the Greater Cursus is that it was built as a procession way somehow related to ritual and ceremony in association with Stonehenge. However there is no evidence of such use inside or nearby the confines of the ditch and bank. In fact, aside of evidence that the ditch was re-excavated during the mid-third millennium BC, the cursus has provided almost no artefacts that could be used to help identify and date either mundane or sacred use of the feature.

As a sacred symbol the cursus must be related to its monumental function. Its purpose was more than to capture Neolithic attention. In fact, there is no evidence it was built to attract anyone's attention. The question is 'who is the intended receiver of the message?'

Although the size of the Greater Cursus is so vast, its east end with Amesbury 42 was readily viewed from the west terminus (today the long barrow can no longer be seen). Its shape, size and placement upon the natural landscape are evidence of its purpose. Certainly the structure stands out when seen from the air amongst the surrounding grassland, woods, and development on Larkhill (Refer to Figures 3 and

Figure 4). In original form with the ditch and bank lined in bright white chalk, it could have been seen from many miles above, yet would have been completely unnoticeable from locations not more than a kilometer or two afield. It cannot be observed from Winterbourne Stoke Down, Stonehenge Down, Normanton Down, Stonehenge Bottom other than its most upper reaches, the River Avon and Bluestonehenge, Woodhenge and Durrington Walls.

The Greater Cursus seems tucked away, far enough north such that most visitors to Stonehenge do not give it much thought. Yet it simply lies across 1.71 kilometers of chalk plateau, in full view for anyone interested, while its purpose has waited discovery for nearly 5500 years. It is like a great sign post indicating the presence of something in the environment ca. 3500 BC that was very important at that time. But now the sign post has been laid to rest, nearly forgotten.

Dr Terence Meaden, a professional physicist, meteorologist and archaeologist, has made significant contributions to research and interpretation of Neolithic and Bronze Age archaeology. His particular interests include unlocking the mysteries of Stonehenge and Avebury. During the 1990s he developed a theory that cursus constructed across Britain were monuments to the Sky God coming down in the form of a tornado during storm events, and touching Earth-the Earth Goddess.

The most intriguing result of Meaden's study of the Greater Cursus is his finding that each of nine long barrows within site of the cursus has its long axis oriented in the direction of one end or the other of the cursus.[7] He used a military compass accurate to half of a degree, and concluded that his measurements were accurate to within a range of one-to three degrees, depending on the condition of the respective barrow. In total, the long axis orientation was measured for nine of sixteen long barrows within five kilometers of Stonehenge (Refer to Figure 10). Results of Meaden's alignment measurements of long barrows 1 through 9 are provided in Table 1 in Section 2.5 Long Barrows.[8]

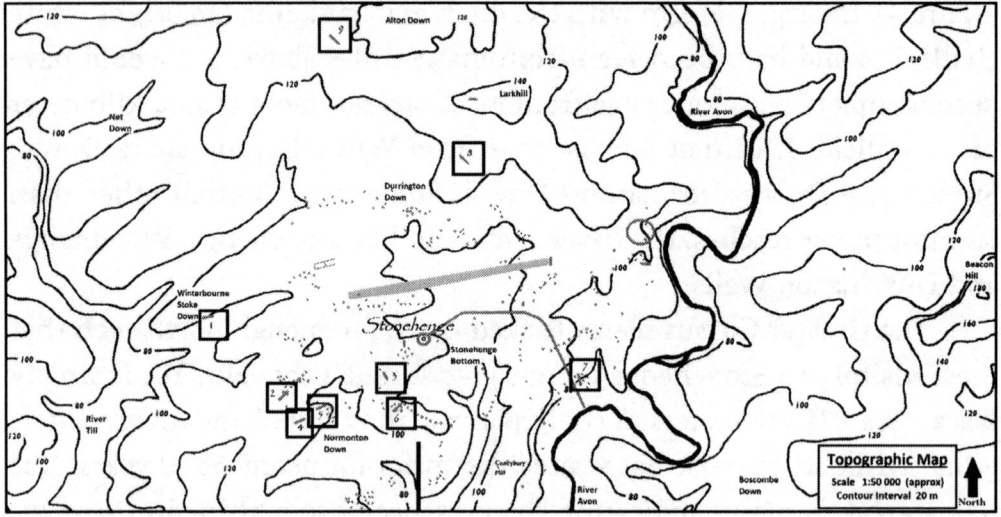

Figure 10: Map showing location of the Greater Cursus and the nine long barrows. Terence Meaden measured the orientation of the primary axis of each long barrow.

Radiocarbon dating of a red deer antler pick discovered at the bottom of the western terminal ditch suggests that the Stonehenge Cursus was first constructed between 3630 and 3375 BC.[9] Each end is about 100 m wide. Nearly 700 m east of its west end the cursus widens to about 150 m. The azimuth of the north side ditch is approximately 84.9 degrees (measured clockwise from due north). The west 700 m of the south ditch has an azimuth of 90 degrees, but turns slightly northward at an azimuth of 83.3 degrees to the east end of the cursus.

About 550 meters northwest of the west end of the Greater Cursus is the Lesser Cursus. With a length of about 400 meters and width of nearly 60 meters it is much smaller than the Greater Cursus. The longitudinal axis of the Lesser Cursus has an azimuth of about 77 degrees. Unfortunately the cursus is little more than a cropmark as it is located in an agricultural field that has been ploughed for many years, rendering the ground surface nearly level. In 1983 excavation of a portion of the Lesser Cursus confirmed it did not have a terminal ditch and bank at its east end. Work done by the Stonehenge Riverside Project later showed the cursus was constructed within the same timeframe as the Greater

Cursus, about 3600 to 3300 BC.[10]

(Refer to Appendix A for explanation of how the shape of the Greater Cursus was derived.)

Long Barrows

A long barrow is an early Neolithic earthen burial mound rectangular in plan and trapezoidal in cross-section. Two examples of long barrows are illustrated in Figure 10. Terence Meaden found that each of nine long barrows within site of the cursus has its long axis oriented in the general direction of one end or the other of the Greater Cursus. Figure 11 depicts the size and location of the Greater Cursus and Stonehenge relative to locations of long barrows 1 through 9. These are the long barrows Terence Meaden identified having each long axis oriented within 3 degrees or less of one or the other end of the cursus.[11] The cursus and long barrows are of similar age, dating to about 3500 BC. At first glance there is no organization to the plan of long barrows about the cursus. So it was quite a surprise to Meaden and other researchers to find direct associations between each barrow orientation and the cursus.

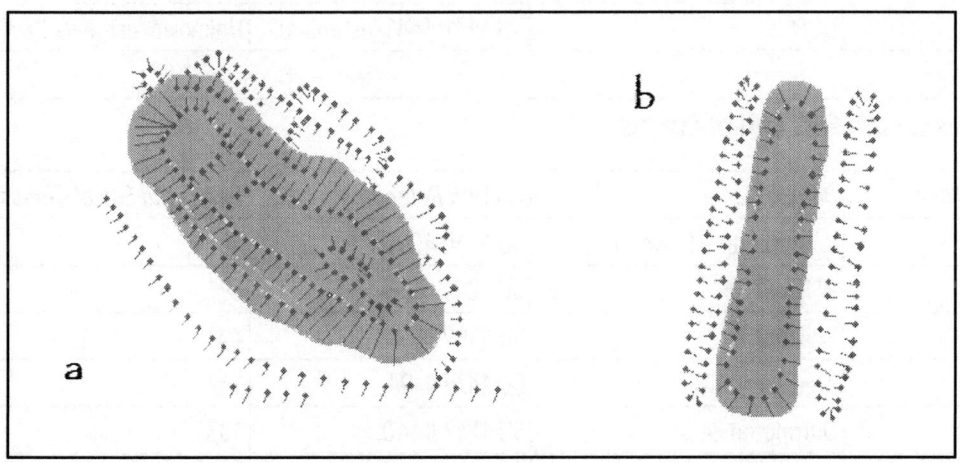

Figure 11: Two examples of a long barrow: a) Durrington 24, b) Amesbury 42

Results of Meaden's long barrow-cursus measurements are listed below in Table 1. On the table those nine long barrows are numbered 1 through 9, the same as Meaden numbered them. Whilst Meaden gave bearing measurements for each alignment, Table 1 provides the equivalent orientations as azimuths measured from 0 degrees north.

Meaden's bearing measurement of 133 degrees (azimuth 133 degrees) for Figheldean 31 (barrow 9) indicated alignment with the east terminal. However this barrow is also located due north of the cursus west terminal, and is listed accordingly.

Table 1: Alignments of the Greater Cursus and nearby Long Barrows[12]

Alignment with West End of Cursus			
Barrow Number	Barrow Name	OS Grid Reference	Bearing to End of Cursus
1	Winterbourne Stoke 53	SU 0917 4280	87°
2	Winterbourne Stoke 1	SU 1000 4151	34.5°
3	Amesbury 14	SU 1154 4176	153°
9	Figheldean 31	SU 1089 4588	180°
10	Figheldean 27(Knighton Barrow)	SU 1247 4438	Not applicable, barrow does not point toward the cursus
14	Watergate	SU 1635 4305	270°
15	UDD	SU 1171 4441 (estimate)	Unknown; estimate 203°

Alignment with East End of Cursus			
Barrow Number	Barrow Name	OS Grid Reference	Bearing to End of Cursus
4	Winterbourne Stoke 71	SU 1010 4090	58°
5	Wilsford 34	SU 1041 4118	59°
6	Wilsford 13	SU 1189 4130	44°
7	Amesbury 140	SU 1418 4194	162°
8	Durrington 24	SU 1247 4440	133°
9	Figheldean 31	SU 1089 4588	133°
10	Figheldean 27(Knighton Barrow)	SU 1247 4438	90°
11	Amesbury 10a	SU 1194 4217	60°

Alignment with East End of Cursus

Barrow Number	Barrow Name	OS Grid Reference	Bearing to End of Cursus
12	Amesbury 42	SU 1374 4318	0°
13	Wilsford 30	SU 1141 4107	90°
14	Watergate	SU 1635 4305	274°

Additional Alignments

Location	Landscape Element	OS Grid Reference	Bearing to Location
Barrow 1	Winterbourne Stoke 53	SU 0917 4280	84.6° to Greater Cursus north ditch and centre of Woodhenge
Barrow 2	Winterbourne Stoke 1	SU 1000 4151	35.5° to Figheldean 27, Amesbury 140 and Amesbury 57 Long Bell Barrow
Barrow 3	Amesbury 14	SU 1154 4176	153° to west terminus of Greater Cursus and east end of Lesser Cursus
Barrow 4	Winterbourne Stoke 71	SU 1010 4090	59° to Amesbury 14, Heel Stone, 22° to east terminus and UDD
Barrow 5	Wilsford 34	SU 1041 4118	65° to Amesbury 14, and Woodhenge alignment with summer solstice sunrise, 18° to west terminus and UDD
Barrow 10	Knighton Barrow	SU 1247 4438	229° to UDD and west end of Lesser Cursus,to Hill 134 and Woodhenge Visual alignments to UDD, Amesbury 14, Coneybury Henge, Amesbury 140, Woodhenge and Larkhill
Barrow 14	Watergate	SU 1635 4305	274° to Woodhenge alignment with summer solstice sunrise, 284° to UDD

Additional Alignments

Location	Landscape Element	OS Grid Reference	Bearing to Location
Barrow 15	UDD	SU 1171 4441	202° to west terminus and Winterbourne Stoke 71117° to east terminus Cursus and Amesbury 57 Bell Barrow 94° to centre of Woodhenge and Watergate Visual alignments to Figheldean 31, Amesbury 14, Coneybury Henge, Amesbury 140, and Hill 134, and Larkhill
Barow 16	Amesbury 57 Bell Barrow (Ratfyn barrow)	SU 1583 4194	270° to Amesbury 140 and Amesbury 14 Visual alignments to Coneybury Henge, UUD, Larkhill, and Watergate
Coneybury Henge	~ 200 m north of top of Coneybury Hill	SU 1340 4160	298° to Heel Stone and west terminus, 66° to Amesbury 140 and Watergate Visual alignments to UDD, Durrington 24, Knighton Barrow, Hill 147, east terminus, Hill 134, Woodhenge and Amesbury 57 Bell Barrow to east terminus
Hill 134	Elev. 134 m, northwest of Durrington Walls	SU 1431 4395	49.9° to pit in Greater Cursus along summer solstice sunrise with Heel Stone, 229° to Heel Stone, 225° to east terminus and Wilsford 13
Larkhill	Elev. 147 m, top of Larkhill, east of Knighton Barrow	SU 1454 4132	166° to east terminal and Amesbury 140 Visual alignments to Figheldean 31, UDD, west terminus, Amesbury 14, Stonehenge, Coneybury Henge, Amesbury 57 Bell Barrow, Woodhenge and Watergate

Table 1 also lists alignments of six additional barrows (numbered 10, 11, 12, 13, 14, 15 in deference to Meaden's numbering of long barrows), a topographic high point north of Strangways (Hill 134, elevation 134 meters (440 ft) above mean sea level), the top of Larkhill (about 1 kilometer north-northeast of Figheldean 27), and Coneybury Henge (about 200 m or 660 ft north of the top of Coneybury Hill). Locations of the landscape elements listed on the table are depicted in Figure 12.

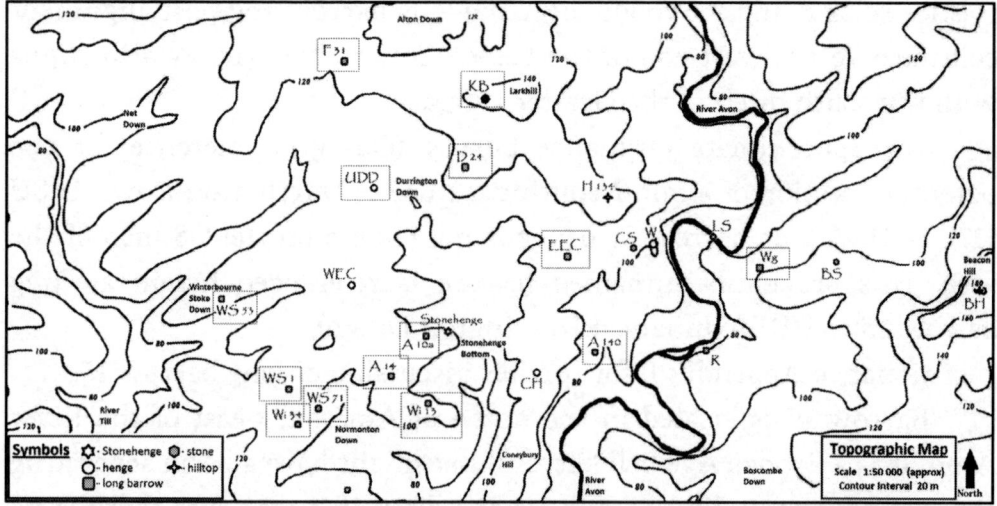

Figure 12: Locations of landscape elements listed on Table 1

The following comments concern long barrows 10 through 16.

Long barrow 10 (Knighton Barrow, Figheldean 27) is north and within site of the Greater Cursus but its axis has an east-west orientation that does not point toward the cursus, so Meaden did not include it during his measurements.

Meaden excluded long barrow 11 (Amesbury 10a) for lack of having ditches that would have assisted in taking accurate measurement. However in reviewing a map he noted a 60 degree orientation of the barrow's axis aligned it with the Greater Cursus east terminus.

Long barrow 12 (Amesbury 42) is immediately east and perpendicular to the east end of the Greater Cursus. It is directly along the lateral alignment of the cursus itself.

Long barrow 13 (Wilsford 30) located at Normanton Down has an equinoctial (east-west) axis and therefore was not included in Meaden's list of long barrow measurements; however the barrow aligns perpendicular to the north ditch at the northwest corner of the Greater Cursus.

Meaden excluded long barrow 14 (Watergate, Bulford I) located east of the River Avon and about three kilometers east of Amesbury 42 because it does not have a line of site to the cursus. Nonetheless, as noted in Table 1 Watergate aligns with two post locations which define summer solstice solar rising at Woodhenge. The long barrow and post alignment continues to the west end of the Lesser Cursus. The barrow also aligns with the south ditch of the Greater Cursus.

The approximate Ordnance Survey (OS) grid reference for the potential location of a mid-Neolithic feature at Durrington Down is SU 1171 4441. A long barrow or henge is not shown on the OS map of the area. This previously unnamed feature is referenced herein as long barrow 15 or UDD (Unnamed Durrington Down).

(Refer to Appendix B for further discussion of long barrow 15.)

Barrow 16 is located in the north of Amesbury east of the River Avon. It is a Bronze Age bell barrow that might have a berm separating the mound from a ditch. However the ditch if it was ever there is no longer apparent. A shallow ditch extends along the south side of the barrow. Skeletal remains of an adult inhumation were found in the barrow. The barrow has not been the site of modern intrusive and non-intrusive archaeological investigation. Thus the earliest date of human activity at that location remains unknown.

Some of the sixteen barrows noted above have been investigated using modern archaeological means and their age has been determined to within a range acceptable to the archaeological community. Dates of construction for other barrows have not been determined. Indeed some of the barrows have not yet been investigated for the presence of artefacts. It is believed each dates to the mid-Neolithic at about the time the two cursus were built.

Based on data obtained from laboratory analyses archaeologists consider the Greater Cursus and Lesser Curses contemporary and built sometime between about 3600 and 3300 BC. A date of 3480 BC is a reasonable estimated date of construction based on the evidence. Similarly, the long barrows are generally attributed to the mid-Neolithic, during the fourth millennium. Currently the evidence points to their dates of construction to be within a similar range as the cursuses, such that 3480 BC is a date that can be applied in general. Given the readily identifiable spatial relationships between the contemporaneous long barrows and cursus, it is not surprising that they form a geometrical network that was intended.

In general round barrows on Salisbury Plain date to about the mid-third millennium and later. Therefore they are not of concern for understanding the Neolithic Landscape. However there are instances when round barrows have been encountered overlying or replacing certain former long barrow sites. This suggests an earlier date for human activity at some round barrow locations, a time that may be much earlier than the date of round barrow construction. We can safely say that orientations and locations of the long barrows and round barrows are evidence of barrow construction after, if not contemporaneous with the two cursus.

While not surprising, it is curious that people would align burial barrows with the cursus, and the Greater Cursus in particular. There are literally dozens of alignments between two, three, even four of the sixteen barrows, two cursus termini, two henges and two hill tops. But beyond simple curiosity we should reasonably expect there was purpose to investing great time and effort accomplishing this network of alignments across Salisbury Plain. Alignments of three or more features are certainly of interest. Each feature has a specific location—a point or node—along an alignment. Alignments may be seen as links between modes.

Considering the local physiographic context, great size of the Stonehenge sacred landscape, and rudimentary surveying techniques that were commonly used during the Neolithic using the unaided eye, we can expect each chain of nodes and links to be constructed to within an accuracy of one or two degrees. And indeed, this is what we find on

Salisbury Plain. However, we should not necessarily interpret lack of better accuracy as error of alignment. It is very possible, and probable, they the alignments were sufficiently accurate to serve their purpose when constructed, since better accuracy could have been easily accomplished.

Since Meaden's discovery, efforts were made to identify rising or setting points of the Sun, Moon, and various stars along alignments created by long barrows and one or the other of the cursus, extending to the horizon. No set of astronomical alignments has been identified that can help us understand the purpose of the network of barrow-cursus alignments. However the fact that each of Meaden's nine long barrows aligns with one or the other cursus terminal suggests a common purpose for the cursus and barrows. As we are about to discover upon further analysis, they are indeed related.

One alignment that stands out immediately includes the west portion of the south ditch and bank of the Greater Cursus. Looking at the Ordinance Survey map 130 (scale 1:25000) of the Stonehenge area, it appears that Watergate long barrow east of the River Avon might be in alignment with the ditch and bank, as well as the site of long barrow Winterbourne Stoke 53, almost 2 kilometers west of the cursus west end (Refer to Figure 4). Neither the cursus nor Winterbourne Stoke 53 can be seen from Watergate. However using basic surveying principles we can easily resolve that matter. Simply, we sight intermediate locations between two known locations along the alignment (Figure 13).

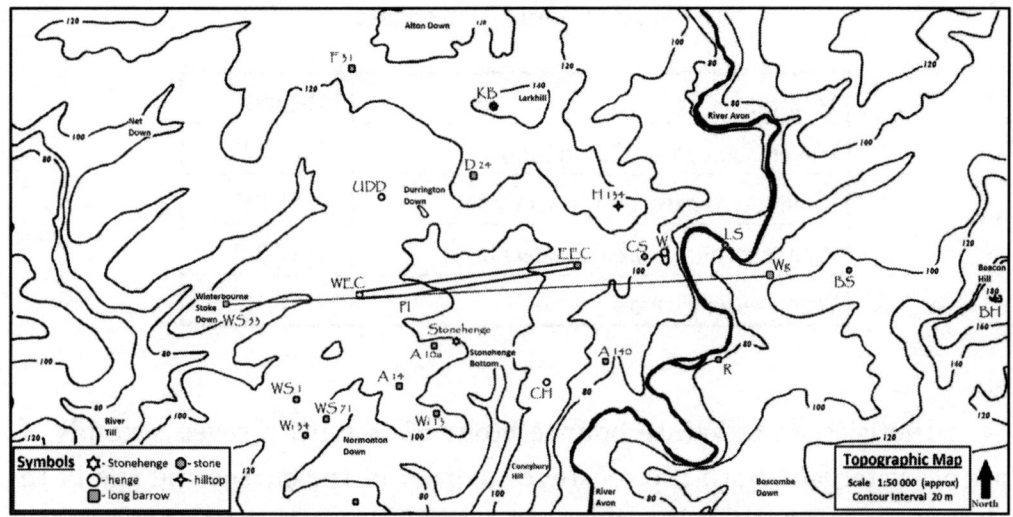

**Figure 13: Alignment of points from long barrow WS53
to long barrow Wg**

To find out if the two long barrows are in fact aligned with the west third of the Greater Cursus' south ditch we need to determine the latitude of each point of concern along the potential alignment. The locations are

- Winterbourne Stoke 53

- the southwest corner of the Greater Cursus

- the point of intersection (PI) in the cursus' south ditch and bank between the section from the southwest corner of the cursus meets the line extending west from the cursus southeast corner, forming an angle of about 84°, and

- Watergate.

The results are shown in Table 2. They are astounding.

Table 2: Latitude of Points between Winterbourne Stoke 53 and Watergate

Location	Latitude
Winterbourne Stoke 53 long barrow	57° 11' 04"
Southwest corner of the Greater Cursus	57° 11' 06"
PI on south ditch/bank of Greater Cursus	57° 11' 06"
Watergate long barrow	57° 11' 11"

The latitude of Winterbourne Stoke 53 is within seven seconds of arc of Watergate. Both the southwest corner of the cursus and the PI in the cursus south ditch line have the same latitude (57° 11' 06"), within the range of latitudes of the two long barrows which are located at the ends of the alignment. Four simple analyses demonstrate how precise the alignment is from one barrow to the other (Refer to Figure 12).

- First we assume the two end points of the alignment are located exactly as designed and the alignment is to be straight between them. In this case the error in alignment at each barrow location is 0° 00' 00"; the southeast corner of the cursus has an error of +0.27"; the PI in the south ditch has an error of -0.39."

- Second we assume the latitudes of Winterbourne Stoke 53 and the south ditch are as planned. We also assume the alignment is intended to cross the south ditch equidistant from the southeast corner and PI. In this case the error in latitude concerns Watergate only, the amount being +0.19."

- Third we assume the south ditch of the cursus was planned to be oriented precisely due east-west, as the latitudes of each end point confirm it is, and that this was the intended alignment from barrow to barrow. In this case the error of Winterbourne Stoke 53 is -2" and the error of Watergate is +5."

- Fourth, we assume Winterbourne Stoke 53 is at the center of a circle with Watergate on the circle, one radius length (about 7.18 km) from the center. The circle's circumference is 45.11 km, and one second of arc is equivalent to 3.5 cm (1.4 in). The largest error in the three cases above concerns Watergate, being +5" off alignment with the south ditch of the cursus. That error is equivalent to 17.5 cm (7 inches) of arc across a distance of 7.18 km, or 2.44 cm/km (or 0.0000244 km/km). A width of 2.44 cm is less than the diameter of a modern day range rod used by surveyors as an aid in determining straight line distances, angles and changes in ground surface elevation.

This is an amazing feat of Neolithic surveying! More so, the alignment is virtually due east-west. It is doubtful that such precision was expected nor required by the people who laid it out about 5500 years ago. However, in tandem with additional findings described herein it can be concluded that the alignment is intentional. It is a surprising demonstration of Neolithic surveying and construction abilities which rival the prehistoric 550-mile diameter sacred hoop extending across the northern Great Plains of North America, built by Native Americans who at the time were living in the context of Neolithic culture (Burley 2012). Just as importantly, the precision of the alignment demonstrates that it was both intentional and meaningful to the people who constructed it.

Figure 14 depicts locations of fourteen long barrows, one round barrow, one bell barrow, two hilltops (Larkhill and Hill 134) and two henges (Stonehenge and Coneybury Henge) plotted about the Greater and Lesser cursus. The long barrows were constructed during the mid-4th millennium BC, at about the same time as the two cursuses, but no pattern to the plan of Neolithic features is readily apparent. Additional information is needed to solve the mystery of the long barrow—cursus alignments. Let's look at other features of the landscape in detail.

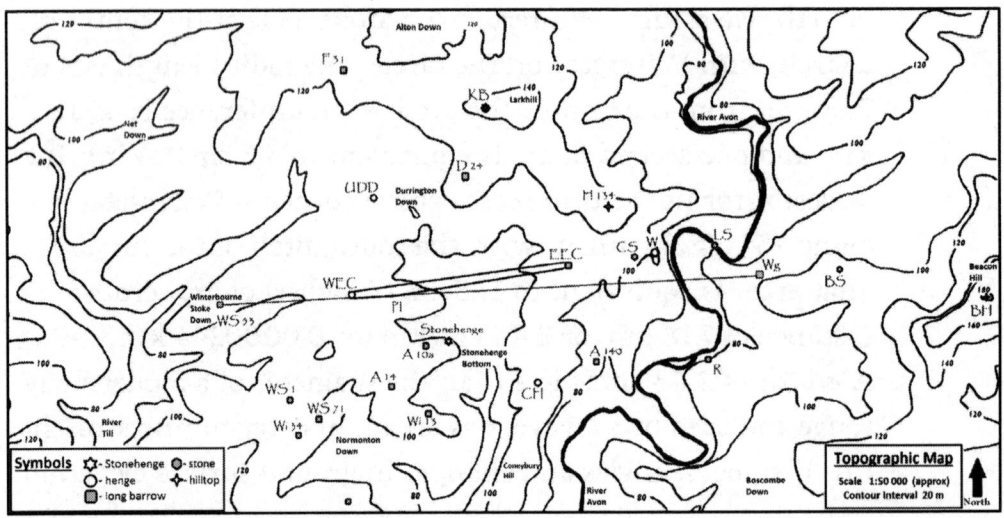

**Figure 14: Fourteen long barrows, one round barrow,
one bell barrow, two hilltops and two henges located about the Greater
and Lesser cursus.**

Henges

It was mentioned above that symbols communicating the cyclical nature of birth, life, death and re-birth are found across the Stonehenge Landscape. Henges and round barrows are obvious examples of the symbolism. Most often greater than 20m meters in diameter, a henge is a circular or sub-circular ditch and bank; it is typical for the ditch to be inside the bank.[13] Figure 15 includes sample plans of several henges. Inspiration for creating these structures, some quite monumental in size, has been attributed to continental Europe with development of causewayed enclosures of various configurations.[14, 15] The source location and purpose of their construction in Britain remain unclear. Locations of the earliest henges have been proposed at Wessex (such as at Avebury and Stonehenge) and Orkney (Ring of Brodgar and Stones of Stenness).[16, 17]

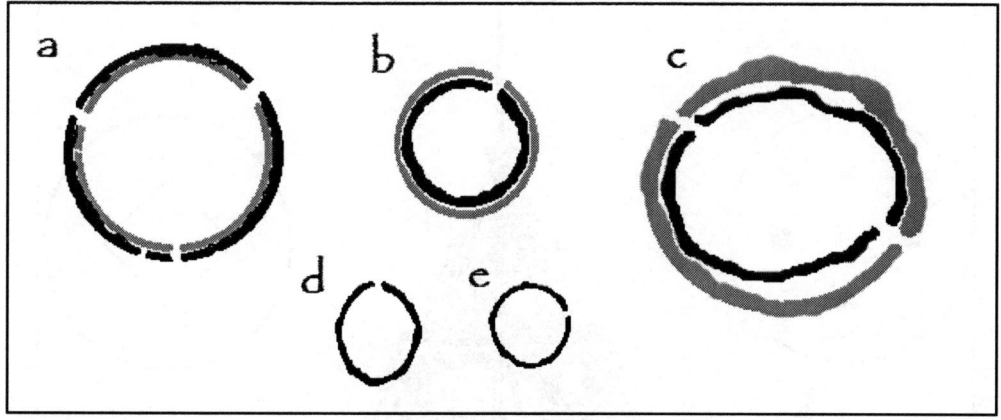

Figure 15: Plans of several henges: a) Stonehenge *(based on Cleal et al 1995)*, **b) Woodhenge** *(based on Cunnington 1929, plate 3)*, **c) Durrington Walls** *(based on Wainwright and Longworth 1971, figure 2)*, **d) Coneybury** *(based on Richards 1990, figure 97)*, **e) Waterbourne Stoke** *(based on David and Payne, 1997, figure 13)*

For ancient and indigenous cultures circles (and spheres) separate interior space from exterior space, inner space of spirit from infinite space beyond. This may explain why there is scant evidence of henges being occupied, since their function is spiritual rather than corporeal. Circles and squares of stone or timber are often indicative of a spiritual function, particularly in wood-framed architecture.[18] Numerous wood-framed Neolithic structures are identified by archaeological investigations conducted across Britain and Ireland. Many of the building remains provide evidence of four posts placed in the central part of the structure so as to form a square. The purpose of such construction is unresolved. However the same geometrical setting of four posts in the central area of a house is found in Neolithic architecture of Central America. The geometry is demonstrated to have sacred meaning. Figure 16 illustrates a architecture of traditional Mayan houses.

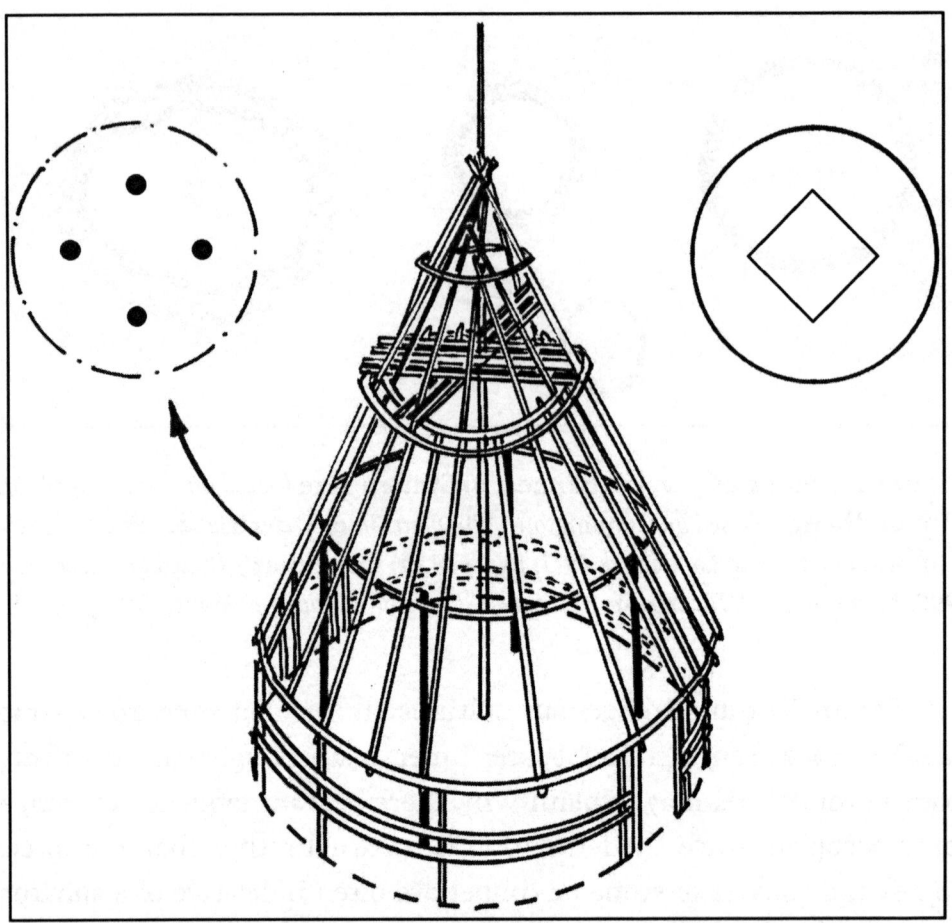

Figure 16: Example of four posts placed as a square as part of a traditional Mayan 'Neolithic' house. The square has sacred symbolic meaning and is related as such to the circle. The same geometrical structure of four posts has been found at many Neolithic sites across Britain. (figure from Burley, 2012).

The center is the unique point surrounded by perfect geometrical symmetry. So burials are not unexpected when encountered in some henges subject to archaeological excavation. For example, a burial near the center of Woodhenge contains the remains of a child. Two burials were discovered near the center of Avebury. The purpose of burials at those locations is unknown, but the context of burial placed near the center of sacred space clearly indicates sacred intent. Bone and cremated remains of humans and animals have been encountered at Stonehenge.

Henge burials have been dated to either prior to or after henge construction.

Henges may be found as features of a larger sacred landscape, Stonehenge being the archetype in this regard. Opposed to earlier burial structures, they are most commonly located in low-lying areas rather than higher topography such as hilltops. However it is a mistake to assume topography was a more important factor than orientation of the henge with regard to entrance and exit locations and astronomical features pertinent to the site. Remember that purification, source, patterns of form, time and place are all vital components of sacred artistry including architecture. Communication of the sacred is symbolized by the circle. Form is evidence of function.

By not recognizing the sacred symbolism of a circle, the full extent of the meaning and purpose of henges and their associated inner structures cannot be realized. What remains are the mundane and scientific explanations of purpose.

- Measuring positions of sunrise and sunset

- Synchronizing the annual calendar for agricultural purpose

- Scheduling rituals rather than celebrating spirituality

- Identifying solar equinox and solstice positions

- Framing specific constellations

Chapter 1 through Chapter 4 provides an outline concerning the context of the Stonehenge Landscape with regard to the people, environment, symbolism and monumental features of the area ca. 3500 BC. We are ready to begin analysis of the Stonehenge Landscape. The purpose is to find out if spatial characteristics of mid-Neolithic elements such as the Greater Cursus, long barrows, and locations of other features of the landscape can help us understand the purpose of the size, type, orientation and location of those structures.

I first learned of Terence Meaden's discovery of the nine long barrow-cursus alignments when I saw a particular map he included in his book 'Stonehenge: The Secret of the Solstice'. The map depicts locations of the long barrows with respect to the cursus. Table 2 of the book lists the bearing of the major axis for each barrow aligned toward the cursus. It quickly appeared to me that I was looking at a map of specific locations and alignments that a land surveyor would make prior to and during a construction project. But it isn't a map of pairs of points connected by a line. It is a map of triads of points creating triangles. Could the purpose of the various alignments between the cursus and long barrows be found by reconstructing the surveyors map ca. 3500 BC?

Chapter 5
A Plan in Mind

Triangulation

When it is desired to determine a specific location on the ground surface by means of land survey, one of the easiest and most common ways is the method of 'triangulation'. Simply, if locations of two points of a triangle are known (surveyors call those locations 'control points') and the angle from the line between those locations (the 'baseline') to a third point is known, then the location of the third point can be determined. Three points not in a straight line form corners of a triangle. They also define a planar surface or area.

Triangulation is a simple, quick and accurate method for plotting points, creating alignments, and defining areas. At its core it is an easy way to measure space, an exercise of fundamental geometry that does not require mathematics beyond adding and subtracting. The Neolithic agricultural package necessitated setting points and alignments, and delineating and mapping plots of land for cultivation. Egyptian records of surveying by triangulation go back 5000 years, to the beginning of ancient history.[1] It was used in ancient Sumeria, India and China.

Even today most map production is based on the setting of control points and baselines from which a series of triangles of known shape and size extend across the mapping surface. That network of triangles may then be subdivided into smaller triangles, increasing accuracy of the map with each subdivision. The process begins with setting control points and baselines surrounding or extending through the area to be mapped.

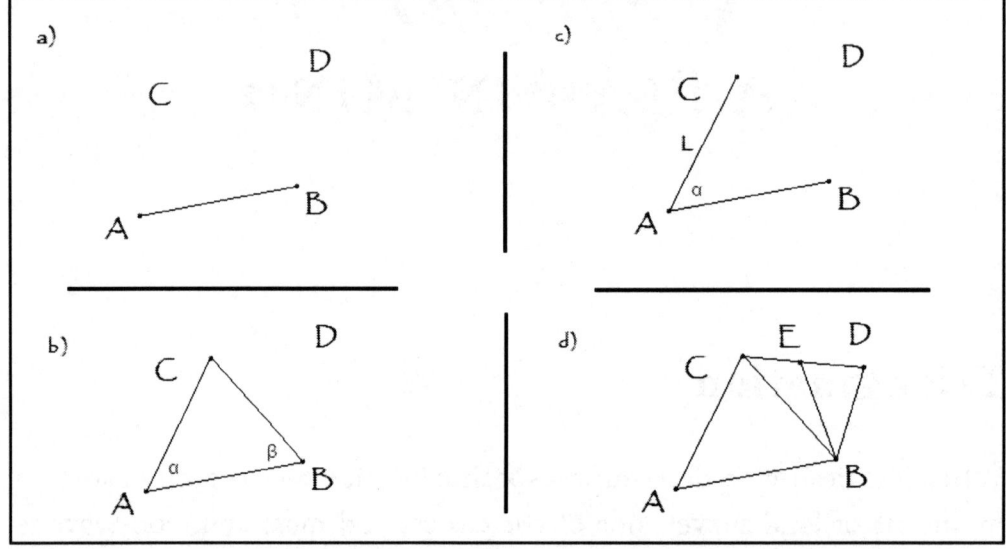

Figure 17: Using triangulation. a) baseline AB, points C and D, b) turn angles α and β to find point C, c) b) using angle α and distance L to locate point C, d) subdividing triangle BCD

As an example of the method, suppose we have two control points A and B (Refer to Figure 17). Those two points define two corners of a triangle, and the alignment of those two points defines a baseline (17a). To locate point C (third corner of the triangle), we turn angle α at corner A, providing the sightline from A to C. Similarly, we turn angle β at corner B, providing the sightline from B to C. The two sightlines will intersect at point C (17b). We can also determine point C if we know angle α and the required length from A to C, or angle β and the length from B to C (Figure 17c). The procedure can be repeated to locate point D. It can also be used for subdividing triangle BCD into smaller areas (17d).

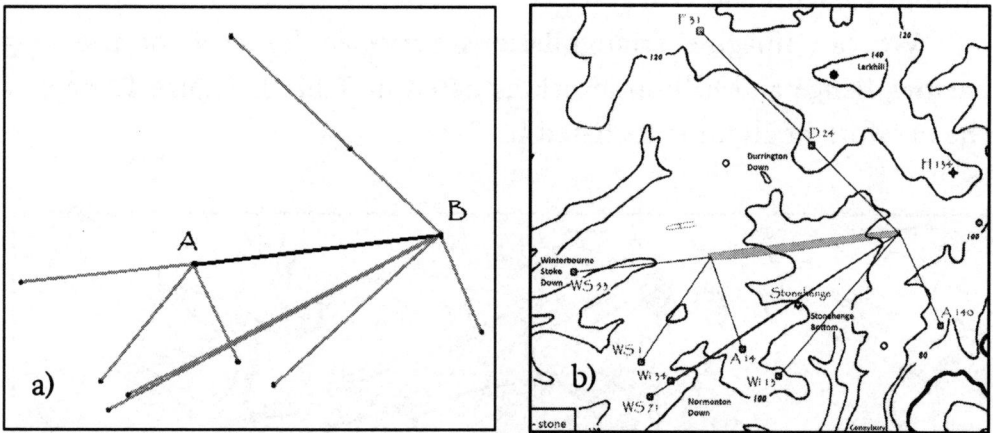

Figure 18: a) Line segment AB and nine points with unique angles and distances to one end or the other of the line segment; b) There are nine long barrows each with the long axis oriented within 3 degrees of the direction toward either the west end or east end of the Greater Cursus. Long barrow Amesbury 42 adjoins the east end of the cursus, oriented perpendicular to its major axis.

Figure 18a shows a baseline with two endpoints and a number of outlying points each having a unique distance and direction to one or the other endpoint. Figure 18b is a plan of the Greater Cursus and the nine long barrows each with a unique distance and direction to an end of the cursus. Obviously the two figures have much in common. It is apparent that the east and west ends of the Greater Cursus are two control points, and the cursus between them is the baseline. Using triangulation the location of each long barrow can be determined. By constructing the baseline (the cursus), any location within sight of the east and west ends can be spatially related to the cursus using triangulation.

What of the other barrows, the henges and hilltops? We have already seen that Watergate and Winterbourne 53 align with the west portion of the south ditch of the cursus. Four additional long barrows are farther from, but do not have a direct line of sight to the cursus. Also note locations of the Coneybury Henge near Coneybury hilltop, and hilltops Larkhill and Hill 134.

We can imagine trianglulations surveyed for each of the long barrow, henge and hilltop locations listed in Table 1. Figure 19 depicts the network of alignments listed in Table 1.

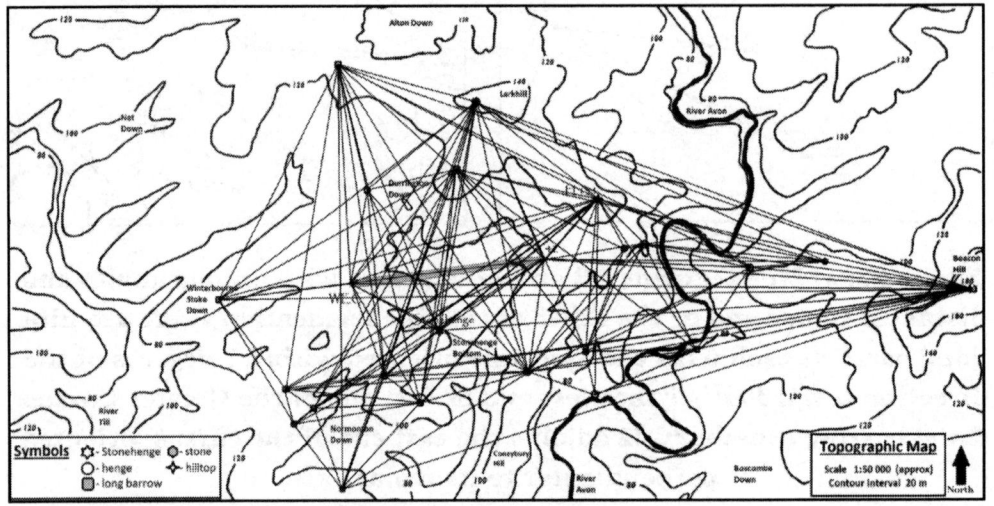

Figure 19: Alignments listed in Table 1 between barrows, henges and hilltops.

Looking at the plan we see most of the alignments are located in the central portion of the network, specifically between the west and east termini of the Greater Cursus. We know we can set or reset any of the points using triangulation. Known angles and distances are all we need.

Network points outside the central area are not generally viewable from many of the locations within the interior of the plan. From a surveying perspective barrows 1, 2, 4, 5, 11, 13, 14, 16 and 9 (and possibly the Lesser Cursus) likely served as control points for constructing the central network, or were extensions of triangulation beyond the core network. In either case we remove those eight points from the plan of alignments so that the core network and baselines are more readily apparent. The resulting network is shown in Figure 20.

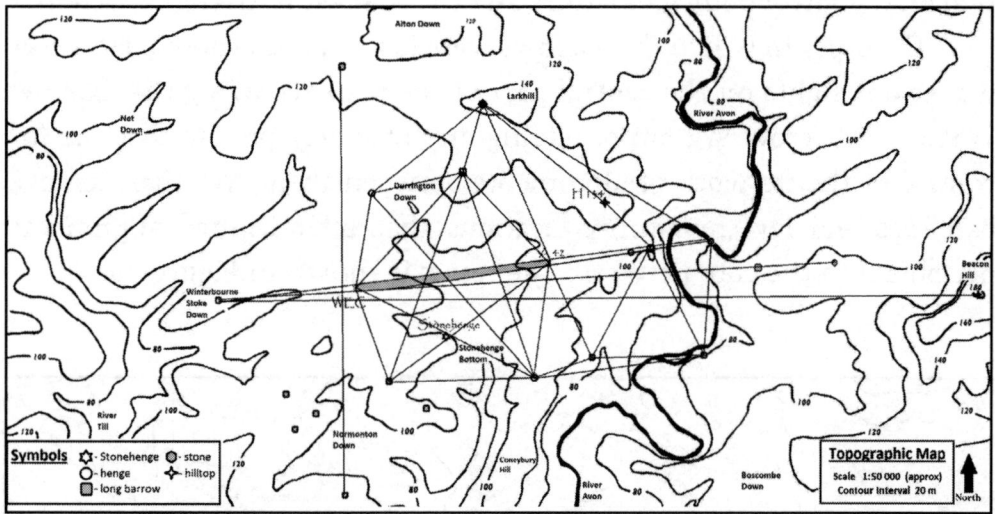

Figure 20: Nodes and links of baselines and core network. Most naked eye alignments between nodes are not shown for clarity.

We've already seen the importance of barrows WS53 and Wg as due west and due east control points of a baseline including the west portion of the cursus south ditch. The north-south alignment of barrow 9 (Figheldean 31, northwest corner of the network) and the west terminus are evidence of an important function of the barrow as one end point of a due north-south baseline. However its significance as a control point may have lessened once the many other points within the network were available to reset the west terminus if necessary. It is quite possible that barrow 9 was located as an extension of the east terminus-Durrington 24 alignment and along the line extending due north from the west terminus, becoming not only a control point but important to the people who constructed the long barrow.

Barrows 2, 4, 5, 11 and 16, and the Lesser Cursus offer alignments to the Greater Cursus termini, but loses some significance for us since the core points of the network provide more than enough control for the plan. Those five barrows and cursus may have been placed to take advantage of, or to create alignments that relate the respective barrow or cursus to the network. In other words they were located by triangulation after control points, baselines and the first set of triangles were set.

The order in which the barrows were located is unknown. However we set our sights on the central part of the plan, knowing that barrow WS53 and barrow Wg are providing an extremely precise baseline for control of the network of alignments between them. We then remove baselines and few remaining locations that offer limited alignments peripheral to the core network. The result is shown in Figure 21.

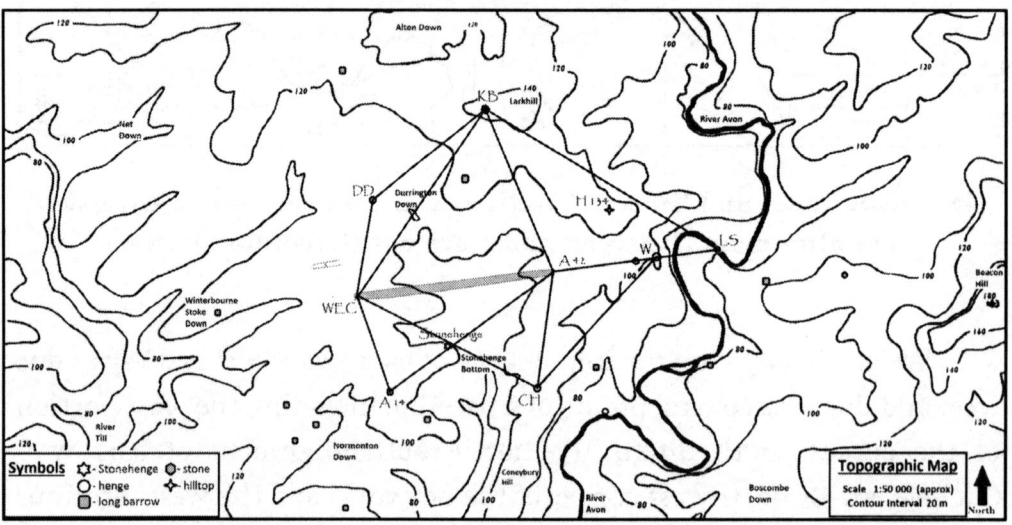

Figure 21: Ten remaining nodes within the core network of long barrows, henges, Greater Cursus and high points. Alignments shown are limited to fundamental triangulations with the cursus termini. Alignments to H134 and Amesbury 140 are not illustrated.

There is something quite remarkable about eight of the ten locations in the network's central area. Excepting barrow 7 (Amesbury 140) and Hill 134, each of other eight locations has direct lines of site to at least 7 points that are located either peripherally or within the central area. We may consider the east terminus as the geographical center of the network. Amesbury 140 and Hill 134 offer control for certain portions of the network, but become less important as the other eight locations provide additional control over larger portions of the area. However we should not discount the importance of Amesbury 140 and Hill 134 to design of the Stonehenge Landscape. They were important in other ways associated with certain features of the area, as we shall see later.

The network of alignments now concerns eight locations in the core of the network: the west and east termini, and counterclockwise from the west terminus: barrow 3 (Amesbury 14), Coneybury Henge, Woodhenge, Larkhill, barrow 10 (Knighton Barrow), and barrow 15 (UDD). The many alignments associated with each point suggests not only the import of those locations and features, but more so an important relationship amongst all of the surveyed locations.

(Refer to Appendix D to find out why the many alignments show in Figure 21, including those between Meaden's nine long barrows and the cursus, should be viewed as two-way alignments, not only toward the cursus or other node, but in the reverse direction as well.)

A Network

Very accurate alignments (measured to within two to three degrees or less) can be visually set between two or more points with the aid of intermediary points at key topographical locations. Baseline WS53-Wg is evidence that a complex, well thought out plan related to the Greater Cursus and nine long barrows was put into effect 5500 years ago. There is every reason to assume the network was intended, conceptualized, planned and constructed. Its purpose must have been to create an effect—perhaps vital in nature—that people would understand and relate 5500 years ago.

Leaving aside Meaden's nine long barrows, of the remaining five nodes in the alignment network one is located at a long barrow on top of a prominent hill, one is at a henge, and three are additional barrow locations. Being human made features, their locations may relate to natural features of the geography. Refer to Figure 21 to see locations of features noted in the discussion below.

From a surveying standpoint (identifying specific locations on the ground surface) topographically high points are most valuable. About 1.3 km (0.8 mi) southwest and 40 m (130 ft) below Knighton Barrow is UDD. The highest elevation in this area of Salisbury Plain is the top of Larkhill. At the hilltop much of the ground surface to the south can be seen other than some stretches of valley bottoms such as along the River Avon. Most of the network alignments can be observed from Larkhill. For this reason it is highly probable that the hilltop served as a critically important control point for the entire network. Each of the other centrally located nodes of the network (including the two cursus termini) is visible from that location. It is a first rate location for using triangulation across the Stonehenge sacred landscape.

Likewise, barrow Durrington 24 is well located for observing the network area since it is high up on the south flank of Larkhill, about 1 km (0.6 mi) from the summit. About 1.3 km (0.8 mi) southwest and 40 m (130 ft) below Knighton Barrow is UDD. This area has been under cultivation for perhaps thousands of years. Barrows and other structures in the area are little more than crop marks, if apparent at all. Yet the location was ideal for setting alignments across much of the plain to the south, from the west terminus to Coneybury Hill.

The physical geography of Salisbury Plain would play a key role in siting the cursus, barrows and henges upon the landscape. Yet the various nodes of the alignment network were located with relative ease using triangulation given the local topography. Perhaps the entire ground surface within the central network of alignments could be seen from one location or another of the central plan.

The numerous alignments available at each location tie together the plan of cursus, barrows, henges and hilltops into a unified structure. Both Amesbury 14 and Coneybury Henge were located to take advantage of the viewshed toward the north, from Winterbourne 53 to Wood-henge and the overlapping viewshed shared between them.

What is that structure, and what does it represent in this Neolithic sacred landscape? The area is an architectural landscape, designed, surveyed and engineered. Geometry and the sacred were understood here, as it was by numerous prehistoric, ancient and indigenous cultures around the world. Geometry and sacred knowledge common to the Neolithic can help us identify and understand the symbolism expressed on Salisbury Plain.

Reverse Engineering

The people who built the many mid-Neolithic features on the Stonehenge landscape provided no documentation of their grand plan. However, the previous discussions provide us the plans and tools necessary to locate and identify the symbolic structure they constructed 5500 years ago. The plans are maps of the hilltops, cursus, long barrows, henges, and other natural and manmade features of the area. The tools are fundamental surveying procedures for setting alignments, turning angles and measuring distances. With the plan before us and knowledge of those basic surveying methods we will decipher the apparently chaotic array of cursus, barrows, henges and other Neolithic features we see on the Stonehenge Landscape. It is a process of reverse engineering, deconstructing the complex of features and alignments until the essence of the design shows through.

Plans

Many thousands of years ago central south England was devoid of any evidence of human activity. By 10,000 years ago this was no longer so. Three pits, and perhaps many more, were excavated nearby Stonehenge by about 8000 BC and large posts or tree trunks were placed in them. During the 4th millennium BC the rate of development on Salisbury Plain increased dramatically as pits were dug and filled with various materials, small wood-framed buildings were constructed, stones and wooden posts were founded below the ground surface, and major features such as long barrows and the cursus began to appear on the landscape. There is evidence of land use at Stonehenge, Woodhenge, on Coneybury Hill and King Barrow Ridge dating to the Mesolithic. Local henge excavation would begin by about 3000 BC.

Figure 22 is a topographic map of the Stonehenge Landscape. The contour interval on the map is 20 meters, and the ground surface elevation ranges from about 75-to 185 m (250-to 610 ft above sea level). During the late Mesolithic and early Neolithic, about 7000 to 6000 years ago, prior to construction of barrows, henges and other manmade features of the area, the hills and valleys at Salisbury Plain appeared very much as they do now, and waterways such as the River Avon to the east and River Till to the west flowed south much as we see them today. Most of the habitat was grassland. This was very much a natural, pristine landscape.

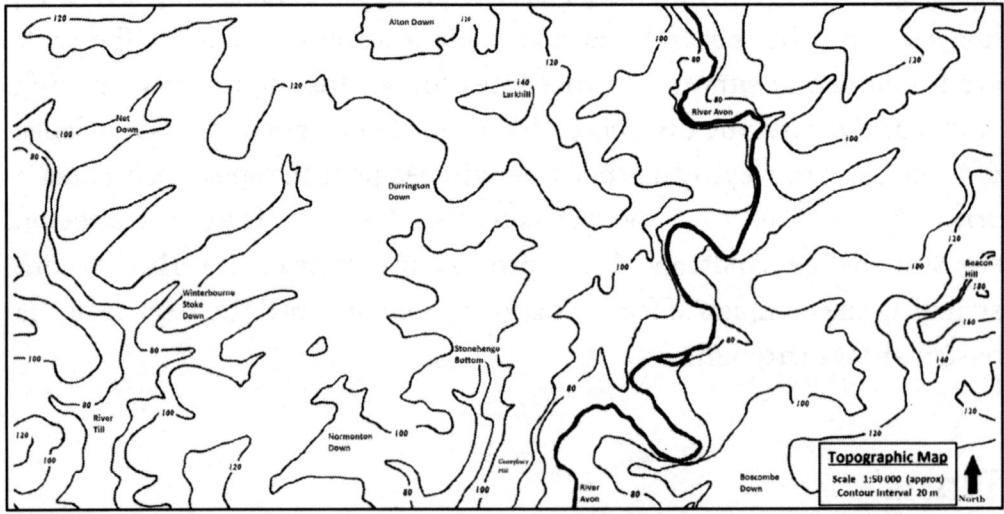

Figure 22: Topographic map of the Stonehenge landscape. Other than names of local physiographic features such as hills, downs and rivers, the illustration is limited to the ground surface contour lines at 20m intervals and channel of the River Avon. At this scale the current landscape is very similar to that of the Neolithic Era.

Archaeologists have found evidence of minor excavations, pits, and post and stone holes dating to the mid-Neolithic at various locations of the landscape. Between 3500 and 2900 BC sites such as Stonehenge,

Woodhenge, Coneybury Henge, the Greater and Lesser cursus were being developed. Long barrows were sited within several kilometers of the Greater Cursus. Figure 23 depicts locations of hilltops, cursus, long barrows, henges, and megaliths located on the Stonehenge Landscape. While not all sites dating between 3500 and 2900 BC are shown, archaeological studies indicate that elements marked on the map are significant features of this landscape.

Figure 23: Locations of Neolithic structures located within about 4km of Stonehenge, including long barrow, henges, single megaliths, and hilltops where archaeologists have encountered evidence of Neolithic activity. Humans have interacted with the landscape for many thousands of years. The map does not show all locations where Neolithic artefacts and structures have been encountered in the area, which may number in the thousands.

Table 3 provides acronyms of features mapped in Figure 23. Those acronyms are included in Figure 24. The table lists each acronym and its respective natural or manmade element of the Stonehenge Landscape. Archaeological sites are listed by location from west to east, and classified in one of three groups—West of Greater Cursus, Between Ends of Cursus, and East of Greater Cursus.

Table 3: Acronyms of Sites Noted on Maps and Discussed in the Text

Acronym	Site Name	Landscape Feature Type	West or East of Cursus and Coneybury Hill
West of Greater Cursus			
WS53	Winterbourne Stoke 53	long barrow	west
WS1	Winterbourne Stoke 1	long barrow	"
WS71	Winterbourne Stoke 71	long barrow	"
Wi34	Wilsford 34	long barrow	"
LC	Lesser Cursus	cursus	"
Between Ends of cursus			
F31	Figheldean 31	long barrow	west
WEC	West End Greater Cursus	cursus terminus	"
DD	Unnamed Durrington Down	barrow or henge	"
A14	Amesbury 14	long barrow	"
Wi13	Wilsford 13	long barrow	"
D24	Durrington 24	long barrow	"
KB	Knighton Barrow	long barrow (Figheldean 27)	on ridgeline
CH	Coneybury Henge	henge	on ridgeline
EEC	East End Greater Cursus	cursus terminus	east end cursus
A42	Amesbury 42	long barrow	on ridgeline
East of Greater Cursus			
A140	Amesbury 140	long barrow	east
BSH	Bluestonehenge	henge	"
H134	Hilltop Elevation 134	hilltop	"
CS	Cuckoo Stone	megalith	"
WH	Woodhenge	henge	"
LS	Lost Stone	megalith	"

Acronym	Site Name	Landscape Feature Type	West or East of Cursus and Coneybury Hill
Wg	Watergate	long barrow	"
BS	Bulford Stone	megalith	"
BH	Beacon Hill	hilltop	"

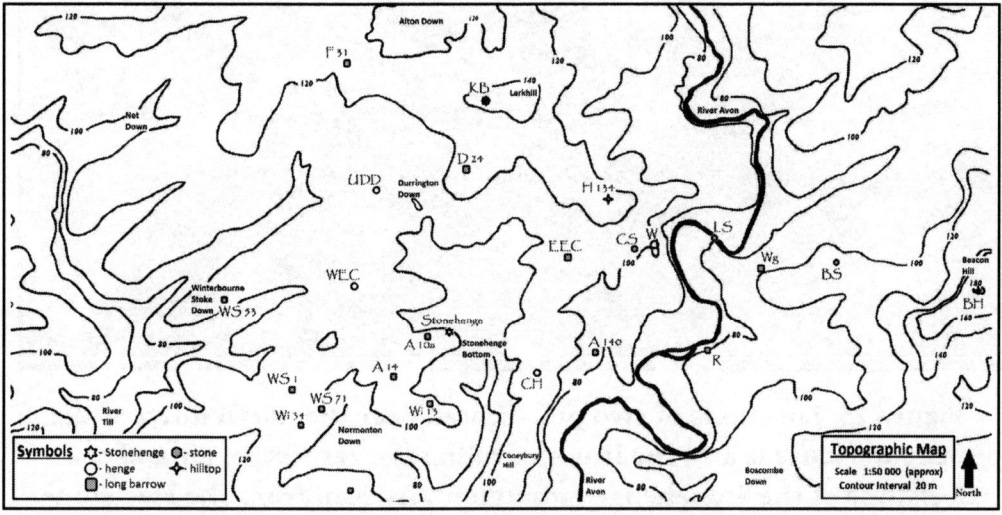

Figure 24: Acronyms of Neolithic sites mentioned in this book. Stonehenge is located near the center of the map. Refer to text for definitions of referenced acronyms.

In 2011 a team of archaeologists and geophysicists discovered evidence of pits at two locations near the north ditch of the Greater Cursus.[2] The findings are an important result of the Stonehenge Hidden Landscape Project led by the University of Birmingham. One of the pits is located on the line between summer solstice sunrise and the Heel Stone at Stonehenge. The other pit is located along the line between summer solstice sunset and the Heel Stone.

The pit locations and alignments to the Heelstone are shown in Figure 25. Each alignment was probably set with the Heelstone serving as the southernmost point, then extending each line toward the respective solar event using the method of triangulation (Figure 26). The findings provide support for the theory that at some point in its development the axis of Stonehenge was oriented toward midsummer sunrise, an alignment documented by William Stukeley in 1720.

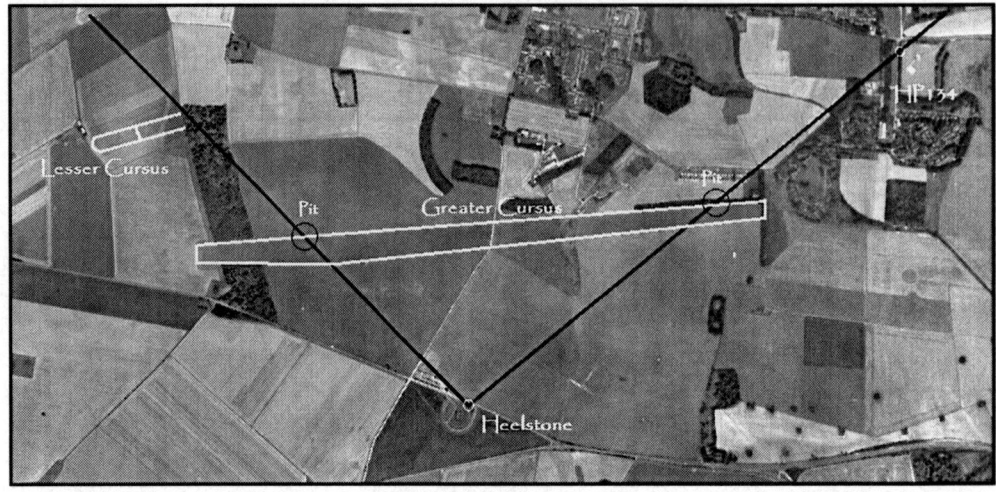

Figure 25: Locations of two pits located near the north ditch of the Greater Cursus and the line extending the respective pit and the Heelstone of the Stonehenge monument. As seen from the Heelstone, the line on the left is aligned with the summer solstice sunset and the east end of the lesser Cursus; the line on right is aligned with Hilltop 134 and the summer solstice sunrise. (aerial photograph courtesy University of Birmingham)

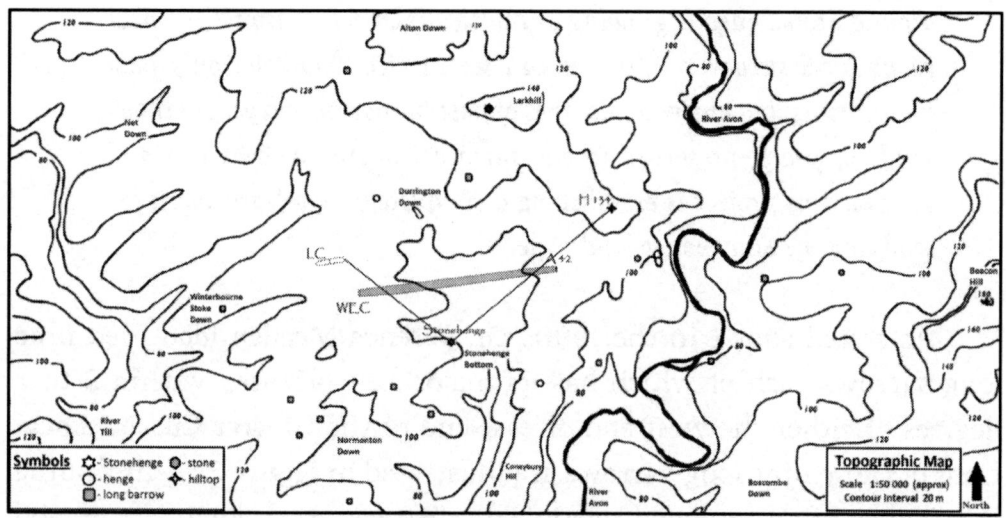

Figure 26: Triangulation of Stonehenge with the east end of the Lesser Cursus and Hilltop H134 on Larkhill. The alignments cross the Greater Cursus, between WEC and long barrow A42.

Discovery of the two alignments led to speculation that they delineate ceremonial procession ways, similar to the idea that the Greater Cursus itself was constructed for use as a procession way associated with ceremonies honoring the dead. Professor Vince Gaffney, archaeologist and project leader from the IBM Visual and Spatial Technology Centre at the University of Birmingham, sensed a connection between the two alignments and rituals practiced by the culture that created them, saying "This is the first time we have seen anything quite like this at Stonehenge and it provides a more sophisticated insight into how rituals may have taken place within the Cursus and the wider landscape . . . . The results from this new survey help us to appreciate just how complex these activities were and how intimate these societies were with the natural world."[3]

Paul Garwood of the University of Birmingham's Department of Ancient History, Classics and Archaeology commented on the discovery as it relates to the Stonehenge Landscape.

"Our knowledge of the ancient landscapes that once existed around Stonehenge is growing dramatically as we examine the new geophysical survey results. We can see in rich detail not only new monuments, but entire landscapes of past human activity, over thousands of years, preserved in sub-surface features such as pits and ditches. This project is establishing a completely new framework for studying the Stonehenge landscape."[4]

As stated above, in the 1990s Dr. Terence Meaden identified nine long barrows each of which has its major axis oriented within 2 to 3 degrees of either the west end or east end of the Greater Cursus. Locations of those nine long barrows are illustrated in Figure 27. This finding is evidence of an intended relationship between each long barrow and cursus. However, it points to three additional relationships of importance concerning the landscape.

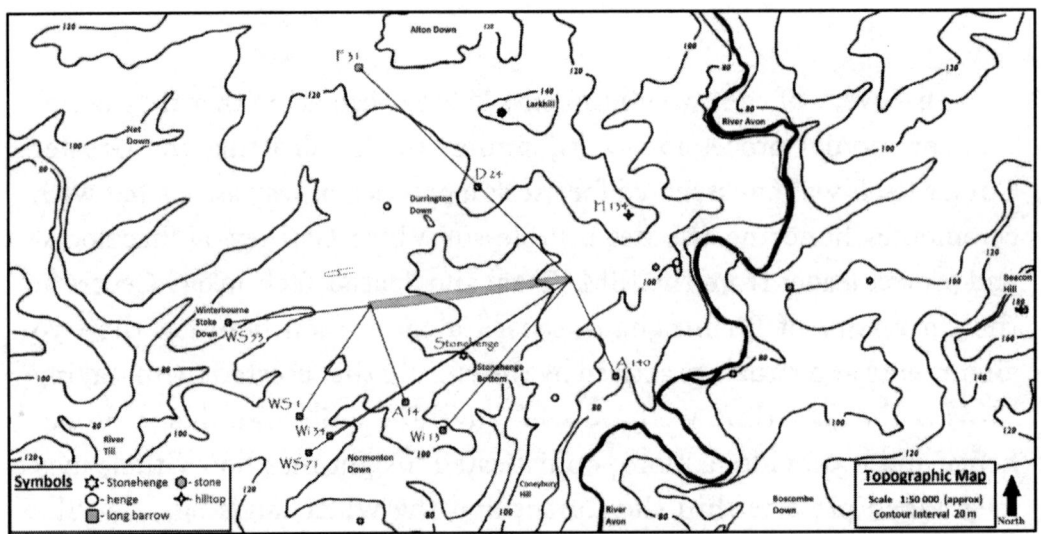

Figure 27: Nine alignments of long barrows with each major axis oriented to within two or three degrees of the direction toward one end or the other of the Greater Cursus. These are the long barrow alignments first noted by Terence Meaden.

First, three barrows are oriented toward the west end of the cursus, and therefore each of the three alignments between long barrow and cursus intersect at one unique location. This is evidence of spatial relationships between the long barrows themselves. Each is located a unique distance from the end of the cursus, with a unique angle turned from one alignment to another from a common point of intersection—the west end of the cursus.

Second, similar spatial relationships are found between the six long barrows oriented toward the east terminus of the cursus.

Third and most importantly, these spatial relationships between monuments are evidence of relationships between the people who built the long barrows, the bodies of people buried within the long barrows, and the purpose of the cursus. Long barrows are oriented toward the cursus. However other than its proximity to the barrows and their alignment to the ends of the cursus, there is no evidence of the cursus in and of itself having any relationship with death of human beings, or death in general.

Figure 28 shows a line connecting each of the nine long barrows to the cursus. Note that the termini of the Greater Cursus had to be surveyed onto the landscape before the long barrows could be oriented toward one end of the cursus or the other. This does not mean the cursus was constructed prior to the long barrow being built, only that the locations for the ends of the cursus had to be known before the long barrows could be oriented toward them. The various monument locations may be considered individual points surveyed onto the landscape, separated from each other by angles and distances.

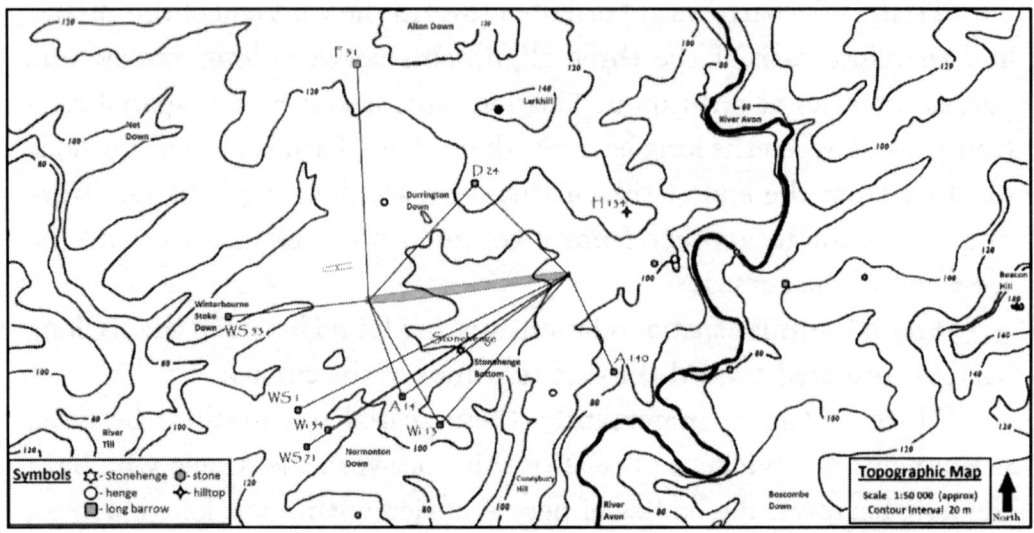

Figure 28: Line of sight alignments between the nine long barrows noted in Figure 21 and ends of the Greater Cursus. Note that line of site triangulations are limited to only three long barrow locations: D24, A 14 and Wi13.

We can now analyze the network of points (nodes) and lengths between nodes (links) as a series of triangulations. In other words locations and orientations of the long barrows about the cursus are evidence of triangulation used for the purpose of siting monuments onto the Stonehenge Landscape. Builders of the Stonehenge Landscape used triangulation to place long barrows and possibly other monuments according to some as yet unidentified plan. Our task is a matter of reverse engineering. We will use the known monument locations to identify triangulations that form the core geometry—the intended geometry—from which further triangulations were based. The plan of the Stonehenge Landscape is revealed when we discover that core geometry.

The next step, then, is to draw additional line of sight alignments between other long barrows with axes oriented toward the cursus termini, and additional lines of site between the cursus termini and significant monuments we know such as Stonehenge, Coneybury Henge, Woodhenge, and so forth. The alignments are depicted in Figure 29.

High points of the topography are also significant as valuable locations from which many triangulation surveys could be accomplished. Those locations include the top of Larkhill at Knighton Barrow and H134.

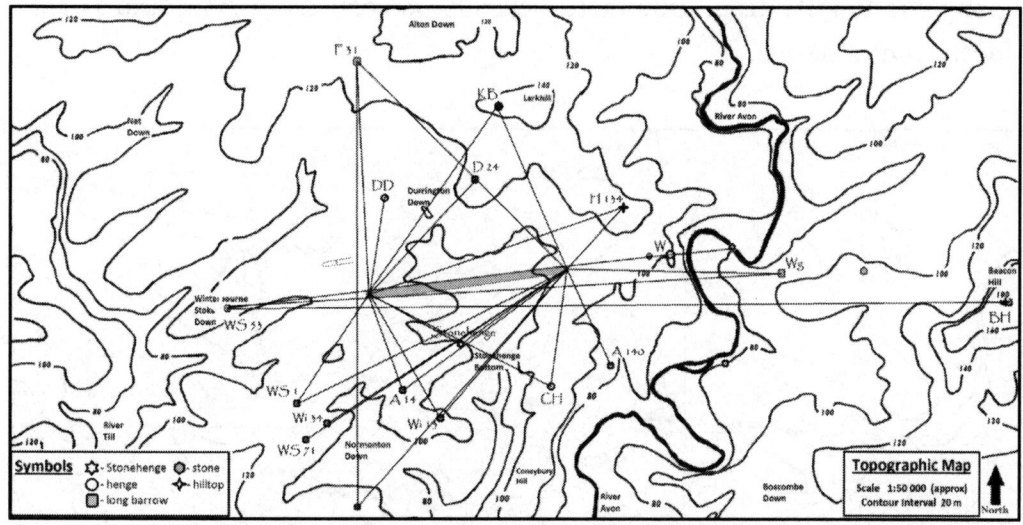

Figure 29: Map of Meaden's long barrow-cursus alignments and line of sight alignments between additional Neolithic features and the cursus. Most alignments form triangulations between the respective feature and ends of the cursus. Note an approximate bilateral symmetry north and south of the cursus. North-South and East-West baselines are shown.

(Refer to Appendix C for further discussion of the numerous alignments between long barrows, henges, cursus, and high point shown in Figure 29.)

(Refer to Appendix D for additional information about triangulation between the long barrows and termini of the cursus.)

Referring to Figure 30, it is evident that A14, CH, WH, KB and UDD provide a unified plan of points related to each other and the cursus. With the addition of WEC they form a hexagon of somewhat irregular shape surrounding the cursus. The polygon exhibits bi-lateral symmetry about the cursus. Stonehenge and EEC are located within the ring of other monuments. Several important facts are associated with these locations. Stonehenge, A14, CH, KB and UDD have lines of sight to both ends of the cursus. KB has a most prominent location at the top of Larkhill. Henges are located at Stonehenge and CH. While WH does not benefit from triangulation with both ends of the cursus, it is located along the longitudinal axis of the cursus, is seen from A42, and is the location of a henge.

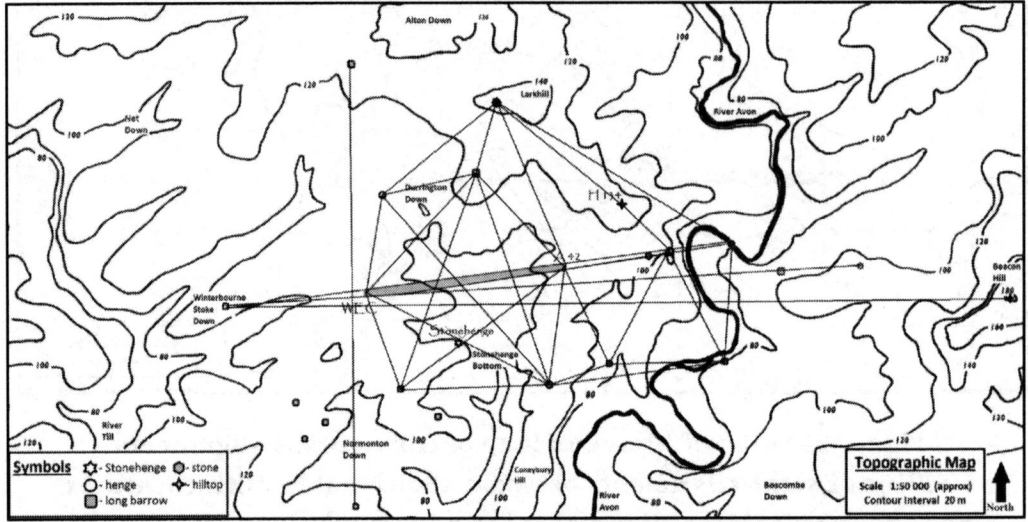

Figure 30: Note the irregular hexagon surrounding the Greater Cursus, formed by line of site alignments between WEC, UDD, KB, WH, CH and A14.

Destruction of features on Durrington Down by ploughing and possibly other means was mentioned above as concerns for identifying the type, size and location of a former Neolithic monument at point UDD. Yet we know a Neolithic structure for that location was possible. Its widespread visibility, proximity to the Greater Cursus, alignment with KB and WS53, relatively short naked eye sighting to the top of Larkhill and KB, and location easily set by triangulation add to the probability that the vicinity of UDD was valuable to completion of a grand plan. Also of note, WS53 suffers comparison with the other monuments as it has no prominent topographic location, is without a henge, and is not served by triangulation with the ends of the cursus. However it remains as a vital control point for the entire network.

The plan of the hexagon surrounding the Greater Cursus at first appears surprisingly uncomplicated, easily achieved, too mundane to serve much purpose within this wondrous landscape. Why would someone bother to construct such simplified design covering 12 square kilometers of rolling topography? How could this be of any importance to them, or us?

In fact answers to those questions are profound. The design is certainly uncomplicated and was relatively easily achieved. Undoubtedly its simplicity of form was beneficial to achieving the intent of the designers and builders. However, it is not the design that is so important, but the symbolism it offers to anyone familiar with ancient and indigenous cultures, including that of central south England during the Neolithic.

Chapter 6
A GRAND PLAN REVEALED

The Greater Cursus and hexagon of monuments that surrounds it are highly charged with a sacred message that has been understood by many Neolithic cultures—prehistoric, historic and indigenous. The knowledge is expressed in a breadth of traditions including mythology, hieroglyphics, decorative motifs in textiles and pottery, and architecture. It is communicated using prehistoric signs and symbols. Meaning and importance of the signs and symbols to functioning of the mid-Neolithic Stonehenge Landscape are detailed below. Here we continue our process of reverse engineering to discover what the geometrical design on the ground was intended to represent, and the source of the design itself.

Figure 31 is a star map of the southern sky at Stonehenge at 3:19 AM on 21 September, 3500 BC. The map was made using Starry Night Enthusiast 4.5. The base map depicts configurations of modern day constellations including Canis Major, Canis Minor, Gemini, Auriga, Taurus and Orion. Stars generally do not appear to move relative to each other. However, they are in motion. It is the great distance between stars, and from stars to Earth, that causes the cosmos to appear static as the entire universe crosses our sky every 24 hours. The result is that the star maps in Figure 31 is appropriate for our needs here, during the timeframe of about 4000 BC to 3000 BC. Table 4 lists notable constellations and stars shown on the map.

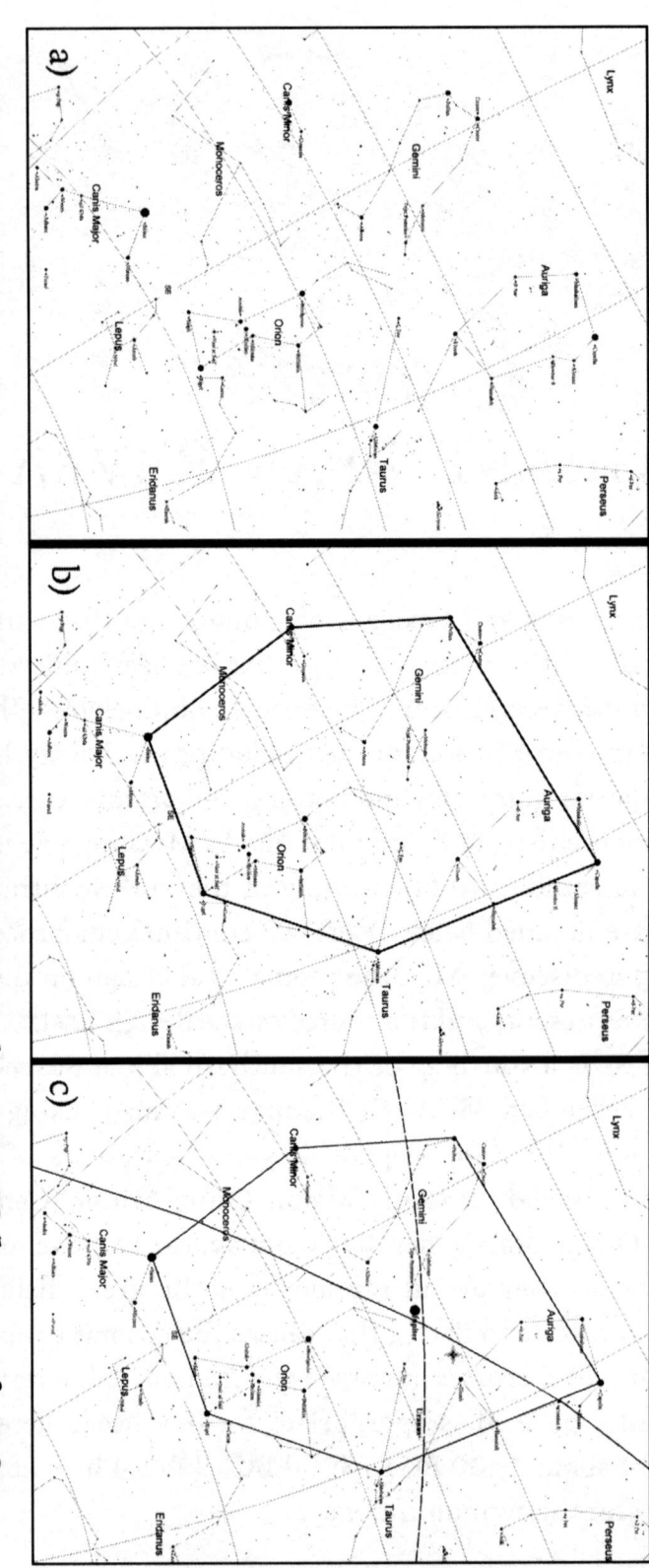

Figure 31: a) Star map of the sky at Stonehenge at 3:19 AM on 21 September, 3500 BC (base map from Starry Night Enthusiast 4.5); b) same star map with outline of Winter hexagon; c) galactic plane, ecliptic and galactic anti-center at the Winter Hexagon

Sirius is the brightest star in the sky. Nine of the stars listed in Table 4 make up half of the eighteen brightest stars in the northern celestial sphere. The other ten stars include a fourth of brightest stars in the southern celestial sphere. Together they form one of the brightest parts of the night sky today, the same as it was during the Neolithic.

There are additional unique features of this area of the sky. The Milky Way extends across the constellations from Canis Major to Auriga. It divides the area into two parts. Watching the constellations rise in the east soon after sunset in late September, the Milky Way cuts a line from Sirius near the horizon to Capella in Auriga. Gemini and Canis Minor appear north of the Milky Way. Orion and Taurus are to the south, although Orion's right arm reaches up and to mid-portion of the Milky Way, into the bright concentration of stars.

Table 4: Significant Stars Shown in Figure 31 Apparent Magnitude

Constellation Name	Star name	Brightness*	Rank
Canis major	Sirius (alpha Canis Majoris)	-1.46	1
Auriga	Capella (alpha Aurigae)	0.08	6
Orion	Rigel (beta Orionis)	0.12	7
Canis minor	Procyon (alpha Canis Minoris)	0.38	8
Orion	Betelgeuse (alpha Orionis)	0.50	10
Taurus	Aldebaran (alpha Tauri)	0.85	14
Gemini	Pollux (beta Geminorum)	1.14	17
Canis Major	Adhara (epsilon Canis Majoris)	1.50	24
Gemini	Castor (binary, alpha Geminorum)	1.58	25
Orion	Bellatrix (gamma Orionis)	1.64	28
Taurus	Alnath (beta Tauri)	1.65	29

Constellation Name	Star name	Brightness*	Rank
Orion	Alnilam (eta Orionis)	1.70	31
Canis major	Wezen (delta Canis Majoris)	1.84	38
Auriga	Menkalinan (beta Aurigae)	1.90	43
Gemini	Alhena (gamma Geminorum)	1.93	45
Canis major	Murzim (Canis majoris)	2.00	52
Orion	Alnitak (zeta Orionis)	2.05	56
Orion	Saiph (kappa Orionis)	2.06	58
Orion	Mintaka (delta alpha Orionis)	2.23	71

*based on logarithmic apparent magnitude

Figure 31c shows several important astronomical features in the same area of sky. These include the galactic plane, ecliptic and galactic anti-center.

Galactic Plane: Our galaxy, the Milky Way, is disk-shaped. Earth is located about half way between the center of the galaxy and the outer stars rotating around the center. Therefore the Milky Way appears as a dense band of stars rotating around Earth. A line drawn across the sky such that it divided the length of the Milky Way into two halves would represent a plane—the galactic plane—rotating around Earth. On edge the plane would appear as a line. A section of this line-the galactic plane-is shown in Figure 31b. Strictly speaking the galactic plane remains ill-defined with no consensus in the scientific community as to its location. The galactic plane is a concept only, a concept that has been studied for thousands of years, dividing the universe into two halves.

Ecliptic: The ecliptic is a trace of the Sun's apparent path around Earth. Of course the Sun does not orbit Earth. Earth completes one rotation on its axis each day, and completes one orbit around the Sun each year. However, if we assumed Earth stood still in space then the Sun, Moon, planets and stars would all appear to be rotating around Earth.

Earth and the other seven planets in our solar system orbit the Sun on nearly the same plane, so the apparent path of the planets rotating around Earth approximates the path of the Sun, the ecliptic. Our Moon also follows this path but the plane of its orbit around Earth is tilted about 5 degrees 8 minutes with respect to the ecliptic plane. Thus it appears to move above and below the ecliptic as it waxes and wanes during the course of its phase cycle of 29.53 days.

We can envision the ecliptic as the trace of a plane with the center of the Sun moving in that plane and an orbit around Earth. This is the ecliptic plane. The ecliptic plane is tilted about 60 degrees with respect to the galactic plane. This results in the ecliptic appearing to cross the galactic plane at two locations opposite of each other. One of those locations appears from Earth to be very close to the galactic center, the other location being very close to the galactic anti-center.

Galactic Anti-center: The Milky Way rotates about its center—the galactic center-which is located in the brightest area of stars along the galactic plane. Imagine the Milky Way as a band of stars rotating around Earth. At any given time the galactic center would be located somewhere along that band either above or below the horizon. If we align the galactic center to the center of Earth, and continue that line in the direction opposite of the galactic center, the line would point to a location in the sky called the galactic anti-center, precisely opposite of the galactic center's location.

In Figure 31b we see the galactic plane crossing the constellations. Every 24 hours the Sun moves on the ecliptic across this part of the sky. The Moon and planets also move along the ecliptic, although the Moon's path extends above or below the line. Not far above the ecliptic and right of the galactic plane is the galactic anti-center.

It is the spin of Earth that produces the effect of the cosmos crossing the sky, night to become day, and day to become night. The Moon orbits Earth to produce the lunar waxing and waning as the triangle defined by positions of the Earth, Sun and Moon continues changing. Earth orbits the Sun giving us just over 365 days per year and four seasons defined by the two solstices and two equinoxes. The planets orbit the sun, appearing to give chase to one another while running their own circuit along the ecliptic path.

Yet with all of that movement some features appear to never change. The Milky Way looks the same. The galactic center and anti-center are always at opposite points of the celestial Sphere. The Sun never deviates from the ecliptic. The two locations where the ecliptic intersects the galactic plane are unchanging. Constellations never appear to change form or location. Everything in the cosmos appears to be moving in orbit around Earth, yet everything is moving together in predictable ways each day, night, lunar month and solar year. And all life on Earth experiences these cycles of time, each life moving through time in the cycle of birth, life, death and rebirth.

Neolithic cultures in Babylonia, Egypt, India, Europe, the Americas and other locations across the Earth recognized those relationships across time and space. They also perceived something special where the ecliptic crosses galactic plane, near the galactic anti-center and surrounded by constellations.

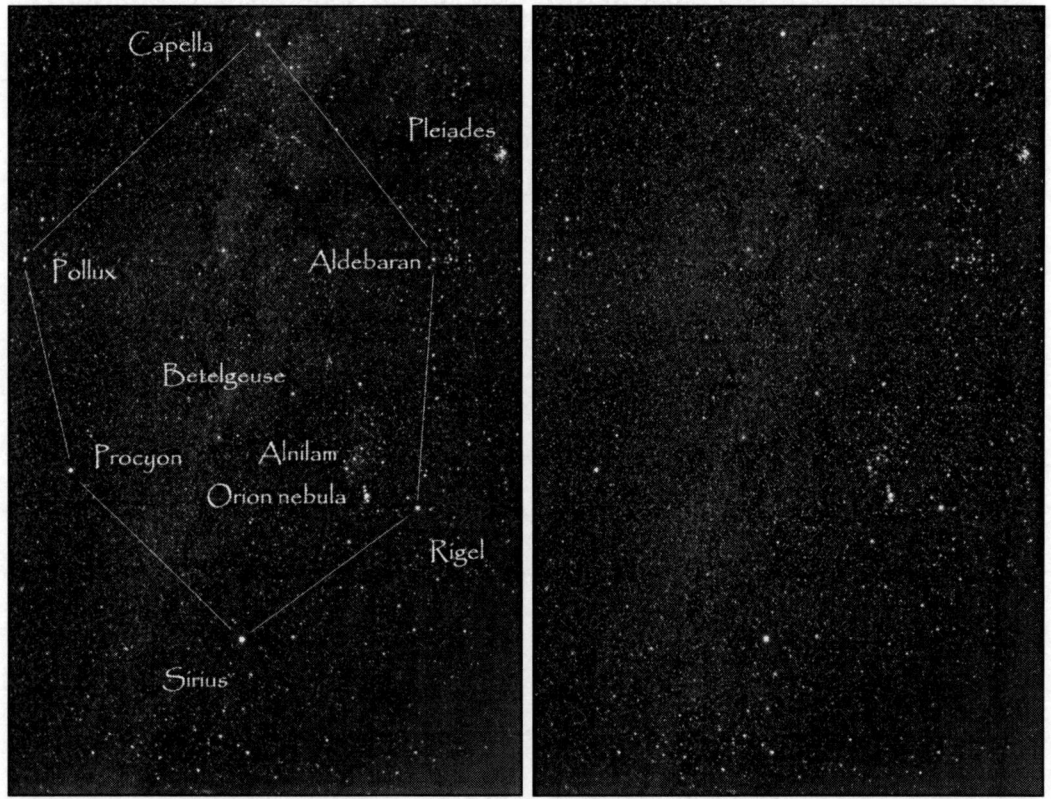

Figure 32: Photograph of the Winter Hexagon. Note the constellation of Orion in the lower right portion of the hexagon. With Orion facing out of the page, his left foot is represented by Rigel. a) with outline of hexagon and stars labeled, b) withouy outline and labels (photograph courtesy F. Ringwald, CSU, Fresno)

The area of the cosmos including almost all of the stars listed in Table 4 is found in an asterism known as the Winter Hexagon. It can be observed from almost any location on Earth. Figure 32 is a photograph of that area of the sky. Significant stars, constellations, galactic plane and ecliptic are shown. There is a wealth of information concerning Neolithic knowledge and cosmography associated with that area of the cosmos. Surprisingly, however, this is not so with regard to the asterism of the Winter Hexagon itself. Undoubtedly this will change.

Figure 33a is a map of the Stonehenge Landscape including the Greater Cursus and the six locations forming the hexagon. Figure 29b is a star map centered on the Winter Hexagon. Comparing Figures 29a and 29b we can see immediately that the spatial relationships between elements of the Stonehenge Landscape correspond to specific features of and inside the Winter Hexagon. Table 5 lists correspondences between cosmos and landscape.

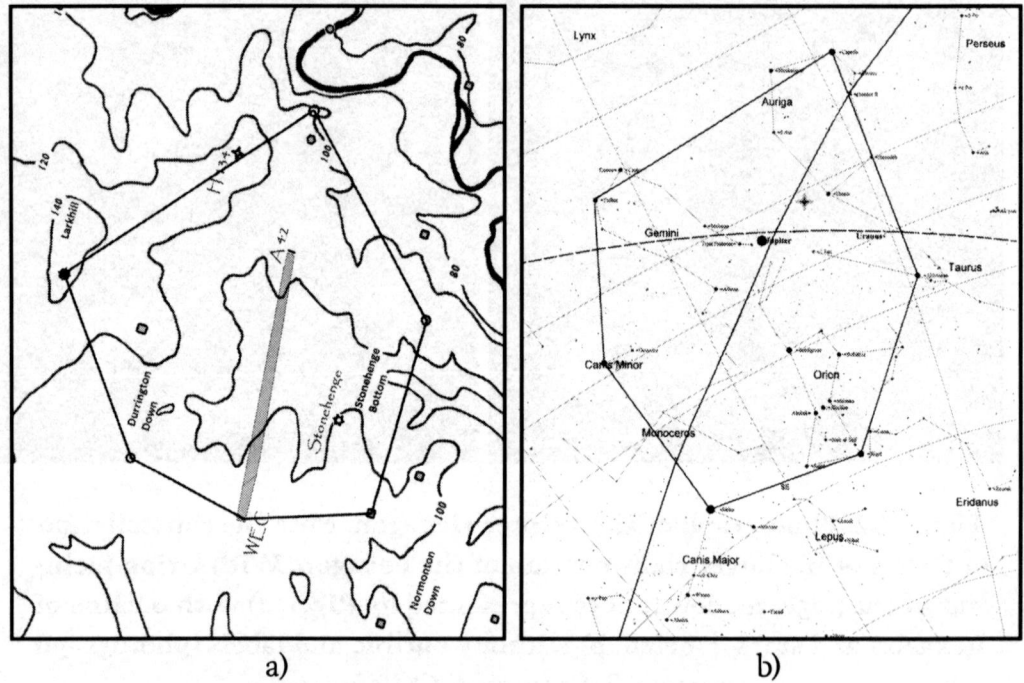

a)   b)

Figure 33: a) Stonehenge Landscape including the Greater Cursus and the six locations forming the hexagon; b) Winter hexagon (based map from Starry Night Enthusiast 4.5)

Table 5: Features of the Stonehenge Landscape Corresponding to Elements of the Cosmic Dome

Landscape Feature	Corresponding Element of the Cosmic Dome
West end of Greater Cursus	Sirius
Amesbury 42	Intersection of ecliptic and galactic plane
Greater Cursus	Milky Way between Sirius and ecliptic
Amesbury 14	Rigel
Coneybury Henge	Aldebaran
Lost Stone (LS)	Capella
Knighton Barrow (Figheldean 27)	Pollux
UDD	Procyon
Stonehenge	Alnilam
Orion Nebula	Long barrow 330 m west of Stonehenge

This correspondence between landscape and astronomical features represents a Neolithic translocation of the Winter Hexagon onto the Stonehenge Landscape. This is the original *Grand Plan* of the Stonehenge Sacred Landscape. The area centers on the intersection of the ecliptic and the galactic plane, the corresponding feature on the landscape being long barrow Amesbury 42 (A42), oriented perpendicular to the cursus.

Figure 34 depicts relative locations and orientations of nine long barrows in the vicinity of the Greater Cursus plotted on a star map of the Winter Hexagon. In addition, the Greater Cursus and respective long barrow and henges that make up the translocated hexagon on the Stonehenge Landscape are shown on the map. Stonehenge plots accurately onto Alnilam, middle star of Orion's belt. By scaling the distance from the west end of the Greater Cursus to Woodhenge, and plotting that distance onto a star map with the west end of the cursus at Sirius and Woodhenge at Capella, the east end of the cursus with adjoining Amesbury 42 long barrow plot precisely at the ecliptic. In addition, plotting the locations and orientations of the two lines crossing the cursus is shown in Figure 21, the lines intersect near the belt of Orion.

(Refer to Appendix E for additional information regarding translocation of stars of the Winter Hexagon onto the Stonehenge Landscape.)

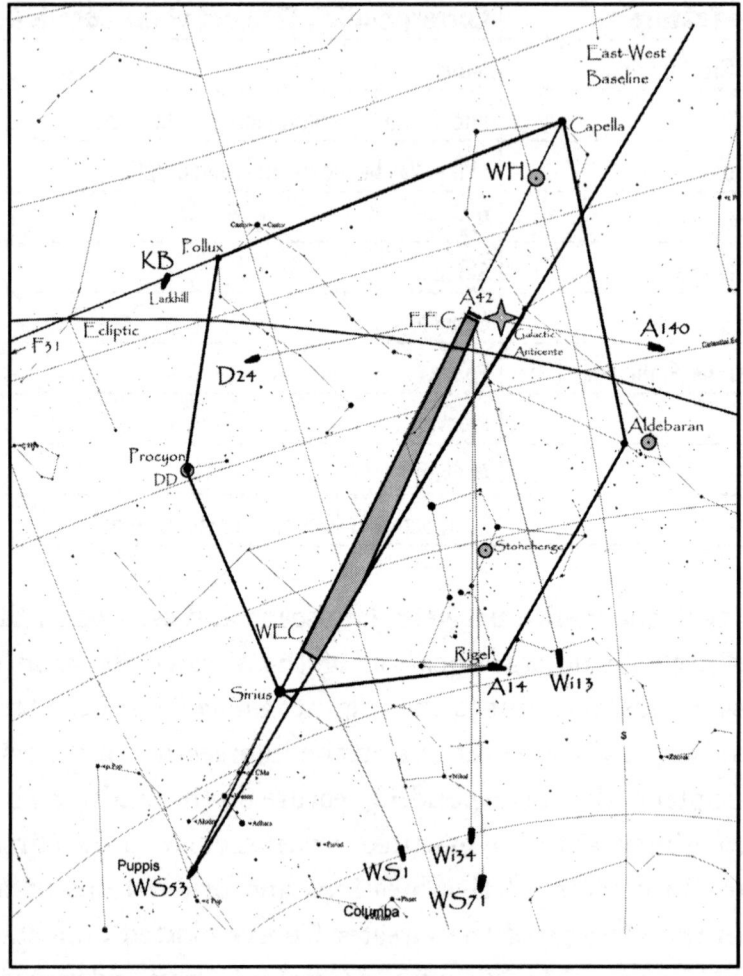

Figure 34: Locations and orientations of nine long barrows, three henges, and other features in the vicinity of the Greater Cursus plotted onto a star map of the Winter Hexagon

The result is illustrated in Figure 35 with the scale used for plotting ends of the cursus based on the distance from Sirius to the intersection of galactic plane and ecliptic. The black stars represent an accurate configuration of the Winter Hexagon, and the white stars the symbolic hexagon built on the landscape. We can see that the relative distance between symbolic Pollux (KB) to symbolic Aldebaran (CH) is greater than the scaled distance between the stars Pollux and Aldebaran. This was the result of the physiographic distance between the top of Larkhill (KB) and Coneybury Henge (CH). Symbolic Pollux and symbolic Aldebaran were to remain at those locations, likely for reasons related to the perceived greater sanctity of the topographic high point at KB, and a lengthy tradition of use at Coneybury Hill Henge dating to thousands of years before translocation of the Winter Hexagon was to happen. Simply put, KB and CH could not be transferred to other locations without affecting the importance and sacredness of those to positions on the natural landscape. That change of scale between Pollux and Aldebaran could have forced the location of symbolic Capella east from the site of the Cuckoo Stone to where Woodhenge was constructed. Looking at the west (left) half and east (right) half of the hexagon, the change of scale is obvious.

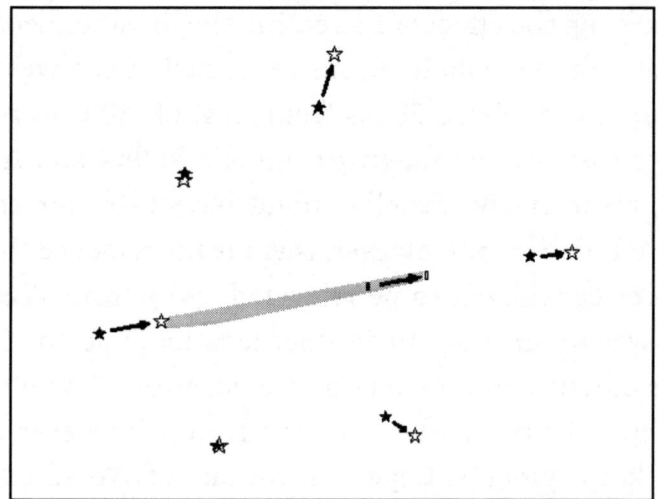

Figure 35: Translocation of star locations to nodes of the symbolic Winter Hexagon. Note that the east end of the cursus (A42) would need to be relocated eastward in the same direction and distance as the west end of the cursus in order for Sirius to plot accurately. However, the size and location of the Greater Cursus remained in place during construction of the symbolic Winter Hexagon surrounding it. Consideration for a westward repositioning of Sirius to the west end of the cursus was never an issue of concern during construction of the hexagon.

Similarly, if Capella was initially planned to be located along the same alignment but at the Lost Stone in the River Avon (LS), then the two ends of the Greater Cursus should have been shifted eastward to new locations as depicted in Figure 32. However the location of the cursus remained as originally constructed. Therefore, symbolic Sirius, represented by WEC, remained located east of where it would have been if there had been need to move sacred Capella from WH to LS. The cursus is located precisely where it needed to be. The view of the intersecting Milky Way and ecliptic would be seen from the west end of the cursus. The location, orientation and length of the Greater Cursus are exactly as they needed to be. And symbolic Procyon and symbolic Rigel (UDD, W14) are located precisely where they should plot on the landscape.

We see the same geometry playing out on the landscape in Figure 36, showing the effect of increasing the distance between Pollux and Aldebaran while symbolic Sirius remained at the west end of the cursus. By moving symbolic Sirius from west of WEC to the west end of the Greater Cursus, and moving symbolic Pollux and Aldebaran to KB and CH, respectively, Capella would have been forced east from Woodhenge to Lost Stone. However, there is no evidence that symbolic Sirius was ever considered to be relocated away from WEC. In other words WEC was never move to another location, and the position and length of the cursus had no effect on the location of symbolic Capella (WH). Note how the triangulations are affected. However the decision was made to keep symbolic Capella at the site of Woodhenge.

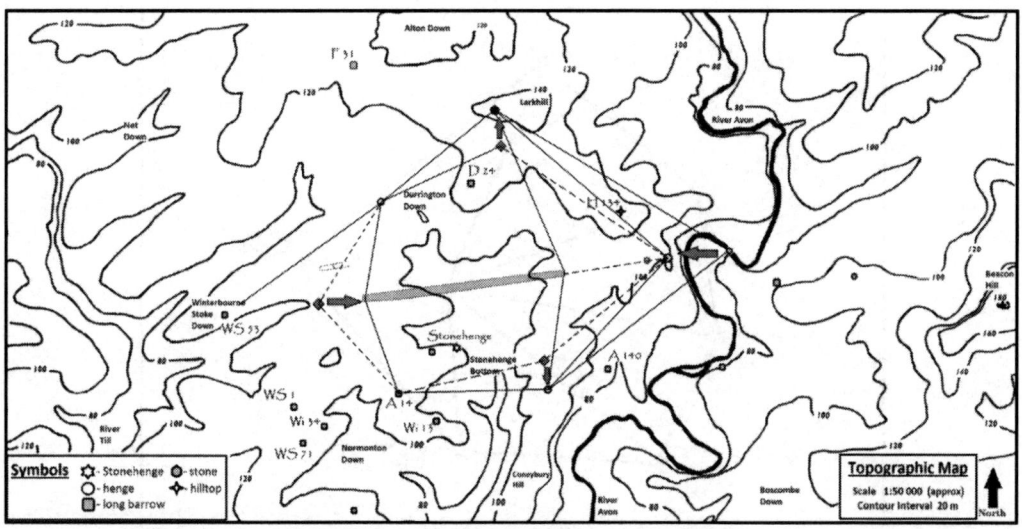

Figure 36: Symbolic Pollux and Aldebaran are farther apart than they should be if translocation of the Winter Hexagon onto the landscape had been precise. This is shown by the two arrows pointing outward to the top of Larkhill and Coneybury Henge. The arrow west of the cursus shows where symbolic Sirius should have been located with respect to Procyon and Rigel (UDD and A14). If the intent was to move Sirius eastward to the west end on the cursus, then this would have forced symbolic Capella eastward from Woodhenge to the position of the Lost Stone in the River Avon. However it appears Sirius was always intended to be situated at the west end of the cursus, thus keeping symbolic Capella at the site of Woodhenge.

Figure 37 provides comparison of the shape of the Winter Hexagon (black stars and grey lines) and the hexagon constructed on the landscape (white stars and black lines). Note that Procyon, Sirius and Rigel are positioned correctly with the intention of Sirius located at the west end of the cursus. However Pollux, Capella and Aldebaran are shifted outward due to the distance between the top of Larkhill and Coneybury Hill Henge being greater than the scaled distance would have allowed. Regardless, the sacred intent of the translocated hexagon appears to have been satisfied without further adjustment.

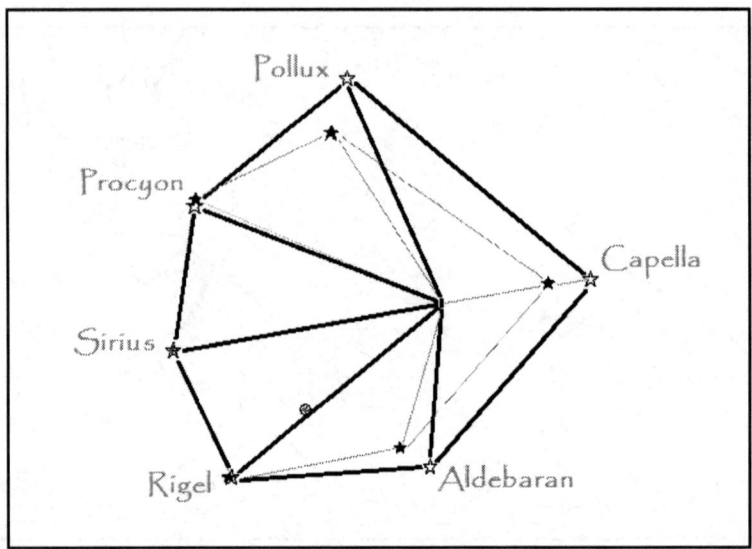

Figure 37: Comparison of triangulations of symbolic Winter Hexagon (bold lines) and accurate plots of Pollux, Capella and Aldebaran (light lines). Symbolic Procyon and Rigel plot quite accurately. Locations of symbolic Sirius and the ecliptic are unchanged at the west end and east end of the cursus, respectively.

In summary, builders of the symbolic hexagon would have created an accurate representation of the Winter Hexagon if 1) the distance from KB to CH was reduced in accordance with the scale used for the two ends of the Greater Cursus, and 2) in so doing the west end of the cursus was moved west to reflect the proper location of Sirius relative to Procyon and Rigel. Most likely the builders decided not to move KB and CH because the top of Larkhill and Coneybury Henge were sacred sites not be desecrated by transferring their importance to other locations for the sake of geometrical accuracy. In any case the intended view of an astronomical event over the east end of the cursus was best accomplished from where the west end of the cursus is located. Symbolic Sirius had to remain at that location.

The differences in size and shape of the Winter Hexagon (represented by black stars) and its symbolic structure on the landscape (white stars) are shown in Figure 38. The two hexagons are in fact rather similar in shape. Similar to design and construction works occurring today, it is likely very few people would have known of the differences between what was proposed and what was actually built. The Stonehenge landscape—the Stonehenge Sacred Landscape—would serve the intended purpose. Figure 39 illustrates the symbolic Winter Hexagon on the landscape.

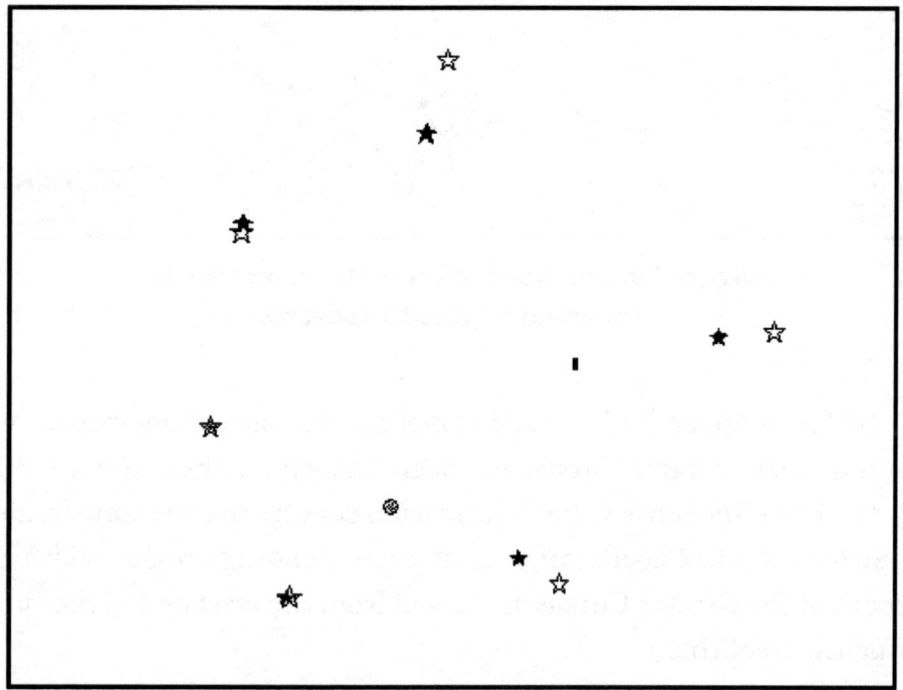

Figure 38: Comparison of relative star locations (black stars) of the Winter Hexagon and scaled locations of monuments representing the symbolic Winter Hexagon constructed on the Stonehenge Sacred landscape. Long barrow Amesbury 42 (representing the ecliptic at its crossing of the galactic plane) is shown at its scaled location immediately east end of the cursus, in center right. Location of Stonehenge is shown by the circle. Note that the cursus (Sirius and the ecliptic-galactic plane) and Stonehenge (Alnilam) remained in place.

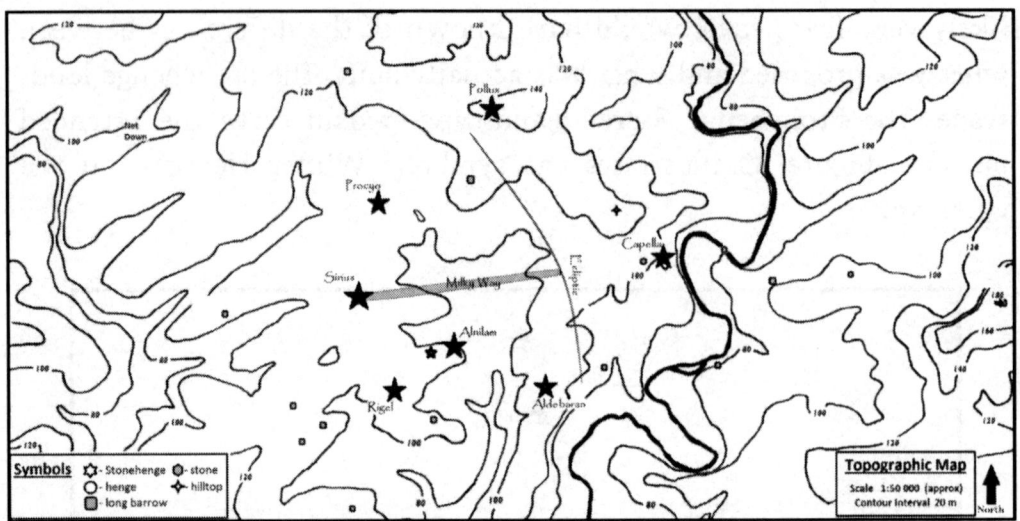

**Figure 39: Symbolic Winter Hexagon on the
Stonehenge Sacred Landscape**

(Refer to Appendix F for additional details concerning reasons why the ends of the Greater Cursus are located as we see them today.)

(Refer to Appendix G for information concerning the time frame of the Sirius-ecliptic-Capella alignment corresponding to the width and azimuth of the Greater Cursus as viewed from the west end of the cursus during the Neolithic.)

Chapter 7
As Above, So Below

The Grand Design on the Stonehenge Landscape is the Winter Hexagon, Milky Way, ecliptic and Orion translocated onto Salisbury Plane. This is clear from the correspondence between locations of long barrows, henges and the Greater Cursus, and the configuration of the Milky Way, galactic plane, ecliptic and stars. It is one of the greatest examples, and possibly the oldest example, of prehistoric hierotopy to be found anywhere, from anytime.

During research for this book a number of startling similarities were discovered between the Stonehenge Sacred Landscape and the World Heritage complex of Neolithic sites at Brú na Bóinne, County Meath, Ireland (Figure 40). There is little need to provide details concerning the triad of great passage tomb mounds at Newgrange, Knowth and Dowth. There are numerous authoritative references addressing construction and use of those renowned structures. However it is notable that evidence of increasing settlement along the Boyne River valley dates to the early Neolithic (c. 3800 to 3400 BC) and the three great mounds date to as early as 3500 BC. This places construction of the passage tombs in the same timeframe as the Stonehenge Sacred Landscape. Knowth and Dowth are believed to be the oldest of the three monuments of Brú na Bóinne.

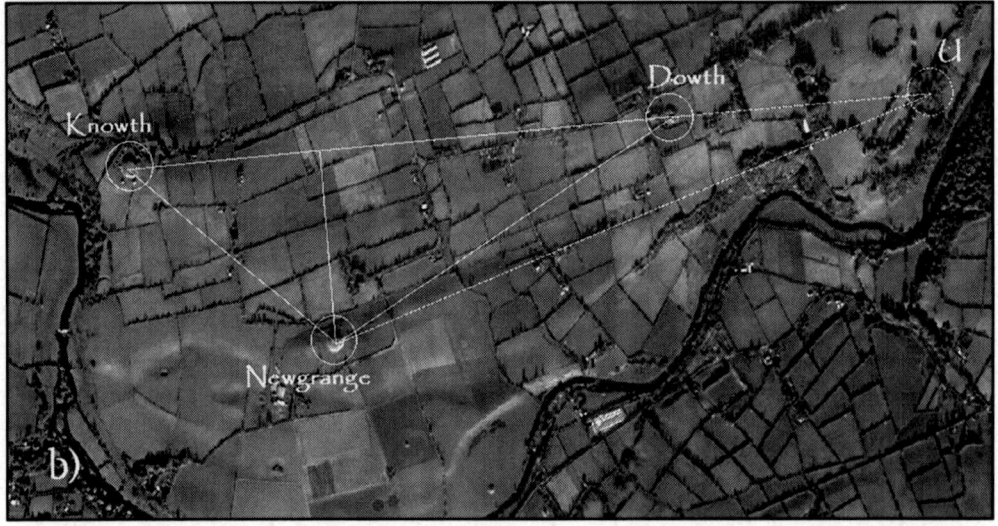

Figure 40: a) Triangle with corners defined by the west end and east end of the Greater Cursus and the Heelstone at Stonehenge; Woodhenge represents location of symbolic Capella. b) Locations of the three great passage tomb mounds of Newgrange, Knowth and Dowth at Brú na Bóinne; U is the equivalent location of symbolic Capella, although archaeological evidence of its potential importance to Brú na Bóinne is unknown as of the date of publication of this book. (top: base photo copyright 2014 Infoterra Ltd & Bluesky, copyright 2013 Google Google; bottom: base photo copyright 2013 Google)

A triangle is formed on Salisbury Plain by the two ends of the Greater Cursus and the center of the Stonehenge monument. Another triangle is created from the centers of Newgrange, Knowth and Dowth. The two triangles are virtually identical in size and shape. Data presented in Table 6 demonstrates the geometrical similarities of the two triangles, which are illustrated in Figure 41.

Table 6: Comparison of the Stonehenge-Cursus and Brú na Bóinne Triangles

Item	Stonehenge-Cursus	Brú na Bóinne
Length of Greater Cursus	1.71 mi	--
Distance between Knowth and Dowth	--	1.69 mi
Azimuth of Greater Cursus (average of north and south ditches)	84.1°	--
Azimuth of line from Knowth and Dowth	--	84.0°
Ground surface gradient west to east along length of Greater Cursus	0.022%	--
• arc equivalent	7.5'	--
Ground surface gradient from Knowth to Dowth	--	0.025%
• arc equivalent	--	7.7'
Distance from center of Stonehenge to		
• Cursus north ditch line	2969 ft	--
• Cursus centerline	2760 ft	--
• Cursus south ditch line	2550 ft	--
Distance from center of Newgrange to line between Knowth and Dowth	--	2697 ft

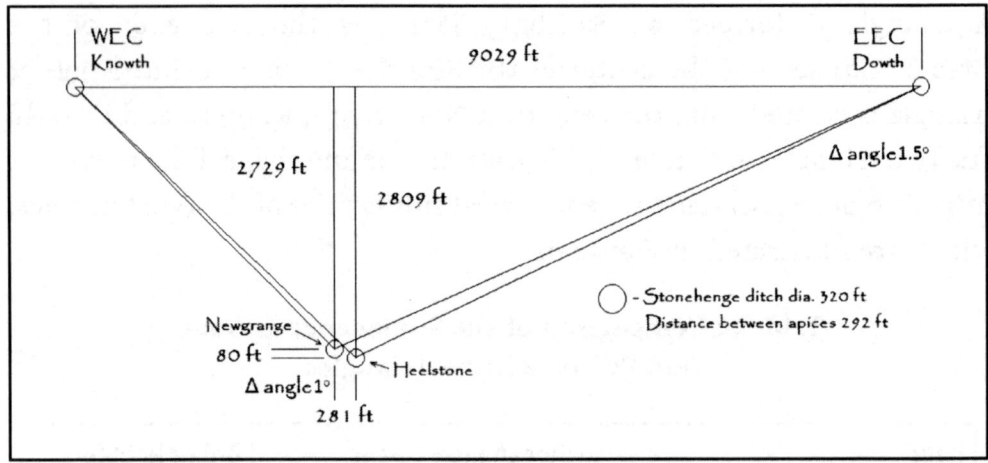

Figure 41: Comparison of triangles formed by the two end points of the Greater Cursus and Stonehenge, and the three passage grave mounds at Brú na Bóinne. The triangles are almost identical when the distance from Knowth to Dowth is scaled to the same length as the Greater Cursus.

From the data in Table 6 notice that the two triangles are not only close to the same size and shape, but the gradient from the west end of the cursus to long barrow Amesbury 42 is almost identical to the gradient from Knowth to Dowth. From the west end of the cursus the horizon at the long barrow has an altitude of 7.5 minutes, while at Knowth the altitude of the horizon at Dowth is 7.7 minutes, a difference of 0.2 minutes or one thirtieth of a degree. Thus the orientation of both triangles is nearly the same relative to the local land surface.

Figure 42 depicts comparison of the Stonehnege and Brú na Bóinne triangles with the distance from Knowth to a location U east of Dowth scaled to the distance from the west end of the cursus to Woodhenge. The east of of the Brú na Bóinne triangle plots at a location overlooking the north bank of the River Boyne, a situation very similar to Woodhenge's location overlooking the west bank of the River Avon. Archaeological studies have been conducted north of U, however research indicates no archaeological investigation of site U (unknown). The great similarity of the Stonehenge and Brú na Bóinne triangles suggests site U should be evaluated for archaeological significance.

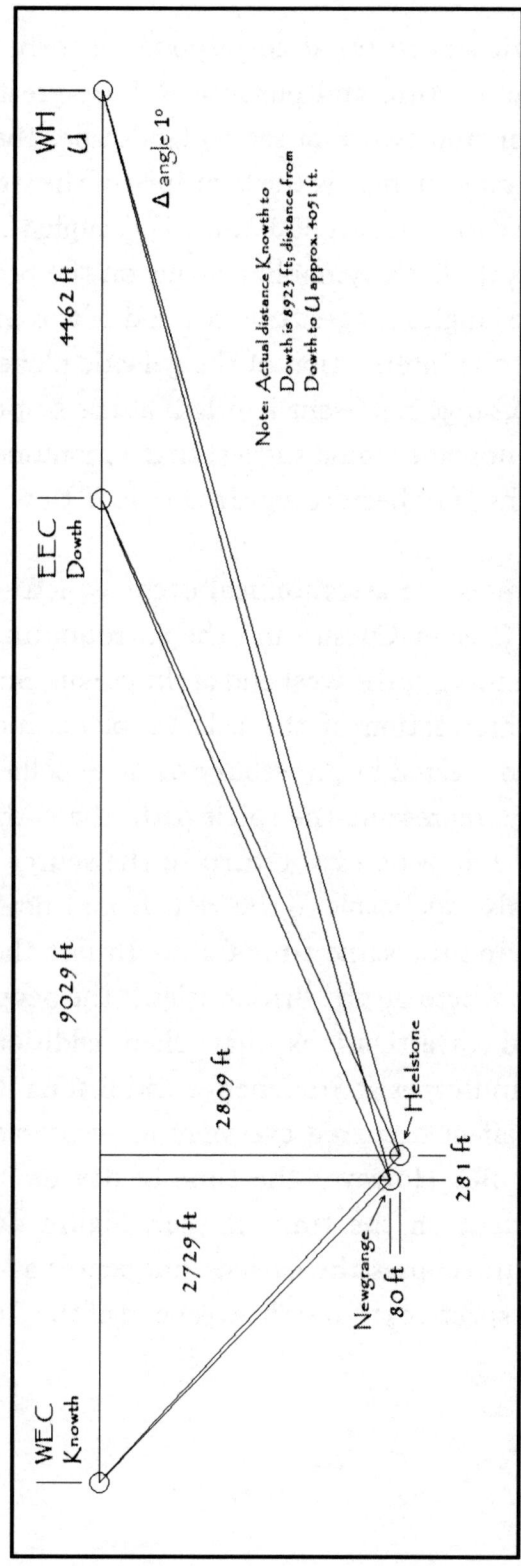

Figure 42: The reason for constructing the Greater Cursus and surrounding sacred landscape at Stonehenge. The spirit path is made manifest as the cursus representing the Milky Way and Amesbury 42 conjuncts with the intersection of the galactic plane and ecliptic locates. Capella watches from above, represented by the location of Woodhenge east of King Barrow Ridge.

The mid-Neolithic structures at corresponding corners of the two triangles differ in architecture and purpose. All are great monuments located within a larger framework of sacred landscape. The west corner of the Stonehenge-Cursus triangle is the terminus of the Greater Cursus, while its equivalent location at Brú na Bóinne is occupied by the passage tomb mound of Knowth. Both symbolize Sirius on the respective landscape. Similarly, the triangles suggest the east end of the Greater Cursus and Dowth represent the intersection of the galactic plane and ecliptic. Stonehenge and Newgrange represent Alnilam at the belt of Orion. The Stonehenge Sacred Landscape would suggest that a monument or marker representing Capella has not been recognized east of Dowth on the Brú na Bóinne landscape.

Figure 43 illustrates the astronomical event which was the cause for constructing the Greater Cursus and the surrounding sacred landscape ca. 3500 BC. Standing at the west end of the cursus, Sirius perceived directly below, the intersection of the galactic plane and the ecliptic appears at the horizon created by Amesbury 42 as Capella is seen above the cursus. The cursus represents the spirit path, the path upon which the spirit of the dead follows on its' return to the source of life in the cosmos. The event is also applicable to the view from Knowth to Dowth at Brú na Bóinne during the same time frame. In fact the effect could have been created anywhere on the British Isles if the people so desired. Future archaeological investigations may shed additional light for comparing the two landscapes at Stonehenge and Brú na Bóinne.

The spirit path effect occurred everyday for centuries during the mid-4th millennium BC. However the time of day or night when it occurred was dependent on the time of year. Figure 44 depicts the moment when the Sun eclipses the galactic anticenter as it crosses the galactic plane. The perspective is from the west end of the Greater Cursus.

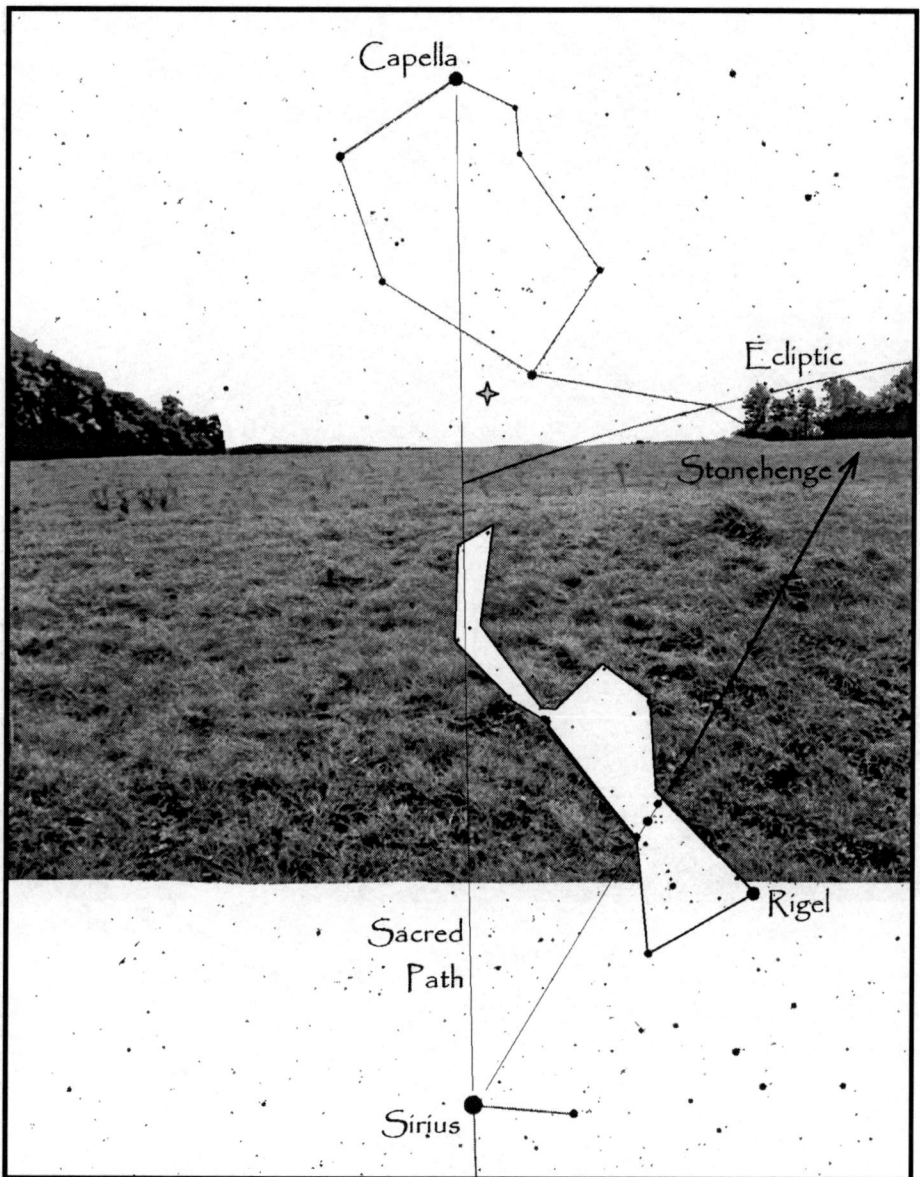

Figure 43: The reason for constructing the Greater Cursus and surrounding sacred landscape at Stonehenge. The viewer stands over Sirius at the west end of the cursus. The spirit path is made manifest with the cursus representing the Milky Way. Amesbury 42 will soon conjunct with the intersection of the galactic plane and ecliptic plane. Orion points to that intertsection from underground (Underworld, Otherworld) as Capella watches from above, represented by the location of Woodhenge east of King Barrow Ridge.

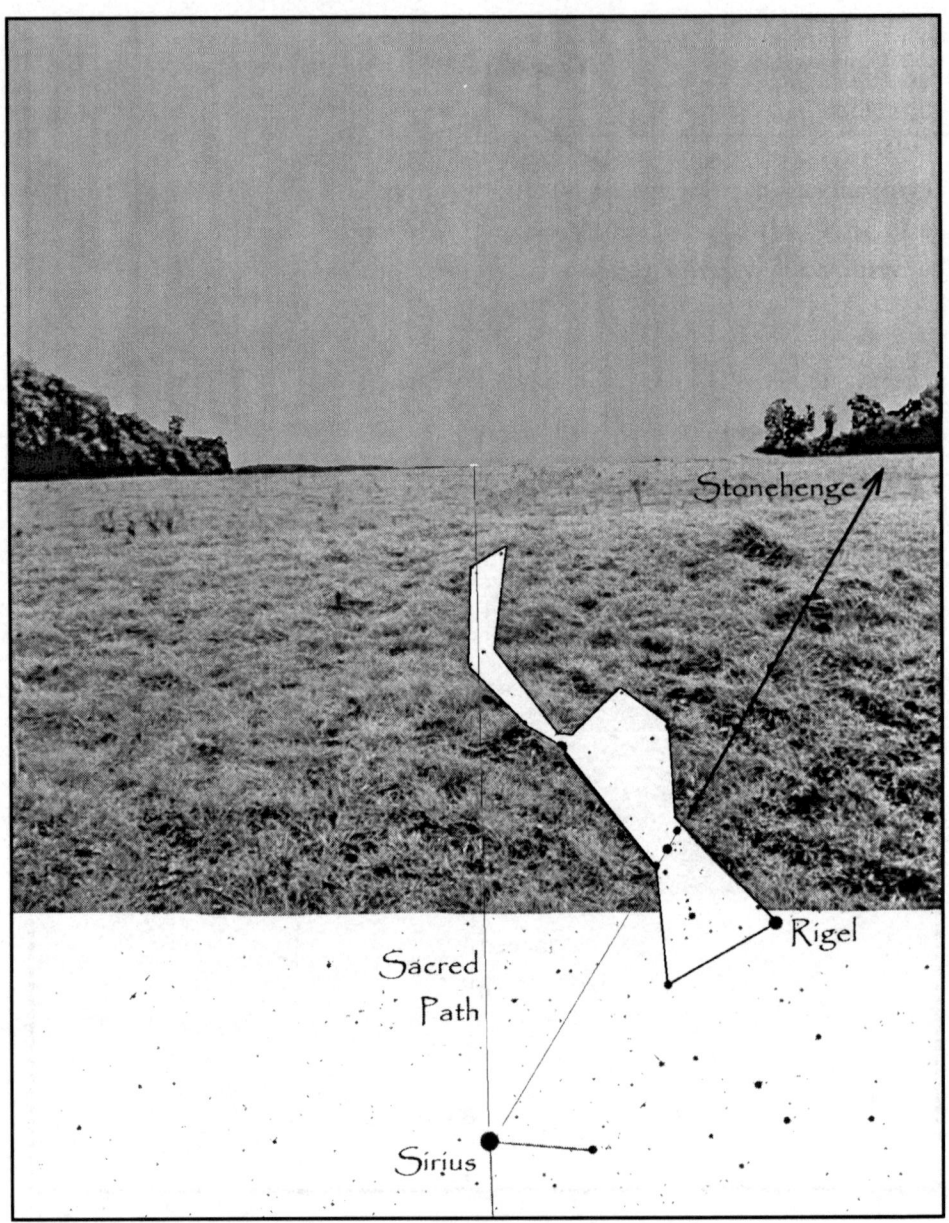

Figure 44: Similar view as in Figure 43, but with the first glint of the Sun appearing over the east end of the cursus. Viewed from the west end of the Greater Cursus ca. 3500 BC, the Sun eclipses the galactic anticenter at Amesbury 42. Soon Capella will not be visible. Still, Capella is observing from above, and Sirius from below. The spirit path lies before the observer.

In Figure 45 Earth has been removed from the field of view depicted in Figure 44. The Sun eclipses the galactic anticenter as it crosses the galactic plane. This is the relative location of the Sun as it appears on June 21 during the 21st century AD. In this position the Sun eclipses the galactic anti-center. By December 21 the sun rises and eclipses the galactic center (center of the Milky Way) as the galactic anticenter sets in the west.

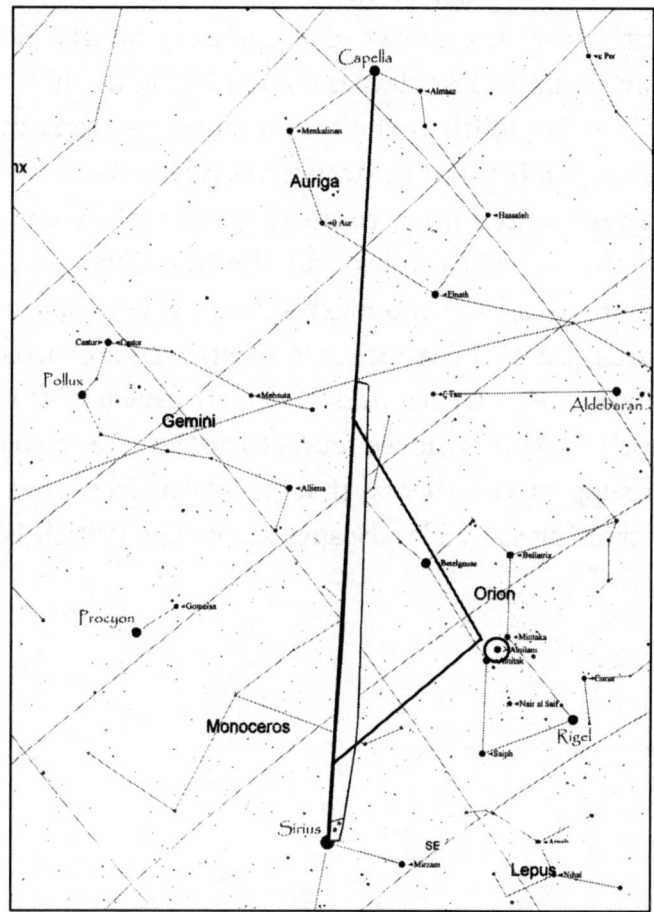

Figure 45: Scaled line drawing of the Stonehenge Sacred Landscape and the night sky centered on the intersection of the galactic equator and ecliptic. If the Greater Cursus is rotated to a vertical position with its west end transferred to the former location of the cursuses east end shown at the east horizon, the point of intersection of the two trenches crossing the cursus is at the Heelstone, and the middle star of Orion's belt—Alnilam—is situated where the center of Stonehegne would plot in the sky.

There is tantalizing evidence of similar spatial relationships between monuments at Neolithic landscapes found across the British Isles, including Avebury, the Isle of Orkney, and in particular at Rudston in the East Riding of Yorkshire. If the Greater Cursus is rotated to a vertical position with its west end transferred to the former location of the cursus east end shown at the east horizon, the Heelstone is found to be the point of intersection of the two trenches crossing the cursus. Another result is that the center of Stonehenge would plot at Orion's center belt star, Anilam. The view is shown in Figure 46.

The Rudston Monolith is the tallest standing stone in the United Kingdom (Figure 47). It is tall in stature yet relatively thin in width and slight in thickness, quite similar to the shape of the Greater Cursus. Like the length of the Greater Cursus and the line between Knowth and Dowth, the azimuth of the monolith's broad side is approximately 84 degrees. The area east of the stone lacks substantial archaeological investigation. However there are features of the area suggestive of a symbolic ecliptic or Capella. If this is indeed found to be the case, then the evidence will strongly support the theory that people in Neolithic Britain and Ireland were creating sacred landscapes across the British Isles.

Figure 46: Rudston Monolith at Rudston, East Riding of Yorkshire, England. View is toward the east at azimuth 84°.

Figure 47: Rudston Monolith representing the spirit road between Sirius and Capella. The Ecliptic crosses the horizon at the center of the stone. The standing stone may represent the spirit road set vertically rather than horizontally like the Greater Cursus.

There is another point of architectural interest suggesting this may have been so. It is the evolution of shape in housing on the British Isles during the late-to mid-Neolithic. The square formed by four posts in the central area of Neolithic houses and communal structures was noted previously, implying potential use of sacred geometrical motifs as part of their design and construction. However from about 4000 BC to the mid-Neolithic (roughly 3500 BC) the peripheral shape of houses evolved from rectangular with a length to width ratio of about 2:1, to being ovals or near circular. This raises the possibility that the tendency toward use of the oval in architecture may be related to the rather ovalulor shape of the Winter Hexagon.

The Winter Hexagon, perceived by ancinet and indigenous cultures as the source of life, is seen as egg-shaped (Figure 48a). It is the symbolic world egg or cosmic egg found in numerous ancient mythologies including many from across Europe (Figure 48b). Of course the egg is source of, and symbol for many forms of life on Earth. Narrative origins of the mythical world egg in Europe are pre-Neolithic, with the most archaic versions related to cultures in northern Europe. Therefore the concept of the world egg on the British Isles may date well into the Mesolithic. The oval shape of the mid-Neolithic house may then symbolize the world egg for the family within. The sacred geometrical relationships between oval, egg, circle and sphere, square and cube become even more apparent.

Figure 48b shows a white marble relief (No. 2676) at Museum Modena. It is Greek and dates to the 2nd century AD. A naked youth stands at the center of oval. The figure is androgynous. Phanes holds a lightning bolt in one hand and a staff in the other. The figure bears wings and a cresecent moon is seen behind. The deity stands on half of a flaming egg shell. The other half of the shell is above the youth's head. A serpent is coiled about the figure. The youth stands at the center of the zodiac, and the winds blow from the four corners of the relief.

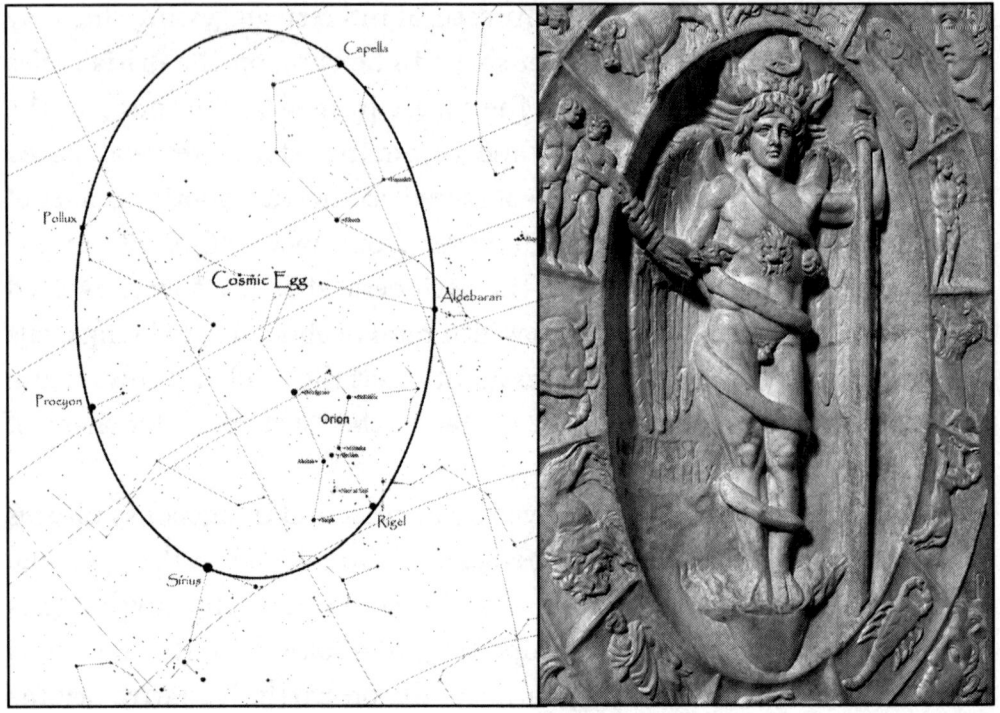

**Figure 48: a) Winter hexagon perceived in the shape of an egg;
b) Greco-Roman bas relief from the 2nd century AD showing Phanes,
the primeval deity of procreation in Orphic cosmogony, enveloped by
the cosmic egg. Note that Phanes is wrapped by a snake, an ancient and
widespread sacred symbol for the Milky Way. Thus we see in bas relief
the source of life within the world (universal) cosmic egg as it is carried
around the cosmos, depicted by the constellations of the zodiac.**

The figure in the relief is Phanes, primeval ruler of other deities, and god of procreation and generation of life. Phanes is the deity of goodness and light, the name meaning "to bring light" or "to shine". The youth emerged from the watery abyss of the cosmos, and gave life to the universe. The relief shows Phanes stands at the crossroads of the galactic plane and ecliptic, surrounded by the cosmos which represents time, changes in time and space caused by the winds.

Numerous attributes of Phanes parallel those of Lugh, the Celtic god of light. The important relationships for us concern the imagery in general of the respective deity. Each is represented in the sky by the constellation Orion, and Orion is found within the confines of the cosmic egg, the Winter Hexagon. This is where life began and where life returns. We know very little of the cosmology and mythology of Neolithic Britain. However the marble relief of Phanes provides a vision of ideas that may have been fundamental to concepts of a cosmic origin of life and return of the spirit back to where it came. That is an area of the sky recreated on the Stonehenge Sacred Landscape. The Greater Cursus and Phanes may each represent the way back to source.

Ever since its discovery in the 18th century, the purpose for the arcing alignment of the Avenue located in a triangular area bounded by Stonehenge, Amesbury 42 and Bluestonehenge has remained elusive. The lengthy, curving alignment appears to make little sense as a route for transporting the dead to Stonehenge for ritual or ceremony. However we now know the Stonehenge Landscape is a product of translocating the Winter Hexagon onto Salisbury Plain. Specific points on the ground were surveyed as symbolic locations of stars, including Alnilam at the location of Stonehenge. We know that for many Neolithic cultures Orion was an important constellation representing the psychopomp welcoming the spirit to the Netherworld.

Chapter 8 presents results of research conducted in 2012, the objective of which was to understand the purpose of the four Station Stones at the Stonehenge monument ca. 2500 BC. An important finding of that research is shown in Figure 49. The size and shape of the Avenue extending northeast from Stonehenge is the product of translocating the right arm of Orion onto the Stonehenge Landscape. Orion's right shoulder is represented by the star Betelgeuse, which on the ground is the location of Stonehenge. Rigel representing Orion's left knee or foot is represented at Amesbury 14.

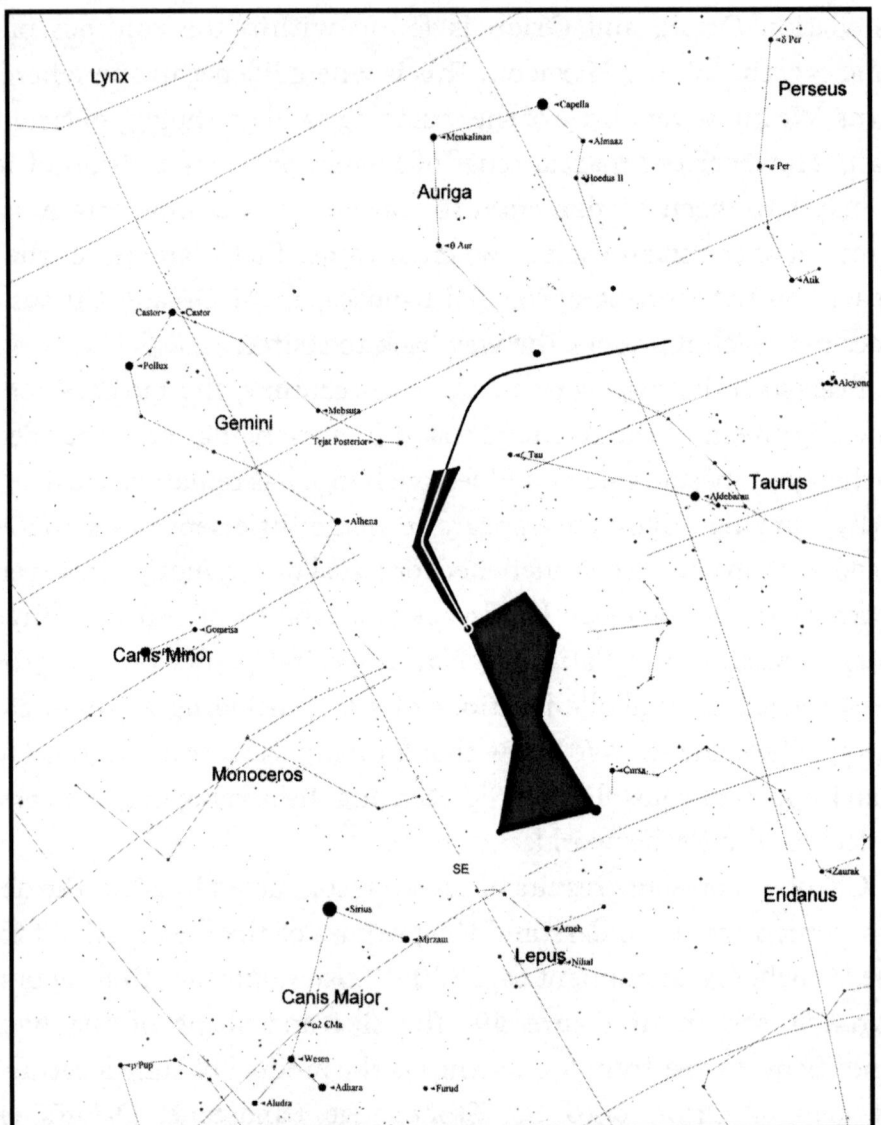

Figure 49: Illustration showing the size and orientation of Orion if plotted precisely with Rigel (representing Orion's left foot) at the location of long barrow Amesbury 14 and Stonehenge the symbolic location of Betelgeuse (Orion's right shoulder). In so doing, the Avenue accurately traces Orion's right arm up (northeastward) from Betelgeuse through μOri to ξ Ori(Orion's elbow), and then east to Chi2 Ori (Orion's wrist). The Avenue then continues through the galactic anticenter, Alnath and parallel with the ecliptic.

The Avenue is an accurate tracing of Orion's right arm and spear or sword (Figure 50). From Stonehenge the Avenue extends northeast and then east, accurately replicating the links between stars that represent Orion's elbow and wrist. It is an accurate tracing of Orion's right arm up (northeastward) from Betelgeuse through Orion's right elbow (between μOri and ξ Ori), and then east to Chi2 Ori (Orion's wrist). The Avenue continues eastward until it crosses the scaled location of the ecliptic where it begins a curve southward and passes through the galactic anti-center and Alnath (the tip of Taurus' upper horn). The curve ends at Alnath and begins a straight section terminating at the west bank of the River Avon. That is the location of Bluestonehenge, discovered in 2009 during the Stonehenge Riverside Project. The Avenue does not continue south across the river, however, the east end of the Avenue is situated at what would be the beginning of a parallel alignment approximately 5 degrees north (above) the ecliptic.

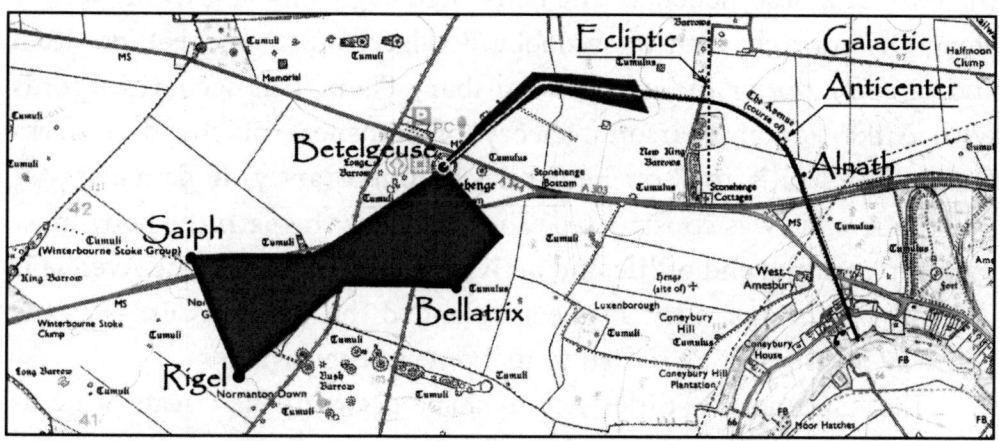

Figure 50: Illustration showing the size and orientation of Orion if plotted precisely with Stonehenge the symbolic location of Betelgeuse (Orion's right shoulder). In so doing, the Avenue accurately traces Orion's right arm up (northeastward) from Betelgeuse through Orion's right elbow (between μOri and ξ Ori), and then east to Chi2 Ori (Orion's wrist). The Avenue then continues through the galactic anticenter and Alnath before ending at the west bank of the River Avon. (base map copyright Crown Copyright/database right 2011. An Ordnance Survey/ EDINA supplied service)

The correspondence cannot be coincidental given all other relationships described herein between the Winter Hexagon, Orion and monuments located across the landscape. Additional evidence for this is presented in Chapter 8. It provides very strong evidence that the Stonehenge Sacred Landscape was constructed as an Earth bound representation of the area of the Winter Hexagon. However between the time when the cursus and hexagon were constructed ca. 3500 BC, and construction of the Avenue and installation of the Heelstone some nine hundred to eleven hundred years later, different scales were used in the transfer of star points to locations on land.

The correlation between the astral geometry of Orion and the Avenue's alignment explains the alignment's purpose. The Avenue is a sacred, earthly, symbolic representation of the right arm of Orion reaching out to receive the body of the dead after it has arrived from its journey downriver from Durrington Walls and then onto the bank of the river at Bluestonehenge. The body then begins its landward journey along Orion's right arm to symbolic Betelgeuse (Stonehenge) for ritual and ceremony prior to burial on Salisbury Plain. This scenario accords with Mike Parker Pearson's theory of transport of the dead from Durrington Walls to Stonehenge. More importantly, it demonstrates *why* the Avenue was constructed. The Avenue is the path the body must take between the end of life and arriving home in Earth. The Avenue is the pathway of mortality. It is equivalent to the Greater Cursus as the pathway for the spirit's return to its home in the cosmos.

There is a notable difference in shape between the Greater Cursus and the Avenue built centuries later. The cursus appears to be very much inorganic in form, constructed of straight lines and sharp corners, like broken ice, sherds of pottery, flakes from toolmaking, triangles formed by the astral nodes and links of constellations. It is the spirit's gateway between Earth and sky. Conversely, the Avenue has no sharp corners. It is organic in shape, curved, flowing, gateway to the end of life made manifest. The difference in design may be intentional and revelatory, with both created to be seen from the cosmos.

The Grand Plan on the Stonehenge Sacred Landscape is a

translocation of an area of the night sky. It symbolizes the Milky Way, Winter Hexagon, Orion, and path of the Sun. Each point surveyed onto Salisbury Plain represented a star. This is the larger context within which ritual and ceremony would take place at individual locations such as Stonehenge and Woodhenge. Each monument was a microcosm of the universe, built as a more intimate context for communication with the Sun and Moon.

The landscape remains symbolic of human relationships with the cosmos and source of life. It demonstrates the strength of relationship between people and Earth. Ditches and banks of cursus and henges, and other elements of the landscape covered in white chalk may have been seen by people several kilometers away. However the Greater Cursus is immense. It size, shape and outline in white, like the henges that would follow, was meant to be seen from above, the cosmos and Creator looking at Earth and seeing a reflection of themselves.

The Stonehenge Sacred Landscape was a means of communicating human understanding of the never ending cycle of life as spirit, and a place where both the body and spirit could begin their journey back to where they came. It relates mortality of the body with eternal life of the spirit. It connects life on Earth with life in the cosmos. Since about 3500 BC it has represented the end of life of the body, and return of life as spirit to the Netherworld and the care of Orion. The Winter Hexagon is where spirits came from, and where spirits return. Upon death the body was interred to Earth, while the spirit took to the spirit path—the Milky Way beginning at Sirius—on its return journey from Earth to the center of the Winter Hexagon. That is where Orion as the psychopomp Sky King or Queen (perhaps both) waited to welcome the spirit in his right hand.

During the mid-Neolithic the Winter Hexagon of the spirit was symbolically replicated on Salisbury Plain. Orion was symbolically translocated as an earthly psychpomp, Earth god or goddess (perhaps both) to receive the body. By 2500 BC Orion made manifest on Earth reached out to the bank of the River Avon to welcome the body home on the Stonehenge Sacred Landscape. As above, so below.

Chapter 8
THE STATION STONES

Mother Earth is a basic anthropological world view which reappears in time in different fields. In many Neolithic and later societies, as in the Mediterranean and other parts of the world including the contemporary lands of the Amerindians and Hindu Indians, Mother Earth sites and sanctuaries are known not only from prehistory but from historical times too. Additionally, there is material evidence from the nature of art and artefacts, and there can be inferential evidence from the character of symbols and images. Some sanctuaries may be identifiable by their shape. At some sites, rocks or standing stones have inscribed images of anthropomorphic form, or megaliths are arranged, or tombs designed, in such a fashion as to imply that a culture of Earth Mother belief may be inferred or is known. In other places, as with geometrized man-made objects such as settlements or necropolises, non-iconic patterns sometimes support the same symbolism.

—Terence Meaden[1]

Introduction

Stonehenge is recognized for its' association with ancient astronomy. Orientation of the henge's central axis toward summer solstice sunrise was first recognized in modern times by William Stukeley in 1720. Since then the monument has been claimed to be an ancient observatory. Stonehenge is well known for the Heelstone (amongst others) across the causeway at the northeast side of the henge, and the theory that those elements of the monument indicate the importance of summer solstice sunrise on design of the Late Neolithic structure. Yet the alignment is approximate at best, and less accurate 4500 years ago than it is today.[2]

Numerous alignments of stones toward astronomical events have been proposed since discovery of the apparent summer solstice alignment. In some cases the purported alignments have been used to date the megalithic construction. An article written by Gerald Hawkins published in 1963 in the journal *Nature*, and Hawkins' book *Stonehenge Decoded* published two years later, added to the fervor for demonstrable alignments. Using the efficiency of computer calculations Hawkins attempted to identify stones aligned with solar and lunar events.[3] He explained how the circle of fifty six Aubrey Holes located inside the henge's bank could be used to predict eclipses. Dozens of solar and lunar alignments were discovered for the time during which Stonehenge was believed to have been constructed, estimated in the mid-1960s to have been about 1500 BC. Unfortunately the megalithic structure is now known to be one thousand years older. All the same, Stonehenge does appear to have been created with certain astronomical events in mind.

The four Station Stones at Stonehenge are often cited in regard to their spatial relationship with the Aubrey circle, the plan of the sarsens and bluestones, and alignments approximate with summer and winter solstices and lunar extremes (Figure 51). The sarsen circle is centered almost perfectly inside the Station Stone quadrilateral. However, the stone's late Neolithic contribution to function in terms of the monument's sacred architecture has been vague at best.

Purpose

This chapter presents methods, results and conclusions of research and analysis conducted by the author in 2012. The objective was to understand the purpose of the Station Stones as integral parts of Stonehenge ca. 2500 BC. This was about 1000 years after construction of the Greater Cursus and long barrows. It was during the late Neolithic when bluestone and sarsen megaliths were brought together, dressed and installed to create the massive structure we envision Stonehenge was first designed and constructed.

Figure 51: SS 93, one of two remaining Station Stones (SS) at Stonehenge. The four stones were located almost along the circle of Aubrey holes, between the megalithic circle of sarsens seen in the back ground, and the ditch and bank serving as the perimeter of the monument and boundary between the sacred and profane.

Stonehenge is the best known example of ancient megalithic architecture in Europe. Many theories explain the intent and use of the monument. Since the seventeenth century most interpretations of the monument's various circles of stones, numerous post holes, and ditch and bank propose the structure was constructed to assist observation of astronomical events. The suggested phenomena include solar risings and settings during solstices and equinoxes, lunar maximum and minimum standstills, and the path of Venus. However, other than a modest number of perceived alignments (such as one between the monument's center and the Heel Stone as an intended orientation toward summer solstice sunrise) the archaeological community has in general been skeptical of such intent. Many of the theories do not address techniques necessary for observing the various roughly defined alignments that are often found to be only approximate.

If the purpose of Stonehenge in its various phases of construction was to provide a means for astronomical observation using alignments built over the course of many centuries, then the question must be asked:

Why was such great effort undertaken time and again, by at least several cultures,

- to plan, design and construct a series of earthen, wooden and lithic monuments (latter ones constructed of stones of megalithic size and mass),

- at times requiring transporting building materials as much as 240 km (150 miles) across difficult topographic and hydrogeologic conditions,

- for the purpose of observing astronomical events that would likely have been known by the mid-fourth millennia BCE (a thousand years before construction of the monument) to occur in regular cycles completed in less than thirty years,

- including the Sun's annual path along the ecliptic, the Moon's 18.6 year cycle caused by lunar precession, and the orbital motion of planets about the Sun?

Such an undertaking hardly makes any sense. The hypothesis for this study was that Stonehenge is more than a remnant of an ancient astronomical observatory, and therefore the Station Stones (SS) may represent more than components used during less than accurate observation of astronomical events, time and time again.

For the purpose of this chapter, reference to the four Station Stones is generally intended to mean each of the stone's locations, rather than the stones themselves. The stones represent corners of a large quadrilateral extending from the northwest side of the circle of fifty-six Aubrey Holes to the southeast side. They do not fit precisely along the circumference, nor are they located over any of the Aubrey holes (Figure 52).

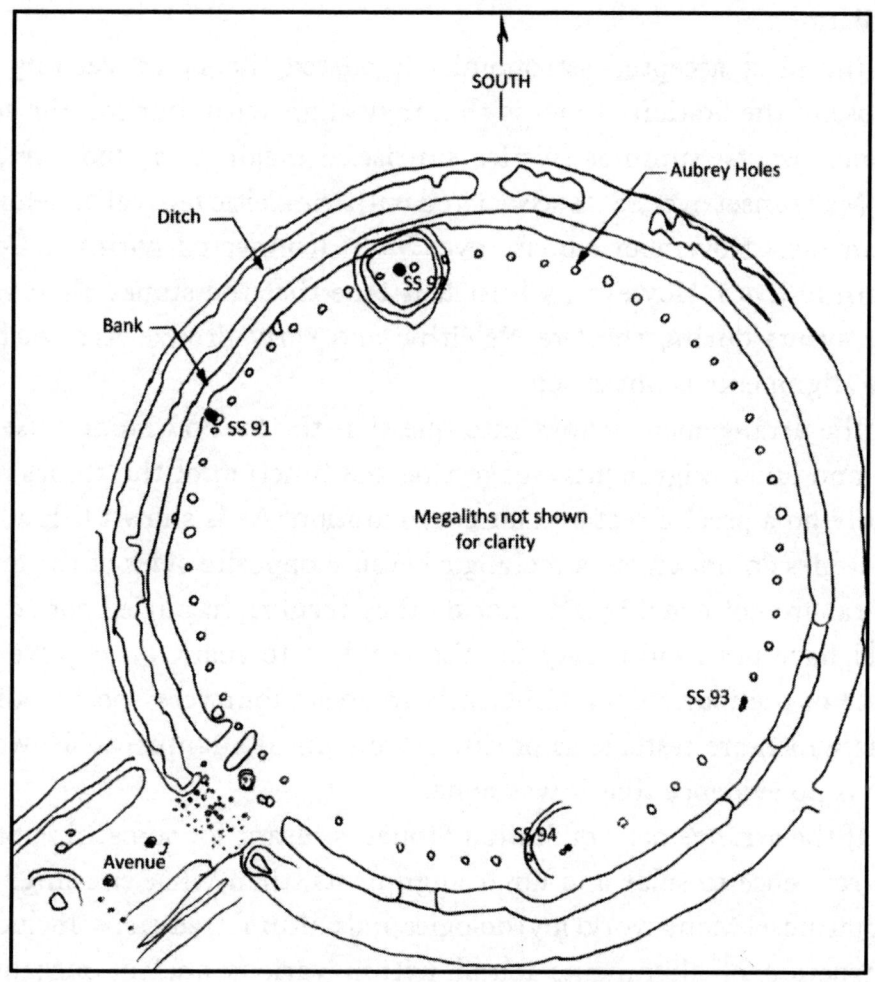

Figure 52: Locations of the four Station Stones (drawing by author based on North, J. (1997), fig.157)

The quadrilateral configuration is unusual in that the monument generally expresses a circular geometry, a shape often symbolizing the sphere of world (meaning Earth, cosmos, universe as it was applied by many ancient and indigenous cultures throughout history).[4] The cosmic dome is above and Earth as the bottom hemisphere is below. Curvilinear banks and ditches, although shallow, surround the former locations of SS 92 and SS 94. Those two stones were removed from the monument for unknown reasons many years ago. The other two megaliths, SS 91 and SS 93, are situated on level ground. Each of the four stones is thought to have stood well above the height of a man at the time of its installation.

The most accepted astronomically-related theory concerning the purpose of the Station Stones is that they align with four specific solar or lunar events: summer solstice sunrise, a major lunar moonset, an early May sunset over SS 93 (associated with the Celtic festival of Beltane), and an early November sunrise over SS 91 (connected with the Celtic Samain festival). However, whilst it is true that the stones align with those events during the late Neolithic and early Bronze Age, each of those alignments is not exact.

The arrangement brings into question the Station Stones' use for solar and lunar alignments, suggesting the function of the stones does not rely on a precise rectangular configuration. As is shown below, the four stones do not create a rectangle because opposite sides of the quadrilateral are not equal length, nor do they form right angled corners. It would have been quite easy for the builders to mark or engrave the surface of the four stones sufficiently to create four very specific alignments which are testable as precise astronomical alignments. However there is no evidence that it was done.

If the arrangement of Station Stones is meant for something other than reference to solar and lunar alignments, then what else might be their purpose? Many world mythologies and cultural traditions, including construction of alignments found within various ancient megalithic structures. Some structures contain information about calendrical concerns that go well beyond measurement of days, nights, months or years, including the cyclical major lunar standstill of about 18.6 years. Some ancient traditions concern precession—the near 25,800 year cycle associated with a wobble in Earth's rotation resulting in the apparent rise and fall of stars and rotation of the equinoctial points through the twelve constellations of the zodiac. Is it possible that the Station Stones are associated with discovery, measurement or monitoring of precession?

With the predominant geometry of Stonehenge being circular, the architectural form is indicative of the monument's representation of a sphere, or spheres within spheres. In so doing it may express the designer's intent to symbolize sacred relationships between people, Earth, cosmos and Creator, in whatever way a creator of the world may be perceived by the culture. The approach applied herein to demystify the architecture of this ancient megalithic monument, specifically the four Station Stones, was first to understand the culture responsible for its design ca. 2500 BCE. Then the architecture of the structure itself was analyzed, and testable characteristics of environment were identified that would connect the structure to the people responsible for its construction.

Analysis
Date of Construction

As with other ancient megalithic structures, approximating the date of construction of Stonehenge might be deduced from the orientation of the structure with respect to its environment, but the reliability of such a conclusion would depend on the precision of alignments and opinion concerning contemporary practices of building orientation.[5] The orientation of a structure may be related to the azimuth of features or events situated along the plane of Earth's surface such as solar or lunar risings and settings. It can be to skyward, to events such as star positions with reference to both azimuth and altitude. Recognizing such messages encrypted into a monument may lead to determining a date (or dates) associated with the structure, as well as understanding the purpose of form it exhibits.

In previous chapters we saw that use of Salisbury Plain and nearby environs for ritual and ceremonial purposes predates the first phase of megalithic construction at Stonehenge by more than a thousand years. At the time of Phase 3 construction in the mid-third millennium, great earthen and timbered structures were being constructed at Durrington Walls and Woodhenge. Figure 53 depicts locations of Durrington Walls, Woodhenge, Stonehenge (DWS) and other major features of the land-scape. The scale of planning, design and construction activities required to achieve those manifestations of a sacred cosmology meant involvement of people from throughout Britain.[6]

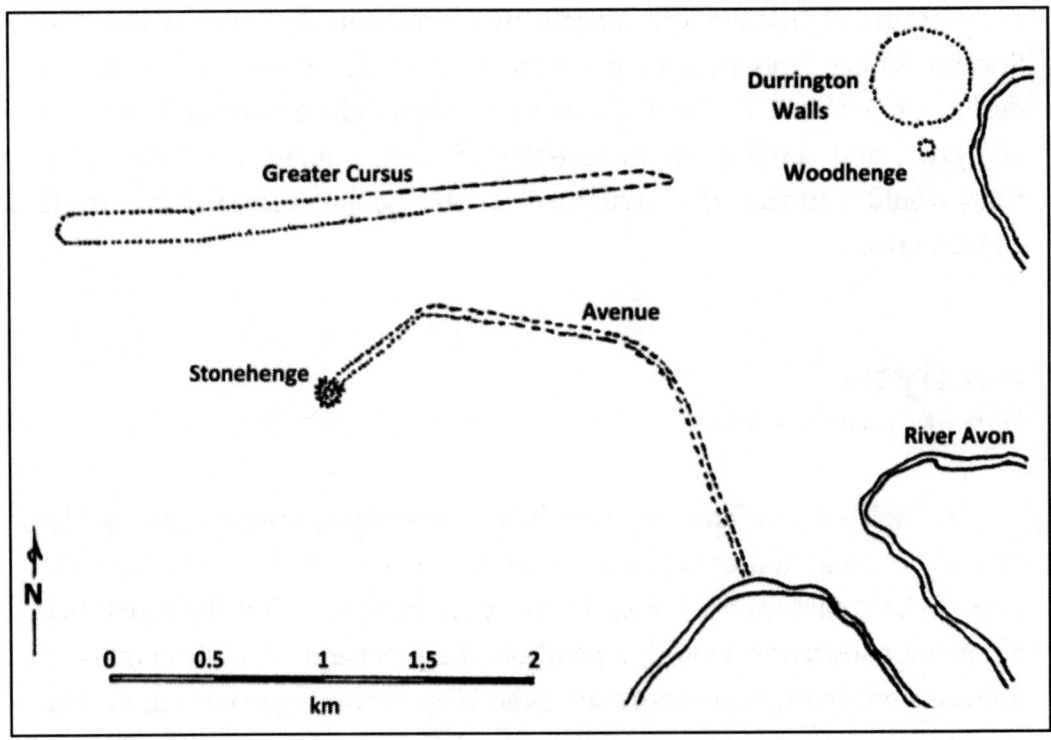

Figure 53: Major features at the Durrington Walls, Woodhenge and Stonehenge (DWS) complex.

Stonehenge was occupied by a henge within which were wooded structures in various configurations until about 2600 BCE when Phase 3 construction introduced megalithic elements to the monument. Phase 3 included erection of the great stone monoliths and trilithons and continued over several centuries. Parker Pearson *et al* (2007) subdivides the Phase 3 period into six sub-phases (3i through 3vi).[8] Table 7 summarizes dates of on-site lithic constructions, other important engineering works at Stonehenge, and evidence of nearby and contemporaneous Grooved Ware/Beaker Ware use, and inhumation rites, during those sub-phases. The Table indicates erection of megaliths beginning with the bluestone arc during sub-phase 3i prior to 2470 BCE, followed by sub-phase 3ii with installation of the sarsen circle and trilithons, the Slaughter stones, and possibly the bluestones inside the horseshoe of trilithons between 2600 and 2400 BCE.

Table 7: Stonehenge Phase 3i—3iv Chronology
(based on Parker Pearson et al (2007))

Sub-phase	Timeframe	Items	Artefacts	Other Sites
3i	Pre-2470 BC	Bluestone arc	Beakers possibly in use	Durrington Walls Southern Circle Phase 1
3ii	2580-2470 BC and 2600-2400 BC	Sarsen circle, trilithons, Slaughter stones, possible bluestones set inside trilithon horseshoe	Beakers possibly in use	Durrington Walls Southern Circle Phase 2, Avenue and settlement, Begin construction of Stonehenge Avenue
3iii	2450-2210 BC	Large pit and features in west, possible removal of bluestones	Beaker inhumation rite begins; artefacts at nearby sites	Woodhenge ditch Beaker-age burial in Stonehenge ditch, Re-cutting Stonehenge Avenue
3iv	2270-2030 BC	Bluestone oval	Beaker inhumation rite continues; artefacts at nearby sites; Grooved Ware ends	Re-cutting Stonehenge Avenue; Round barrows

Approximate solar and lunar alignments indicated by the Station Stones are related to the circular array of sarsen megaliths occupying the central portion of the monument. That would place the time frame of erecting the Station Stones in the mid-third millennium, during sub-phase 3ii. A mid-sub-phase 3ii date of 2500 BC is applied herein for the approximate time when the four Station stones were installed.

It is likely that Durrington Walls and Woodhenge were contemporary with the sarsen and bluestone circles at Stonehenge, and that the monuments were used for specific applications within one complex of ceremony and ritual. The Durrington Walls henge bank and ditch, and both Northern and Southern Circles encircled by them, were constructed about 2500-2400 BC. The Southern Circle at Durrington Walls and the megalithic circles at Stonehenge were re-formed and rebuilt between ca. 2500-2000 BCE. Also, the same solar axis is evident in the construction of the timber oval at Woodhenge and the Avenue at Stonehenge.

Perspective

For many ancient cultures the constellation that seemed to be in human form is Orion. Much has been said in previous chapters about Orion's relationship with the Stonehenge Sacred Landscape. It is not possible to detail the importance of Orion at numerous Neolithic sites located across the British Isles, such as the enormous Thornborough Henges in North Yorkshire, England, which appear to represent the three stars of Orion's belt. With many references readily available on the topic, forthwith are brief descriptions of two sites.

Long Man of Wilmington

There is at Wilmington in East Sussex a figure perfectly placed to mark Orion's apparent movement across the ridge above (Figure 54). John North dates the Long Man to the mid-fourth millennium BC based on the geometrical configuration of the Long Man of Wilmington and nearby Windover Hill long barrow, and azimuths and altitudes of stars including Rigel and Kappa Orionis.[9] The figure is located on a north-facing 30° grassy slope. It is a trenched outline of a human holding a vertical staff in each hand. Christopher Hawkes and others have suggested that the staffs might represent spears.

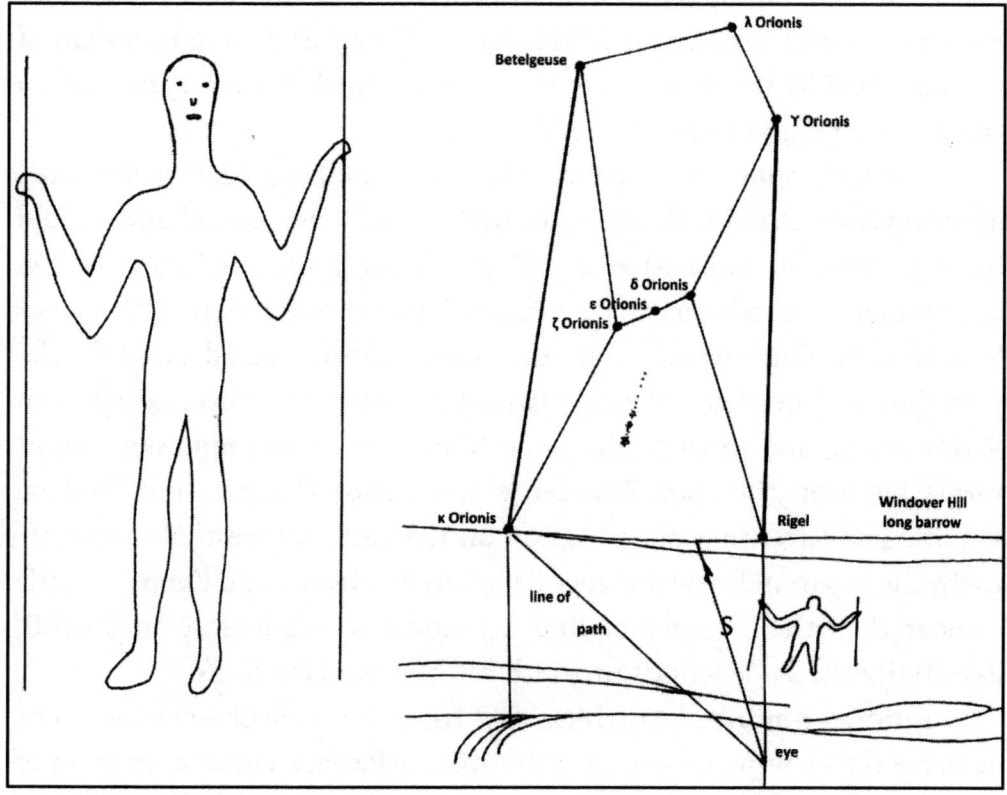

Figure 54: Sketch of the Long Man of Wilmington, East Sussex (left) and Orion depicted above the Long Man ca. 3500 BCE (right). Illustrations based on North, J. (1997), figures 82 and 84)

Lengths of the staffs are 70.3 m (east) and 71.8 m (west). They are spaced at 35.6 m at the top of the figure and 34.8 m at the bottom, providing a height to width ratio of about 2:1 (Note this is the same ratio as the length to width of early-to mid-Neolithic houses mentioned in the previous chapter). Viewed orthogonally from the air the figure is out of proportion compared to the natural height:width ratio of the human body. However, when viewed from a near level position the Long Man tends closer to normal proportions and the height to width ratio of the staves approaches 7:5 or 1.4:1. It is this human figure confined by the two staffs that North finds similar to the constellation Orion. The staffs "point the way to an understanding of the functioning of the giant, whose human form merely confirms what is to be deduced without reference to him at all in the first instance." They are also reminiscent of the staff held by the procreative Phanes enveloped by the cosmic egg on the bas relief depicted in Figure 48.

North demonstrates that ca. 3480 BCE the Long Man represented a translocated Orion walking upon Earth, while the constellation could be seen overhead. Stars Rigel and Kappa Orionis appeared moving east to west along the southern horizon modified by construction of Windover long barrow. Envisioned in human form, Orion would straddle the meridian and be seen moving ('walking') along the horizon between Rigel's rising and setting. The Long Man's two staffs represent alignments between the stars Betelgeuse and Kappa Orionis, and Gamma Orionis and Rigel that bound Orion on the east and west. Not surprisingly, the apparent lineal distance between Betelgeuse and Kappa Orionis compared to the distance of Kappa Orionis to Rigel is about 2.0:1.0, essentially the same length to width ratio as the two staffs.

Another finding of North's is that from the same observation point as above for viewing Orion, ca. 3500 BCE, Aldebaran and other stars of the lower (east) 'horn' in the constellation Taurus (including Alnath) could have been seen rising above the horizon at nearly the same moment. This suggests great value placed on those two astral displays, a culturally perceived relationship between the constellations Taurus and Orion. Those two constellations, in tandem with Sirius in Canis Major, are known to be related in cosmographies of many cultures throughout time, whether they were perceived as a bull, warrior and dog, respectively, or other symbols of import.

Skara Brae

Artwork and symbols incised or impressed on Grooved Ware (GW) often include parallel lines, cross-hatching, spirals, and lozenges. Spirals were carved onto stonework found in passage tombs in Boyne Valley, Ireland, where GW culture might have first taken hold (Figure 55). In Great Britain the areal extent of stonework and pottery exhibiting such symbolism ranges from the Orkneys to mainland Scotland, and from Yorkshire to the lowlands of southern England.

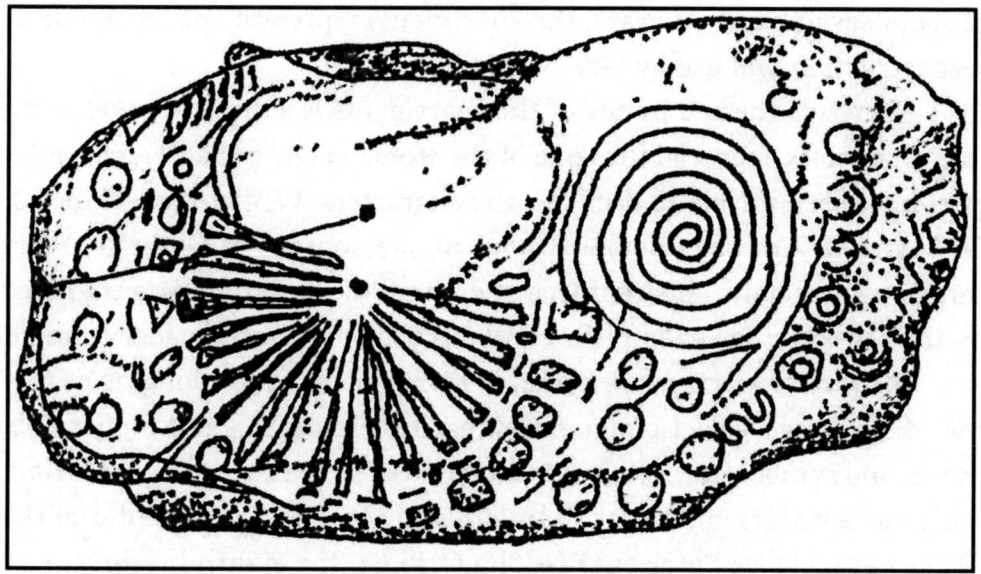

Figure 55: Grooved Ware symbols carved on kerbstone K15 at Knowth, Brú na Bóinne, Ireland

The characteristic shape of GW pottery in tandem with the breadth of standard motifs associated with GW culture appears to have matured in the Orkneys, where the northern end of the ancient and well-established Atlantic sea route is known. Aubrey Burl concludes that GW symbols such as meandering and straight lines, lozenges and small dots, although often discovered in passage-tombs, do not resemble anything of modern significance, yet the symbols must have had importance in ancient rituals. The Orkney pottery is dated as early as about 3400 BCE, and Grooved Ware became a tradition in southern England by about 2800 BCE.

Skara Brae is a cluster of ancient one-room apartments located on the west shore of the Isle of Orkney north of mainland Scotland. The late Neolithic settlement was occupied from about 3180 to 2500 BC. The apartments are connected by covered walkways that were filled with midden material creating a semi-subterranean environment for the residents. All but one of the single room apartments was furnished with stone slabs to create central hearths, box-beds and dresser shelving. One unit was used as a workshop. Occupied in three phases over the course of about seven hundred years, the apartments represent the last phase of reconstruction and use by GW people.

Alongside the bed in one of the apartments is a dry stack wall with four characters engraved into one of the stones (Figure 55a).[10] Archaeologists have been unable to decipher the characters. Whilst significance of GW symbols has been demonstrated in the context of GW ritual and ceremony, it is quite apparent that the intent of the symbolism engraved on the bedside stone exemplifies GW culture in a much broader context.

The four characters are symbols representing stars along or nearby the Milky Way's galactic plane. Comparing Figure 56a and Figure 56b, the second symbol from the left is interpreted as the constellation Orion, with the belt stars of Alnitak, Alnilam and Mintaka at the center of the 'X'. Orion includes Betelgeuse (Alpha Orionis, the eighth brightest star in the night sky) and Rigel (Beta Orionis, sixth brightest star in the night sky). The hook extending to the right and down from the 'X' represents links between stars comprising Orion's right arm reaching into the adjoining galactic plane, and stars located in the west horn of Taurus leading to Aldebaran. Note the similarity of the hook of the 'X' in Figure 56a and the Avenue at Stonehenge in Figure 53.

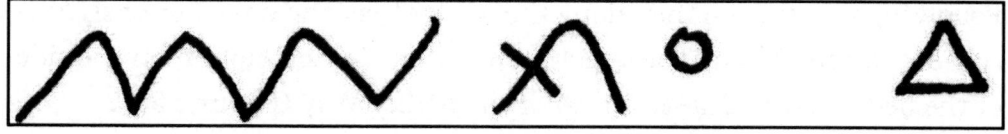

a)

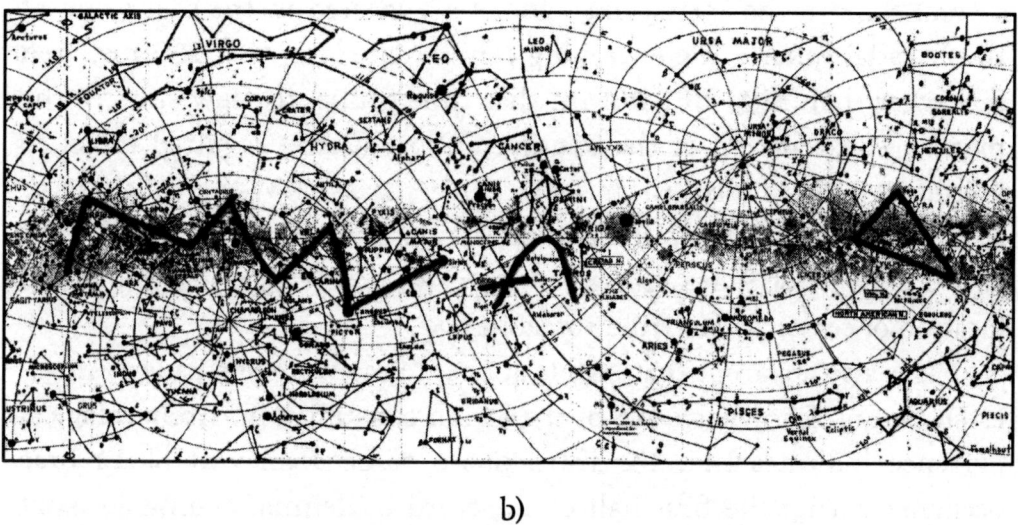

b)

Figure 56: a) Engraved figures on stone at Skara Brae, b) Map of Milky Way showing relevant star locations

The next symbol to the right is a small circle interpreted as the star Capella (Alpha Aur), brightest star in the constellation Auriga and third brightest star seen from the northern hemisphere. The symbol at the extreme right represents the Summer Triangle constellation of Deneb (Alpha Cygni, nineteenth brightest star), Vega (brightest star in constellation Lyra, fifth brightest in the night sky, and second brightest in the northern celestial hemisphere) and Altair (brightest star in constellation Aquila and twelfth brightest in the night sky). The fourth character is the figure on the left. After backtracking along the Milky Way from the Summer Triangle to Capella and then to Orion, we begin tracing across a number of bright stars and constellations starting with Sirius, followed by Canopus, the False Cross, the Southern Cross, Centaurus, Triangulum Astral, Scorpios and Sagittarius. The major stars in those parts of the Milky Way are corners of a spring-like figure with seven segments.

Following this line farther along the Milky Way the next star of significance is, again, Altair. The conclusion is that the inscription on the side of the bed at Skara Brae is a map of the Milky Way (Figure 56b).

The symbols at Skara Brae are important because they document knowledge of stars located along the entire galactic plane. However, several stars in the spring-like symbol are located in the south half of the celestial sphere. The engraving cannot date later that 2500 BC and no earlier than 3180 BC. Within that time frame, to view stars in the modern constellation of the Southern Cross (Crux) required travel to latitude 24° N, at least as far south as the coast of Western Sahara or Mauritania along the west horn of Africa. The engraving is evidence that occupants of Skara Brae were either well-traveled or learned of the location of certain stars from someone else.

It is also apparent that people at Skara Brae were particularly interested in, and knowledgeable of the Orion constellation. Archaeological evidence indicates that the third phase of occupancy at Skara Brae occurred during the first half of the third millennia, ending at about 2500±150 BCE, about the same time that Stonehenge Phase 3 construction (including the Station Stones) began.

Common Neolithic Interest in Astronomy

Star locations provide a means of relating the observable night sky to geographic position—vital knowledge for seafarers as well as migratory people such as Mesolithic hunters and gathers transitioning to Neolithic agriculturalists. The four astronomical symbols at Skara Brae, in tandem with numerous circles of standing stones across the British Isles, suggests that GW culture was greatly interested in astronomy, cosmology and cosmography. Those interests are common with Neolithic cultures around the world, including in the Middle East, Africa and the Americas. Sumerian and predynastic Egyptian interests in astral events, and the relationship between those events and the respective cultural cosmogonies and mythologies, are well known. The portion of the sky of greatest interest in Sumeria and predynastic and Old Kingdom Egypt was in and around the Winter Hexagon, including the Milky Way, ecliptic and Orion.

Less well known are the interest and capability of the pre-Columbian Lakota tribe with regard to astronomy and its relationship with tribal cosmology and mythology. In brief, each year the Lakota migrated across and around the Black Hills of South Dakota, Wyoming and Montana. The migration was conducted in accordance with specific annual events seen in the night sky. Stars were accurately mapped on buffalo hides which were cared for as sacred documents. The star symbol was a triangle pointing up, touching the tip of an inverted triangle, similar to the shape of an hourglass. Each inverted triangle represented a star. Each adjoining triangle represented a specific location on Earth. Lakota cosmology demonstrates extensive understanding of the mechanics of the solar system and cosmos in general, including knowledge of precession of the equinoxes.[11, 12]

The Lakota paid particular attention to the area of the Winter Hexagon, a particularly important part of the night sky. They replaced Aldebaran with the asterism of the Pleiades for one of the hexagon's six points (Figure 57).[13] Castor and Auriga β are shown along the subcircular constellation. The area's importance is remindful of the design and purpose of the Stonehenge Sacred Landscape ca. 3500 BC.

The circle of stars is called Red Running Path (Lakota: *Ki Inyanka Ocanku Sa*). On Earth it is represented by a ring of red sandstone and shale that surrounds the Black Hills of South Dakota. In the middle of the path is *Hocoka*, the center, womb of the universe, the intersection of the galactic plane and ecliptic at the right hand of Orion. The earthly equivalent of Hocoka is *Pa Sla* (Bald Spot), a gently rolling grass-covered plain at the center of the tree-covered Black Hills. Pa Sla is the center of the sacred world of the Lakota world. It is also represented by Wind Cave, where the Lakota arrived on this world.

Hocoka is understood to be the galactic core. The galactic anticenter is very close to center of the Milky Way-ecliptic intersection point and may be considered coincidental with that intersection. It is only about four degrees of the ecliptic and about one degree from the galactic plane. This area is the center of the universe, and the center of the cross is the center of the Sacred Hoop. Perhaps the most important symbol for many Native American tribes, the Sacred Hoop represents home, the world and universe.

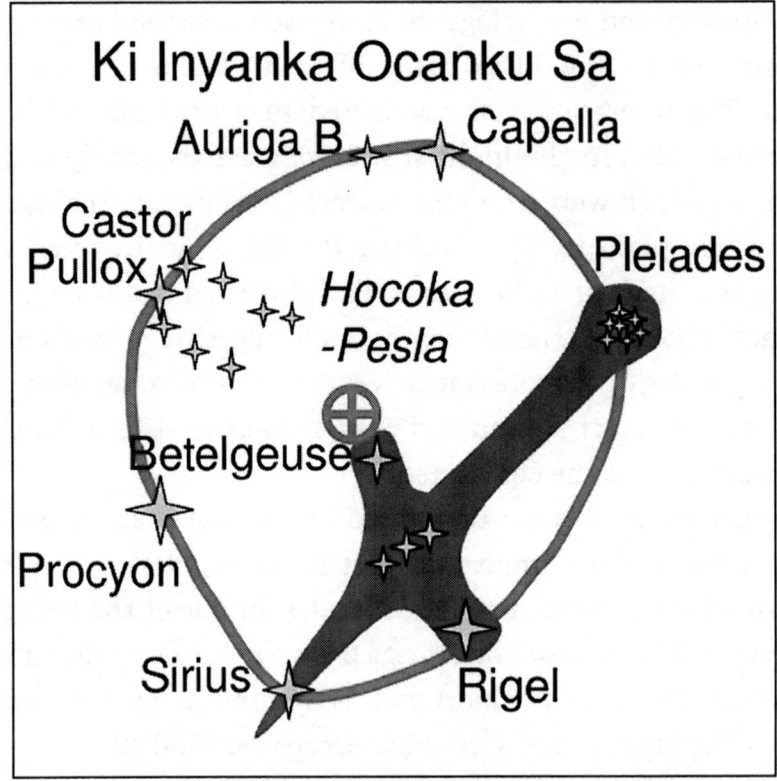

Figure 57: Lakota constellations and asterisms centered on the intersection of the galactic plane and ecliptic near Orion's right hand. The Lakota identified specific physiographic features of the natural landscape that correlated with the configuration of constellations depicted here. (Courtesy Victor Douville, Sinte Gleska University, 2011)

At conception a soul emerges from Hocoka and enters an embryo to give life to a baby. The brown form inside the Red Runnig Path in Figure 56 is a spirit animal (Tayamni) emerging from Hocoka as a buffalo embryo. The Pleiades represent its head, Orion's belt the ribs, Betelgeuse and Rigel its feet, and Sirius the tail. Thus Figure 57 is a representation of a soul which has entered a spiritual body at birth from the womb of the universe.

The Milky Way crosses the Red Running Path, from Sirius to Capella. Like the Greater Cursus, it is Wanagi Tacanku, Path of the Spirit, or Ghost Trail (wanagi is the soul or spirit after death of the body). The Red Running Path and its' center parallel the cosmogeographical importance of the Winter Hexagon and intersection of the galactic plane and ecliptic. For the Lakota, the cosmic hexagon is represented on Earth by the Black Hills, He Sapa:Heart of Everything. At the center of the Black Hills is Pe sla: Bare Place, Bald Spot, center of the Lakota world, center of the heart of everything that is. At Salisbury Plain this location is at the east end of the Greater Cursus, Amesbury 42.

Figure 58 illustrates the cosmological context within which the Red Running Path is located.[14] The figure includes a depiction of a rotating Earth and its cycle of precession (hocoka hektakigle: center of rotating circle; that which returns to where it came). The Lakota recognized that Earth has a wbble as it spins which results in the North Pole appearing to point to the edge of a circle in the cosmos, going around that circle every 26,000 years. That is the precessional cycle.

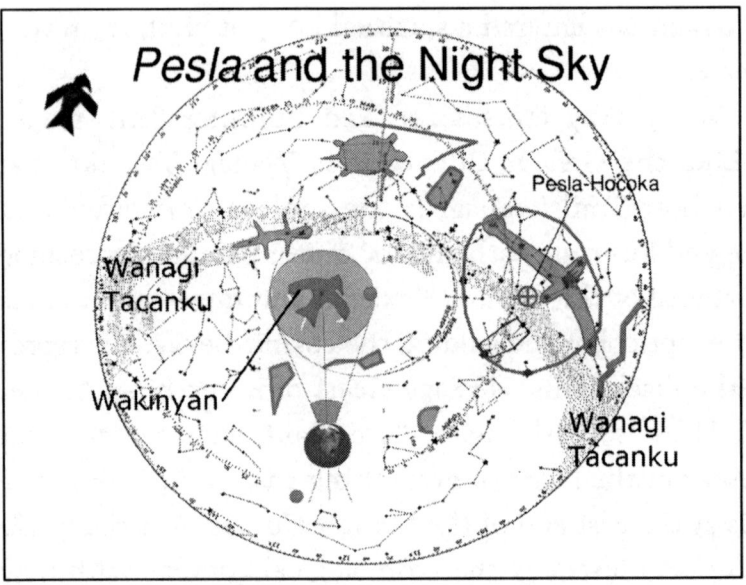

Figure 58: Life in the Lakota world revolves around the center of the Black Hills in South Dakota, the heart of everthing that is. The heart of Life in the universe is found in the heart of Wakinyan (Flying Mystery) which flies around the center of the earth's precessional cycle, the center of everything in the universe. (Courtesy Victor Douville, Sinte Gleska University, 2011)

Inside hocoka hektakigle is the Thunderbird (Wakinyan: Flying Mystery) soaring in a circle completed once each precessional cycle; and at the center of thunderbird is Wakinyan Tacante, the heart of Wakinyan, the celestial center of everything in the universe. Its earthly equivalent is He Sapa, the Black Hills.

Although living in a Neolithic world until the mid-19th century, it is readily apparent that the Lakota like many indigenous tribes of the Americas were careful observers of the sky. The Milky Way was interpreted to be the Spirit Path along which spirits of life came to Earth, and where they return. The astronomical equivalent of the center of their world was at the center of the galactic cross, and all things in the universe revolved around the center point of earth's axial precession. There is potential for similar knowledge expressed on the Stonehenge Sacred Landscape.

Contemporary Astronomy and Calendar Development

Design of Stonehenge Phase 3 was directed toward constructions relating an observer to the geometry of space within a circle, alignments of points, and symmetry expressed through architecture of the monument. These were achievements of people knowledgeable of the slow churn of astronomical events not limited to those at the horizon, but above the horizon—events displayed across the cosmic dome. They capably transferred observations of infinite four dimensional space and time to constraints of Earth's two dimensional surface. With longitude of little significance to astronomical observation, the greater concern is latitude whereby angles between winter and summer solstice risings and settings, and angles between solar and lunar events are unique.

There is no evidence indicating the definition of the moment of astronomical rising or setting at the horizon as applied circa Stonehenge Phase 3 development. There are no records, the monument is in disrepair, and alignments of stones toward specific astronomical events are approximate at best. For purpose of this study rising and setting are defined as first glint, the moment that an orb first appears upon the horizon. That is the definition applied when using astronomical software during the analysis. Atmospheric refraction is not accounted for, assuming that astronomic events of concern ca. 2500 BCE were based on naked eye observations.

Precession causes the angle between solar solstice rising and setting to change over time, but quite slowly. Observation and recording of the sun's risings and settings over a period of 366 days would be sufficient to plot and predict locations of similar events for many years that follow. Lunar extremes change month to month, although they do not exceed limits of the moon's major and minor standstills that cycle through a period of about 18.61 years. Almost nineteen years of diurnal data would be necessary before a full set of lunar rising and setting positions could be known and predicted, let alone solar and lunar eclipses requiring an understanding of the path of the ecliptic and the relationship between solar and lunar locations over time.

Accurate determination of the day and season of the year during the Neolithic likely involved identifying the alignment (azimuth) of an observer's location with respect to sunrise or sunset on a given date. However, there are other means of time keeping that were important to many ancient and indigenous cultures, one of those being heliacal risings and settings of planets and stars. Just as observation of the Sun provides a measure of space and time between dawn and dusk, planets and stars can serve as reference points to the spatial and temporal aspects of Earth and the cosmos between dusk and dawn.

By careful and considerable attention to solar, lunar, planetary and astral movements over time, a record can be constructed of the pathways and intersections of those bodies. Such observations lead to understanding the mechanics of the solar system and galaxy, and the relationship between the two in space and time. That understanding can lead to an ability to recognize and predict the time of year when certain planets, stars and asterisms first rise (their heliacal rise) just before sunrise, and the setting of those same bodies (heliacal setting) immediately after the sun sets. Other important events may include a body's last (acronychal) rising after sunset and first (cosmical) setting before sunrise.

Evidence of calendar development resulting from recognizing the relationship between the Sun's changing rising and setting positions on the horizon, as well as risings and settings of stars, has been documented for ancient cultures including Maya, Egyptian and others. There is no reason not to expect this to have been the case in southern England during the third millennium BC. John North outlines his reasoning behind this being the situation at Stonehenge.

> *Modern commentators often seem to imply that the 'modern' way of calendar reference—with respect to solstice and equinox, defined in terms of the circles of the celestial sphere, the equator, and the ecliptic—is the natural successor to the labeling of the seasons in terms of the first and last risings and settings of named stars. It is not*

even approximately known when people first got a feeling for this latter sort of 'astronomically' defined calendar—which is an inessential byway of astronomical science—but it is likely to have come in some form at a very early date . . . it seems almost inevitable that when stars were observed over long periods, it would very soon have been noticed that they were not to be seen during certain period of the year. The two different traditions would therefore have gone naturally hand in hand—the more exact—a tradition of marking places on the horizon where rising and setting took place, and the other a tradition of correlating different sorts of seasonal weather with first and last sightings.[15]

The year can be perceived divided into quarters based on observations of summer and winter solstices, vernal and autumnal equinoxes, and determining the number of days between those events supplemented by recognizing heliacal risings of stars of cosmographical importance, with particular concern for scheduling agricultural activities. It is then a simple matter of dividing the year into eights, twelfths, sixteenths, or other subunits satisfactory to the needs of the culture.

Aubrey Holes, Station Stones and Sarsens

Burley (2012) details the universal importance of spherical geometry relating to numerous circular symbols and sacred architecture from around the world.[16] In that respect Stonehenge appears no different. The following is a brief review of spatial and metric characteristics of the Aubrey Holes, Station Stones and megalithic sarsens that surround the center of the monument.

The Aubrey Holes are named for John Aubrey who observed several slight depressions of the ground surface during a survey of Stonehenge in 1666. He concluded that each depression represented a former location of a stone. The fifty six holes are earth-filled pits arranged in a circle about 87 m (285 ft) in diameter. Today the location of each pit is marked by a concrete disc. In 1919 William Hawley used a metal rod to probe filled pits located in the northeast portion of the ring near the Slaughter Stone. He found those holes to be "at regular intervals of 16 feet [4.9 m] . . . To these we have given the name of 'Aubrey Holes' . . ."[17] During subsequent investigation Hawley located each of the fifty six pits and excavated fill from some but not all of them. The numbering scheme he applied to the pits remains in use today, beginning with Aubrey Hole 1 in the northeast portion of the henge near the south side of the Avenue, and continuing clockwise to number 56 across the Avenue from number 1. Pits 1 through 32, 55, and 56 have been excavated; numbers 33 through 54 have not.

The Aubrey Holes are situated about 19 ft (5.8 m) inside the bank enclosure. The holes are located along a circle with uniform radius. The radius of the circle based on Alexander Thom's measurements to the center of the pits is about 141.80 ft (43.22 m). It is not known if the builders used a length measured to the outer edge, inner edge, or center of each pit or post location.

Excavation of Aubrey Hole 5 near the east cardinal direction and Hole 21 near the south entrance yielded animal bones and long bone pins in matrices of chalk fill. Other pits contained cremated remains apparently placed after the holes were initially excavated and filled, and possibly refilled. Radiocarbon dating of a charcoal sample obtained from one of the pits provided a date of about 2400 BC, while analysis of eight samples of antler, animal bone and bone gouge taken from the peripheral ditch and associate with GW during the second phase of Stonehenge yield a combined date of about 2860 BC. That timeframe was prior to installing stones at the monument. Fragments of bluestone and sarsen have been encountered at the tops of the holes from later construction phases.

The four Stations were named by E.H. Stone in 1923, nearly a century after Rev. Edward Duke concluded that the short sides of the quadrilateral appeared to be Stations for observing midsummer sunrise and midwinter sunset. The longer sides were later found to approximate an alignment toward the northernmost setting of the moon, and toward the midsummer southern moonrise in the southeast.

The Station Stones (SS) are numbered 91 through 94 beginning with the Station located in the southeast quadrant of the Aubrey circle and moving clockwise about the henge. SS 91 and SS 93 remain on-site and appear to have been left unsmoothed by the builders. Both are sarsens. SS 91 is recumbent near the henge bank, but had only a slight leaning in the eighteenth century. SS 93 stands erect although incomplete as a result of undocumented attempts to break and remove it. Stones 92 and 94 were removed many years ago, their former locations near the centers of topographically subdued sub-circular swales. Station 94 is located between Aubrey Holes 45 and 46, its filled hole discovered in 1978 by Atkinson and Thom. Assuming that the nearby bank rose to a height of about 2 megalithic yards (5.44 ft, or 1.66 m) when the Station Stones were in use, North suggests that SS 92 must have been similar in size to SS 91, quite large, each of the four stones attaining a height of about 5.4 ft (1.6 m) to 8.2 ft (2.49 m).

The 'rectangular' setting of the four Stations is not common in the British Isles. Beyond Stonehenge, there are three others across Britain and Ireland, and two in Scotland. However, none of those others are configured with similar assumed astronomical precision along the sides and diagonals. Crucuno, a megalithic quadrilateral near Carnac in the Morbihan of Brittany, includes long sides oriented east-west toward the equinoctial sunsets, while the northeast-southwest diagonal aligns with midwinter sunset. Its length to width ratio of 40:30 megalithic yards (1 megalithic yard (MY) equals 2.72 ft or 0.829 m). Crucuno is well known and certainly planned. The rectangle does not lie within a henge or constructed circle.

Aubrey Burl's assessment of the four Station Stones is important for understanding their value to the builders of Stonehenge.

"Squares and oblongs with their straight sides and their diagonals have the potential to contain a dozen sightlines—to the Meridian and Quarter days; to the sun and moon rising and setting at their midsummer and winter extremes; even to a hill or distant mountain that was venerated by its society . . . It does not follow that such constructions were for an astronomical exploration of the skies. Most sightlines are too short for precision, and most foresights of clumsy stones too inexact. *It was not science but symbolism that was the cause of the quadrilaterals.* King Arthur's Hall, the Fortingalls, Crucuno and the Four Stations all had sightlines, but their comparative crudity imply that *it was a poetic rather than analytical vision of the cosmos that induced man to lay out the alignments.* As the Thoms and Merritts observed, 'It should be understood that Crucuno, unless it had foresights some distance away, could never have been more than a symbolic observatory'. . . True of Crucuno and the Four Stations, the conclusion would be just as relevant to the sarsen circle of Stonehenge that was to follow." [emphasis added][18]

Debate over use of the Station Stones to delineate solar and lunar alignments generally centers on the ability of the quadrilateral's size and shape to provide accurate sight lines for such observations. Based on geometrical orientation of the quadrilateral, moonrise alignments viewed along the edges of the stones appear to have been nearly 4 inches (10 cm) off lines that would have been observed at the time of Stonehenge Phase 3, errors that John North finds too imprecise to be acceptable at that time. Aubrey Burl suggests replacing wooden poles with rough stones with girths of up to 9 ft (2.6 m) would explain why opposite sides of the quadrilateral are not of the same length nor parallel, thus reducing precise astronomical alignments.

The Station Stones' short alignments (SS 91—SS 92, and SS 93-SS 94) are close to the summer solstice axis. Their longer alignments to the southeast (SS 94—SS 91, and SS 93—SS 92) approximate the southern limit of full moon rise. The northwest alignments, toward the northern limit of full moon setting at midwinter, are less accurate by several degrees in part due to lunar parallax. This has led to the conclusion that midsummer was more significant than midwinter for the Phase 3ii builders. Similarly the approach to the Southern Circle from Durrington Walls Avenue is about 1.5 degrees from aligning accurately with midsummer sunset.

Sir Flinders Petrie may have been the first person to observe that the four Stations formed a quadrilateral symmetrical about the NE-SW axis of the monument, and that its two diagonals crossed near the center of the henge at 45°±06' such that the Aubrey Hole circle was envisioned to be divided into sixteen segments of 22.5°. John North concludes that the circle of Aubrey Holes served as the foundation upon which locations of the four Stations were conceived as a rectangle. Excavations for installing SS 92 and SS 94 impacted Aubrey Holes at those locations, evidence that the Stations were constructed after the circle.

Sir Norman Lockyer furthered that idea by suggesting that the henge expressed the builder's concept of the year divided into sixteen periods. That idea led to the thought the architecture of Stonehenge might be related to Late Neolithic festivals that evolved into traditional Celtic festivals during the Iron Age. While excavating the Stations, Colt Hoare and William Cunnington encountered cremated bone where pit SS 94 mixed with Aubrey Hole 46. SS 92 yielded only chalk fill. During a re-excavation of SS 92 Hawley found the pit partially overlying Aubrey Hole 19 and extending to Aubrey Hole 17. These findings show that the Stations are younger than the Aubrey Holes.

The circle of sarsens and the four Stations quadrilateral are co-centered. As a result, sunset on May 1st (Celtic festival of Beltane) could have been observed along a line from the center of the monument to one of the Stations, and sunset on about November 1 (Samain) over another Station. Similarly, observations in the two opposite directions would indicate timing of the festivals of Imbolc in February and Lughnasadh in August. Thus orientation of the quadrilateral has been considered to be proof of an intention by the builders to construct Quarter Day alignments.

The approximate right angle between the solar axis and lunar extremes at the latitude of Stonehenge Landscape was applied in architecture at Woodhenge and Durrington Walls, and therefore should not be unexpected at Stonehenge. With the orientation of sides set by specific astronomical alignments, and the decision to place the Stations along the ring of Aubrey Holes, the only parameter remaining was the shape of the resulting quadrilateral. With an Aubrey circle radius of 141 ft 7 in (43 m or 52 MY) a square would have four sides each 100 ft 1 in (30.5 m or 36.8

MY), equivalent alignment lengths for observing solar or lunar events.

As constructed the Station Stone quadrilateral has a length to width ratio of almost 2.4:1 resulting in an angle of 22.62° between diagonals, 7.2' more than the 22.5° angle noted above. Atkinson found the two diagonals to measure 104.55 MY (SS 91 to SS 93) and 104.83 MY (SS 92 to SS 94), with a mean radius of 52.35 MY. Actual lengths of the quadrilateral measured during surveys conducted in 1973 and 1978 are: SS 91 to SS 92-112 ft 10 in (34.7 m); SS 92 to SS 93-262 ft 3 in (79.9 m); SSS 93 to SS 94-107 ft 4 in (32.7 m); SS 94 to SS 91-263 ft 3 in (80.38 m). Those side lengths produce corner angles of 89.5°, 89.5°, 91.1°, 91.1°. Using the average length and width of the measures sides, the resulting right-angled rectangle is about 262 ft 9 in x 110 ft 1 in (80 m x 33.5 m) producing an angle of 22.7° between diagonals of length 284 ft 10 in (86.8 m or 104.73 MY). That diagonal length is 1.71 feet (0.521 m) greater than the measured diameter of the Aubrey circle.

In summary the Station Stone quadrilateral does not have opposite sides that are parallel nor of equal length, the resulting four corners are not right angles, the two diagonal lengths are not equivalent, neither the diagonals nor their mean are equivalent in length to the diameter of the Aubrey circle, and the breadth of lines between stones are not indicative of accurate solar or lunar alignments they have been attributed (including midsummer sunrise, midwinter sunset, northernmost moonset, and midsummer southern moonrise). The Station Stone quadrilateral is not a rectangle.

Distances between SS 91 and SS 92 (112.8 ft) and SS 93 and SS 94 (107.3 ft) both exceed the 97.5 ft diameter of the circle of sarsens. As a consequence, sight lines between SS 91 and SS 94, and SS 92 and SS 93 would be no closer than about 4 feet (1.2 m) from the sarsen ring. That allows those two alignments to have been used for astronomical observations across the monument and toward the horizon, but there is no evidence those observations were made.

Burl suggests that the two diagonals between the four Stations were used to determine the center for the sarsen ring constructed soon afterward, and that the builders simply neglected to remove the stones afterward.[19] Richard Atkinson states that the stones would have been too large and measurements from them could not have been made with precision. He concluded the stones produced *"permanent and symbolic memorials of an operation of field-geometry which if it were repeated today, would tax the skill of many a professional surveyor."*[20] [emphasis added] In either case, the sarsen circle is situated between the two lunar sightlines and was likely constrained by the diameter of the Aubrey circle and shape of the Station Stone quadrilateral.

Archaeoastronomy at Stonehenge, Sub-phase 3ii

1—Orientation of Station Stones compared with solar and lunar events

The fact that size, shape and location of the four Station Stones did not produce accurate site lines toward previously mentioned solar and lunar events should alert us to the idea that the Stations were not placed to represent those astronomical alignments. It would have been far easier to install narrow posts adjusted as necessary to create accurate alignments—the short sides of a rectangle oriented toward the summer solstice rising and winter solstice setting, the long sides aligned toward the southern limit of full moon rise and the northern limit of full moon setting at midwinter. As it is however, the Station Stone quadrilateral does not provide those alignments, the sightings being off by a quarter degree (equivalent to the apparent arc length radius of the sun or moon) or more.

Review of data in Table 8 on page 153 indicates alignments formed by the Station Stone quadrilateral were not equivalent to any of the referenced solar or lunar risings or settings between 3500 and 1500 BCE. Further,

- Solar summer rising: The mean short side alignment was 0.1° less than the summer solstice rising in 3500 BCE, with the difference increasing as the years go by. By 2500 BCE the difference increased to 0.28°.

- Solar summer setting: The mean long side alignment was 0.72° more than the summer solstice setting in 3500 BCE, with the difference decreasing as the years go by, although no less than 0.34° by 1500 BCE.

- Solar winter rising: The mean long side alignment was 8.77° more than the winter solstice rising in 3500 BCE, with the difference increasing to 9.14° by 1500 BCE.

- Solar winter setting: The mean short side alignment was 0.53° less that the winter solstice setting in 3500 BCE and increased to 0.91° by 1500 BCE.

- Lunar maximum rising north: The mean short side alignment was 8.63° more than the lunar maximum rising in 3500 BCE, with the difference decreasing as the years go by, although no less than 8.21° by 1500 BCE.

- Lunar maximum rising south: The mean long side alignment was 3.72° less than the southerly lunar maximum rising in 3500 BCE, with the difference decreasing to no less than 3.26° by 1500 BCE.

- Lunar maximum setting north: The mean long side alignment was 0.88° less than the northerly lunar maximum setting 3500 BCE, with the difference decreasing to no less than 0.46° by 1500 BCE.

- Lunar maximum setting south: Mean short side alignment was 11.89° more than the lunar southerly maximum setting in 3500 BCE, with the difference decreasing as the years go by, although no less than 11.44° by 1500 BCE.

Table 8: Extreme Risings and Settings at Stonehenge, 3500 to 1500 BCE (Data from North, 1996, pp. 475, 570-571)

Solar (αo measured from North)					
Year (BCE)	Obliquity	Summer Rising	Summer Setting	Winter Rising	Winter Setting
3500	24° 04' 20"	49.19	318.61	130.56	229.62
3000	24° 01' 42"	49.28	318.70	130.48	229.71
2500	23° 58' 50"	49.37	318.79	130.39	229.80
2000	23° 55' 45"	49.47	318.89	130.29	229.90
1500	23° 52' 29"	49.57	318.99	130.19	230.00

Lunar (αo measured from North)				
Year (BCE)	Max. Rising North	Max. Rising South	Max. Setting North	Max. Setting South
3500	40.46	143.05	320.21	217.20
3000	40.55	142.94	320.12	217.30
2500	40.66	142.83	320.01	217.41
2000	40.77	142.71	319.90	217.52
1500	40.88	142.59	319.79	217.65

Current Station Stone Quadrilateral Alignments (αo measured from North)					
Short Sides		Mean Alignment	Long Sides		Mean Alignment
Sta. 91–Sta. 92	Sta. 93–Sta. 94		Sta. 91-Sta. 94	Sta. 92–Sta. 93	
49.12	49.06	49.09	139.43	139.23	139.33

From this information we can see that in 2500 BCE alignments provided by the Station Stone quadrilateral best fit summer solstice rising (Δ-0.28°) followed by summer solstice setting (Δ 0.54°), northerly maximum lunar setting (Δ-0.68°), and solar winter setting (Δ—0.71°). Assuming a Station Stone average width of 3 ft (0.9 m) (Burl assumes an average stone girth of 9 ft (2.7 m), equivalent to 1.2 arc degrees for a circle with radius of 284 ft (86.6 m), we may expect that the stones would likely align with those four solar and lunar alignments to some measure, particularly given that the width of the sun and moon is about a half arc degree as viewed from Earth.

It is possible the built-in accuracy of the stone alignments was such that the designer simply required the stones to completely impede direct observation of any part of either orb at the moment of rising or setting. If this was the case then the system would have provided as much as 0.75° leeway (one and a half apparent sun or moon diameters) between precise alignment and apparent alignment given that the only requirement was that the stones hide the orb for just an instant. The four alignments above appear to satisfy that requirement but the results would be certainly less than necessary for accurate measurement.

Having each Station situated near the circular arrangement of Aubrey Holes poses additional concerns. A unique radius can be determined for the Aubrey circle even though the fifty-six holes have a breadth of pit diameters and spacings. However we do not know if the intended diameter was related to a specific edge or location within each pit. Also, locations of the Stations have not been determined to be along the radius of any circle of specified radius, let alone the arrangement of Aubrey Holes.

We also know that the Station Stone quadrilateral is not a rectangle because the opposite sides are not parallel, not equal in length, and the four corners are not right angles. Just as important, the quadrilateral does not reflect circular symmetry expressed by the ditch and bank, and various pits and arrangements of sarsens and bluestones. However the center of the quadrilateral is co-centered with the circle of sarsens. The geometry of the four Stations concerns issues not necessarily limited to previously accepted solar and lunar alignments, yet it is related to the sarsen circle and possibly the horseshoe of sarsen trilithons.

2—Geometrical purpose for the long axis orientation of the quadrilateral

If we remove all considerations other than having four non-collinear points on the ground surface for which intersection of the two diagonals defines the center of the monument, then we have elements of a planar surface surveyed onto the landscape, and a specific location at the center through which a line perpendicular to that plane extends into the ground and out toward the zenith (Figure 59).

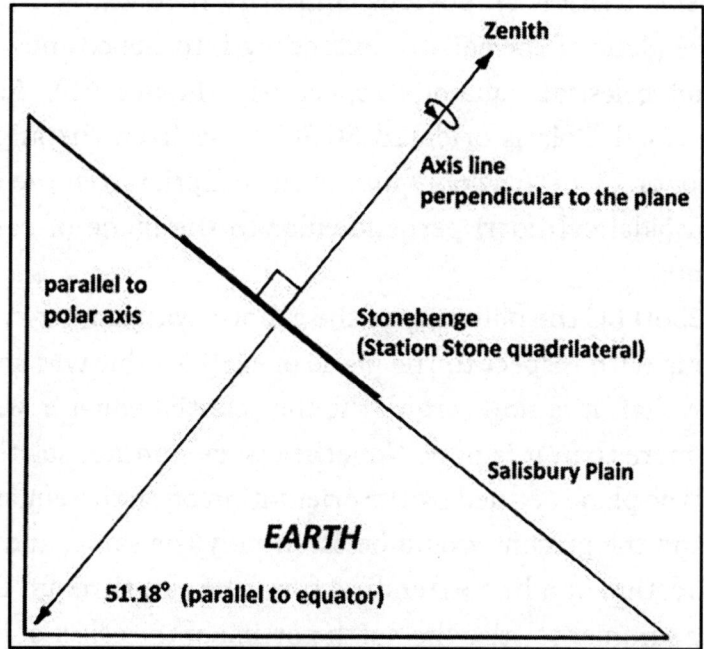

Figure 59: Planar surface perpendicular to pole pointed toward the zenith

If the quadrilateral represents a plane, then the question is which plane? There are two elements of the geometry that are readily apparent. One is the plane is tangential to Earth at the center of the sarsen circle (center of the monument). The other is orientation of the long axis of the quadrilateral is toward the southeast. Of course, the two long sides of the quadrilateral are not parallel, but closely approximate each other's alignment. If the intention of the designer was satisfied with such approximation, then to the nearest degree of arc from the center of Stonehenge (the intersection point of the two diagonals) the mean alignment of the two long sides bears an azimuth of 139.33° from due north. It is important that this azimuth concerns the approximate orientation of the two long sides of a plane indicated by the locations of the four Station Stones, and not an alignment as generally applied to presumed sightlines at Stonehenge. This being the case, is there any geometrical (earth measured) planar surface of which this azimuth can apply?

Keeping in mind the configuration of a line extending perpendicular to a plane, there is an obvious similarity here with that of earth's poles and the plane of the equator extending into the cosmos, the celestial pole and celestial equator, respectively (Figure 60). At summer solstice the North Pole is oriented 66.56° away from the alignment of Earth to Sun, or 23.44° (the obliquity of the ecliptic) from the line (actually an ellipsoidal cylinder) perpendicular to the plane of earth's orbit about the sun.

Circa 2500 BC the obliquity of the ecliptic was about 24°, so the tilt of earth's axis with respect to the plane of earth's orbit was about a half degree more than it is now. Similarly, the celestial equator was about a half degree more than it is now. Nonetheless, at summer solstice the dip direction of the plane defined by the orientation of earth's equator during 2500 BCE and the present would be essentially the same, and co-planar with the direction of a line extending from the sun through Earth.

During summer solstice the north portion of the celestial pole points toward the axis of rotation of the solar system. It points away from that axis at winter solstice, and perpendicular to that axis during vernal equinox and autumnal equinox. In other words the line between Sun and Earth during vernal equinox and autumnal equinox extends along the line of strike of the celestial plane. From this sequence it is readily apparent that the orientation of the equatorial plane changes continuously—virtually one degree per day-with respect to the direction of the line between Earth and Sun, returning to the same orientation on an annual basis.

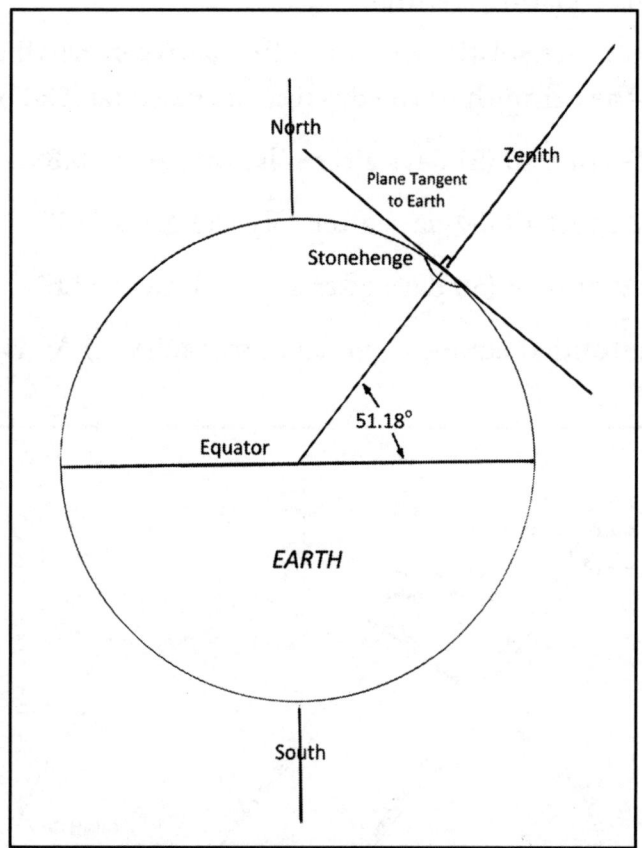

**Figure 60: Plane tangent to Earth at Stonehenge, and
perpendicular line pointing toward zenith**

As an example, we assume that summer solstice occurs six hours before noon local time. At summer solstice the orientation of the dip line of the equatorial plane and the line between Sun and Earth will be coplanar, while the local zenith will be oriented within a plane 90° to those lines. There are 94 days between summer solstice and autumnal equinox, when the same dip line is perpendicular (90°) with respect to the line between Sun and Earth. Therefore, the difference in azimuths ($\Delta\alpha$) between the line extending between Earth and the sun, and the dip line of the equatorial plane, may be approximated as:

$$\Delta\alpha \approx \frac{\text{number of days since summer solstice x 90 degrees}}{94 \text{ days}}$$

Using this equation we find:

- At summer solstice $\Delta\alpha$ of the line between Earth and Sun, and the azimuth of the dip line of the equatorial plane, is 0°

- On August 10 (51 days after solstice) $\Delta\alpha$ is 48.8°

- On August 13 (54 days after solstice) $\Delta\alpha$ is 51.7°

- On August 15 (56 days after solstice) $\Delta\alpha$ is 53.6°

- At autumnal equinox (94 days after solstice) $\Delta\alpha$ is 90°

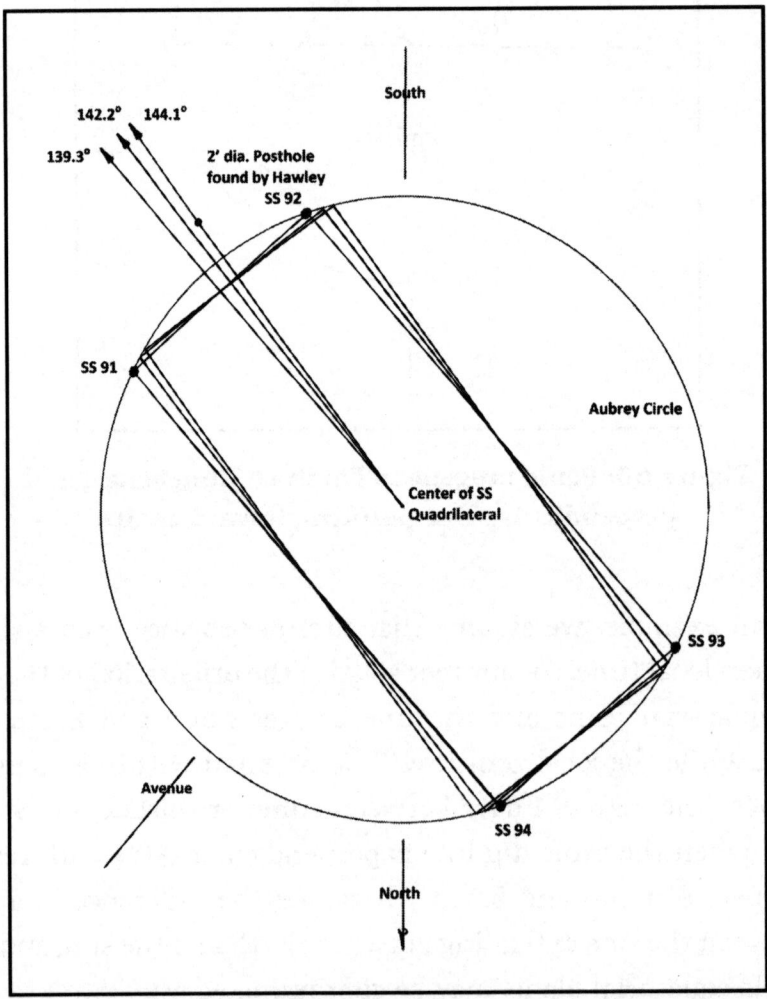

Figure 61: Azimuth of equatorial plane on evenings of August 10, 13 and 15, beginning at Station Stones and rotating clockwise

The calculations provide a measure of arc length between two points on earth's orbital plane. We must add 90° to those values to arrive at the azimuth (relative to North) of the dip slope on the equatorial plane during the chosen dates. Therefore, azimuths of the dip of the equatorial plane on the mornings of August 10, 13 and 15 are 138.8°, 141.7° and 143.6°, respectively. Increasing the number of days since summer solstice by one half (12 hours)-sunset on the evenings of August 10, 13 and 15-yields equatorial dip slopes with azimuths of 139.3°, 142.2° and 144.1°, respectively (Figure 61).

During the 1920s William Hawley encountered 'the largest post-hole yet found' at Stonehenge.[21] The filled pit is located at azimuth 144°, has a diameter of 2 feet (0.6 m) and a depth of 2.5 feet (0.8 m). Situated close to the edge of the circular bank along the south side of the henge, two additional post holes were located nearby. Nine human cremations were discovered south of the post holes. Burl (2007) suggests that the three posts may have been installed during GW occupancy of the site, and that when viewed from the center of the henge they appear to align with the rising midsummer moon.[22] North (1997) lists northerly and southerly maximum lunar risings between 3500 BCE and 2000 BCE ranging from about 143.05° to 142.71°.[23] Those values are within 0.55 to 0.89 degrees of the dip azimuth of the equatorial plane calculated for August 15. However they are 0.95 to 1.29 degrees less than the azimuth of the large posthole discovered by Hawley.[24] Those values would place the alignments about 1.5 to 2.3 feet east of the east edge of the 2 foot diameter post as viewed from the center of the monument.

For comparison, the equatorial dip slope calculated for August 15 is 0.4 degrees from the azimuth of that posthole, placing it upon the edge of the post. Increasing the number of days since summer solstice by one half (12 hours), or the evening of August 15, yields an equatorial dip slope of 144.1°, equivalent to 3 inches from the center of the post. As such, the dip slope at dusk on August 15 provides an alternative purpose of the posthole, and it provides greater precision than the alignment of three posts toward the rising midsummer moon.

3—Purpose of the Station Stone Quadrilateral

The azimuths of the northern and southern long sides of the Station Stone quadrilateral are 139.43° and 139.23°, respectively The mean azimuth of 139.33° is equivalent to the dip direction of the equatorial plane at sunset on August 10. In and of itself, the mean long axis azimuth does not appear to be of much help in identifying the purpose of orienting the Station Stone quadrilateral in general accordance with the dip of the equatorial plane 51 days after summer solstice. However, further analysis of the cosmic dome at that time of the year ca. 2500 BCE reveals astronomical events observable in the southeastern night sky that accord with a cosmography that has been sacred to many other ancient and indigenous cultures. Those events were above the horizon, oriented toward azimuths within about 22.67° (the angle between Station diagonals) of the mean long side orientation of the Station Stone quadrilateral.

This analysis applied Starry NightTM Enthusiast, version 4.5 to view a model of the pre-dawn sky at Stonehenge during 2500 BCE. On August 2 first glint of the sun occurred at about 3:53 AM and so we begin observing the night sky about 35 minutes earlier, when the sun is almost 7° below the horizon. At that time, at azimuth (α) 128.8°, Alnitak (the eastern of Orion's three belt stars) was rising at an altitude (h) of 9.4°, while Aldebaran in the constellation Taurus was at α 142.9°, h 30.3°. Sirius, the 'dog star', was below the horizon. The closest star to the horizon in Orion was Saiph at α 128.4°, h 1.5°, potentially observable in a clear pre-dawn sky. At that moment the complex of stars in Orion could have been seen in their entirety minutes before the sun made its appearance at azimuth 52.0°. That was the morning of Saiph's heliacal rising after summer solstice.

Thirteen days later, on the morning of August 15, Sirius made its heliacal rising at α 126.5°, h 1.25° while the sun was about 6.25° below the horizon (Figure 62). At that moment, with Sirius barely visible over the horizon, Orion could have been seen above and to the right, including Saiph (α 140.6°, h 8.2°), Alnitak (α 142.0°, h 16.0°), Alnilam (α 143.1°, h

16.8°), Mintaka (α 144.2°, h 17.75°), Betelgeuse (α 137.5⁰, h 25.1°), Rigel (α 148.9⁰, h 10.0°) and the other stars that make up the constellation. Aldebaran was farther up and right (α 159.8⁰, h 34.8°) as the Pleiades (α 175.5⁰, h 41.2°) approached the meridian. On that morning the sun appeared at azimuth 56.0°.

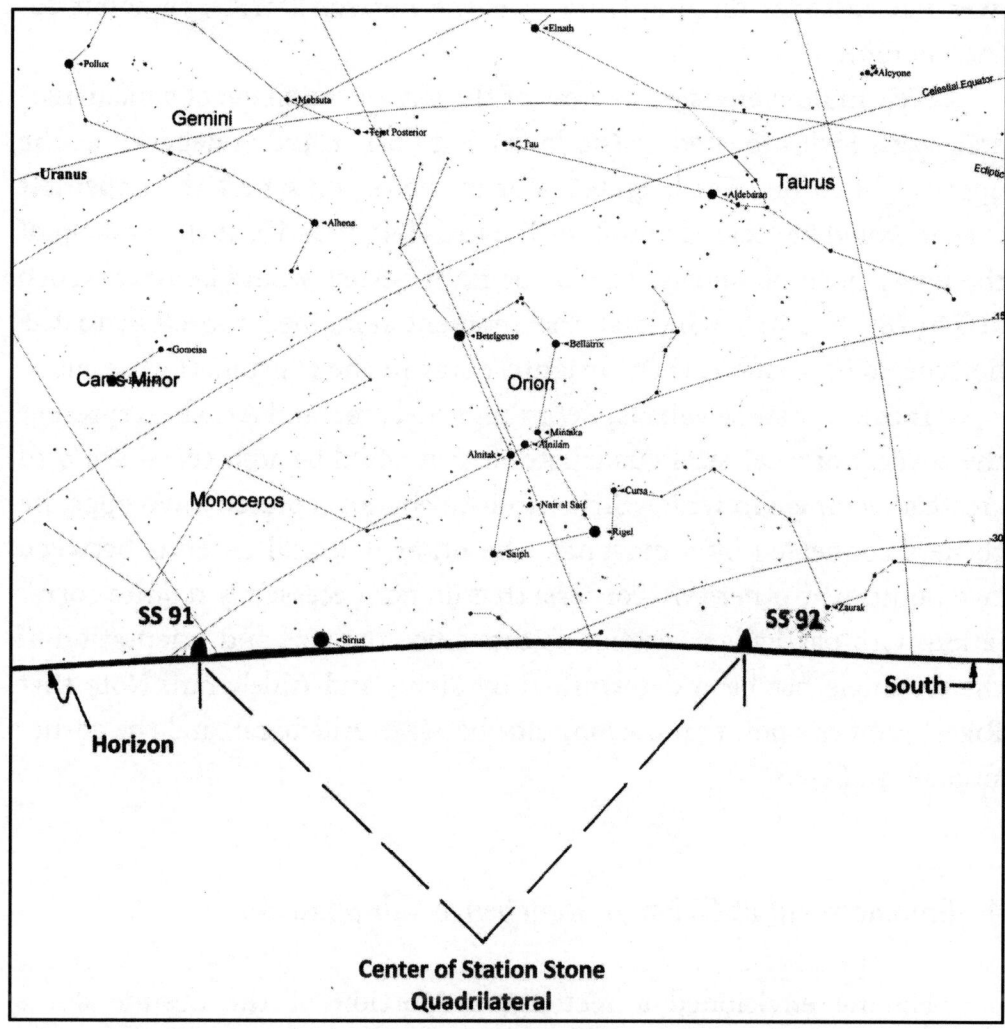

Figure 62: View of southeast sky between SS 91 and SS 92 before sunrise, August 15, 2500 BCE

To summarize, on the morning of August 2 Orion's heliacal rising was accomplished with Saiph's first appearance after summer solstice. On August 15, when Sirius made its heliacal rising, Orion's three belt stars were located between azimuths of 142.0 and 144.2 degrees, and altitudes of 16.0 and 17.18 degrees; Aldebaran was at azimuth 159.8°, altitude 34.8°. At that moment, if we had been positioned at the center of Stonehenge, we would have seen between Station Stones 91 and 92 that portion of the cosmic dome between Sirius (east) and Aldebaran (west) at altitudes ranging from near the horizon (Sirius) to about 35° (Aldebaran).

We can now envision an area of the sky in the shape of a quadrilateral, with Sirius located at the lower left corner and Aldebaran at the upper right corner. The brightest star in the region where the upper left corner would be located was Zeta Tau (α 141.4°, h 39.1°), at the east tip of the lower horn of Taurus. The lower right corner would be near Arneb (α 144.78°, h 0.25°) which at the moment remained too close to the horizon to be seen but is the brightest star in the constellation Lepus.

Those four stars—Sirius, Zeta Tau, Aldebaran and Arneb—represent the corners of a celestial quadrilateral that could be adjusted slightly to create a rectangle in which Sirius and Aldebaran represent two opposite corners connected by a diagonal. The other diagonal extends between two points (the other two corners) that do not necessarily require correlation with particular celestial objects since the size and orientation of the rectangle has been determined by Sirius and Aldebaran. Note that Rigel becomes a point on the long side between Aldebaran and the corner situated in Lepus.

4—Emplacement of Orion at Stonehenge Sub-phase 3ii

Having envisioned a rectangular portion of the cosmic dome between SS 91 and SS 92 as a planar feature framed by Sirius and Aldebaran at opposite corners, we can easily map each of the star locations within the rectangle. Sirius is located at the bottom left corner and Aldebaran –appearing directly above SS 92 as seen from the monument's center-at the upper right corner. Conceptually the cosmic rectangle is then rotated so it's' plane is parallel to the ground surface and centered on Stonehenge, then brought down onto the monument (Figure 63).

This translocation of the rectangle symbolically and accurately emplaces Aldebaran and Sirius at SS 92 and SS 94, respectively. Using Aubrey Burl's estimated girth of 9 ft (2.6 m) for the four stones, and average diameter of 281.5 ft (85.80 m) between opposite stones, the error in translocating the rectangle onto the ground could be over one degree and the rectangle's corners would still set on each of the four megaliths. In other words, the Station Stones are large enough serve as symbolic corners of the rectangle even though themselves do not form a rectangle. This gives reason for the stones not being corners of a rectangle, rather than markers offering inaccurate alignments toward the horizon.

Stars inside the rectangle are then plotted onto the ground, potentially using the diagonal between SS 92 and SS 94 as the baseline for the survey (prior to construction of the bluestone and sarcen structures in the central portion of the monument). Pairing Aldebaran with SS 92 is a decision easily made since the star is observed directly above that Station location by default

Sirius must be represented by SS 94 because the stone's location is the corner opposite of SS 92. The ground surface surrounding Station Stones 92 and 94 include shallow sub-circular ditches highlighting those two locations. This may emphasize the importance of SS 92 and SS 94 in the symbolic emplacement of sacred celestial space onto Earth. SS 91 and SS 93 did not receive the topographic adornment given the other two Stations because the two corresponding corners of the rectangle are not representing stars or other astral bodies. This may provide additional reason for the builders not ensuring construction of a proper rectangle with the four Station Stones.

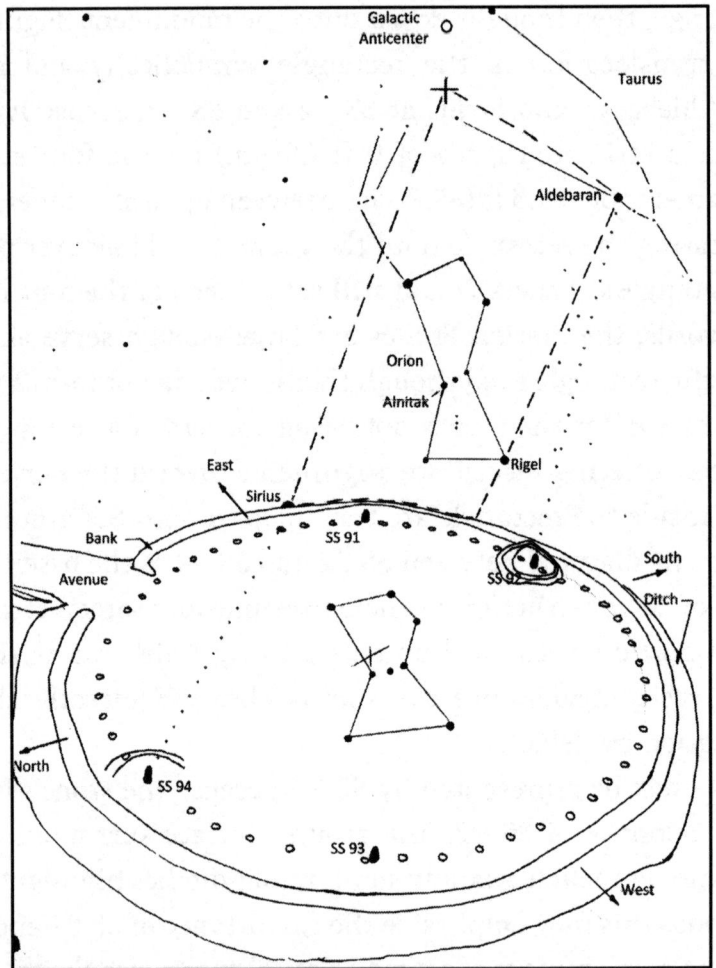

**Figure 63: Translocating Orion to the ground surface
at Stonehenge (drawing by author)**

Several surprising and important findings are immediately apparent once the various stars of Orion are plotted onto the plan of Stonehenge (Figure 64).

- Three stars (Meissa, Rigel and Saiph) representing the head and two feet of the constellation plot onto the plan of Z-Holes (nos. 7, 18 and 22) east and west of the monument's center.

- Two additional stars (Betelgeuse and Bellatrix) representing Orion's shoulders plot onto the ring of sarsens (nos. 5 and 9) east of the center.

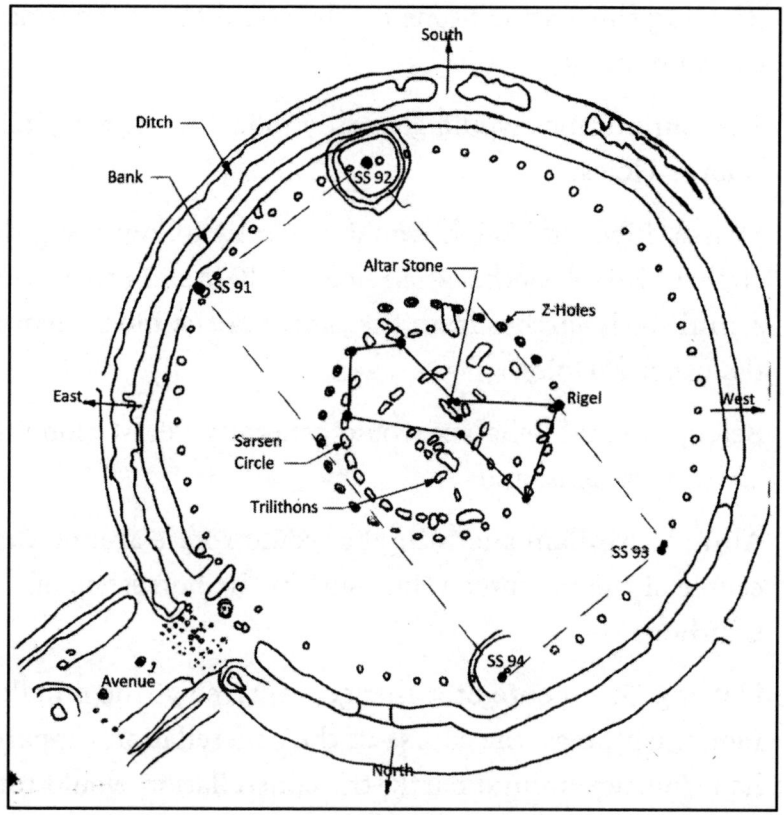

Figure 64: Orion located in the rectangle defined by the four Station Stones ca. 2500 BCE. Note star locations along the Z-Holes and ring of sarsens. (Drawing by author based on J. North (1996), fig. 157)

- The three belt stars (Alnitak, Alnilam and Mintaka) are located in the central portion of the monument—inside the horseshoe of sarsen trilithons and in the vicinity of the Altar Stone.

- Rigel is located along the line between SS 92 and SS 93.

- The center of the Station Stone quadrilateral, and therefore the celestial rectangle, plots at a point within 10 feet (3 m) east of the Altar Stone and along the northeast-southwest axis of the monument. As regards the figure of Orion, this point may be inferred to be the approximate location of where Orion's navel might be envisioned.

- Rotating the Station Stone quadrilateral about the center of the monument,

- The four Stations would generally follow along the circle of Aubrey Holes;

- Meissa, Rigel and Saiph would generally follow along the circle of Z-Holes other than holes 9, 10, and 11 that are located significantly farther from the center of the monument than the other Z-Holes;

- Betelgeuse and Bellatrix would generally follow along the circle of sarsens; and

- Alnitak, Alnilam and Mintaka would rotate around the center of the monument but within the horseshoe of trilithons.

- Plotting Orion onto Stonehenge, centered at the middle of the monument, over the course of the constellation's apparent 24 hour journey around Earth, the constellation would rotate around the monument twice (720°), just as the hour hand rotates around the face of a clock in 24 hours.

5—Astronomical alignments from center of the henge

The azimuth of the dip slope of Earth's equator on the evening of August 15th ca. 2500 BC was 144.1°, between the azimuths of SS 91 (α 115.3⁰) and SS 92 (α 161°) when viewed from the center of the monument. Table 9 lists azimuths of stars visible between and above Station stones 91 and 92 as viewed from the center of the henge.

Table 9: Azimuths at Sirius' Helical Rising, August 15, 2500 BCE
—Viewed from Center of Stonehenge—

Object	Azimuth (degrees from North)	Remarks
Station Stone 91	115.3	
Sirius	126.2	Equivalent to SS 94
Betelgeuse	137.5	
HIP26574	140.4	Galactic anti-center (approx.)
Saiph	140.6	
Zeta Tauri	141.4	
HIP26762	141.8	Equivalent intersection of diagonals, center of Stonehenge
HIP26736	141.9	Equivalent to SS 91 (approx.)
Alnitak	142.0	
Meissa	142.8	
Alnilam	143.2	
Alnath	143.3	
TYC5929-308-1	143.4	Equivalent to SS 93 (approx.)
Mintaka	144.0	
Arneb	144.7	
Bellatrix	145.8	
Rigel	148.9	
Aldebaran	159.8	Equivalent to SS 92
Station Stone 92	161.0	

Several important stellar alignments result from those orientations.

- The southwest edge of Z-Hole 22, upon which Saiph plots, is the beginning of a sightline azimuth of 139.9° and 10 percent gradient past sarsen 22, through trilithons 57-58, grazing bluestone 69 and the Altar Stone, and through trilithon 53-54, toward winter solstice sunrise (within 0.1° azimuth) ca. 2500 BCE (Figure 65). That azimuth approximates (within about a half degree) those of the two long sides of the Station Stone quadrilateral. The megaliths would have prevented observing sunrise along that alignment. However, the alignment intersects the large posthole discovered by Hawley near the southern ditch bank at azimuth 144° (measured from the center of the monument). Therefore it is possible that the huge post could have been seen from Z-Hole 22 along this alignment, which, as described above, might represent the azimuth of the dip line for the equatorial plane on the evening of August 15, 2500 BCE.

- From SS 93, Sirius appears just above Stone H, located between Aubrey Holes 13 and 14.

- From either the center of the henge or SS 94, Aldebaran at altitude 34.75° would have appeared above SS 92.

- From the center of Stonehenge prior to erection of the circle of sarsens-or standing at the translocated position of Saiph (Z-Hole 22), or at Station 93 looking toward SS 92, or from SS 94 to SS 91—a near vertical line (88.6° from level horizon) extended from the ground surface at azimuth 139.3° to HIP26574 (α 140.4°) where the galactic anti-center is approximately located.

- Extrapolating a line from TYC5929-308-1 (equivalent to SS 93 of the 'rectangle') through HIP26762 (equivalent to the intersection of diagonals at the center of Stonehenge), the alignment is within 0.5° of azimuth of HIP26574.

- Similarly, extending a line from Arneb through HIP26828 (equivalent to SS 93 and SS 91, respectively, prior to realignment of the celestial quadrilateral to a rectangle), the alignment is within 0.6° of azimuth of HIP26574.

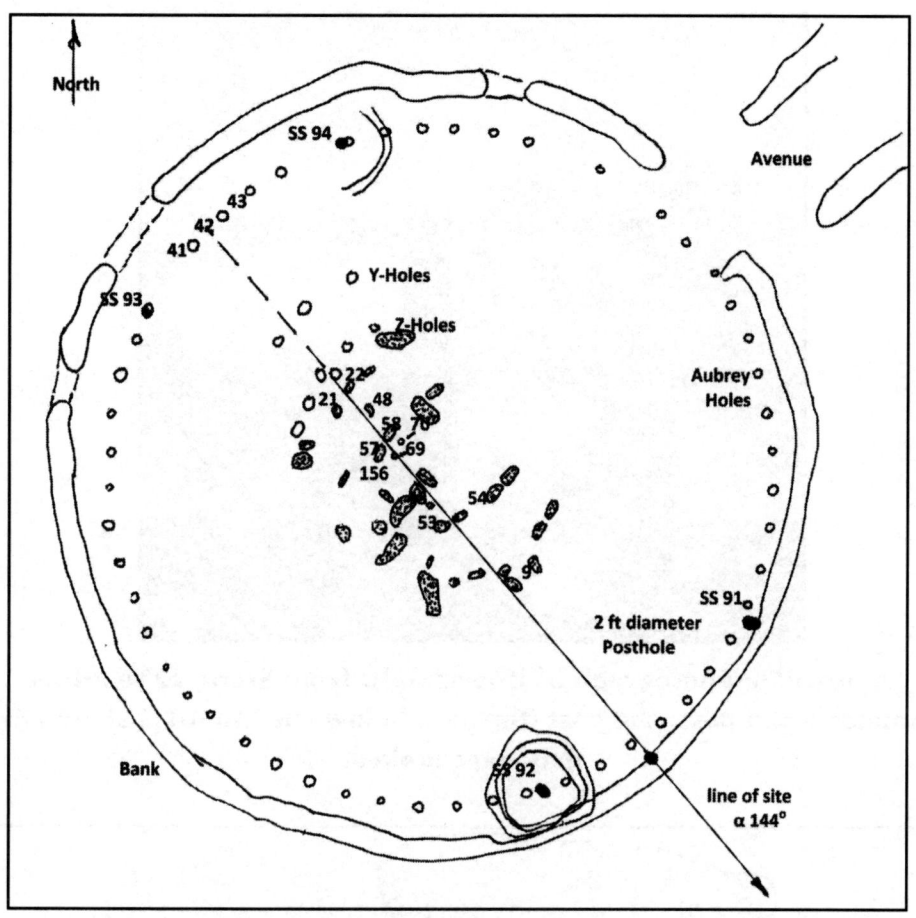

Figure 65a: Plan view of Stonehenge showing line of sight from location of Saiph at Stone 22

Figure 65b: Photograph of line of sight from Stone 22 to 2-foot diameter wood post; the post (top seen below the Moon) is shown as it may have looked.

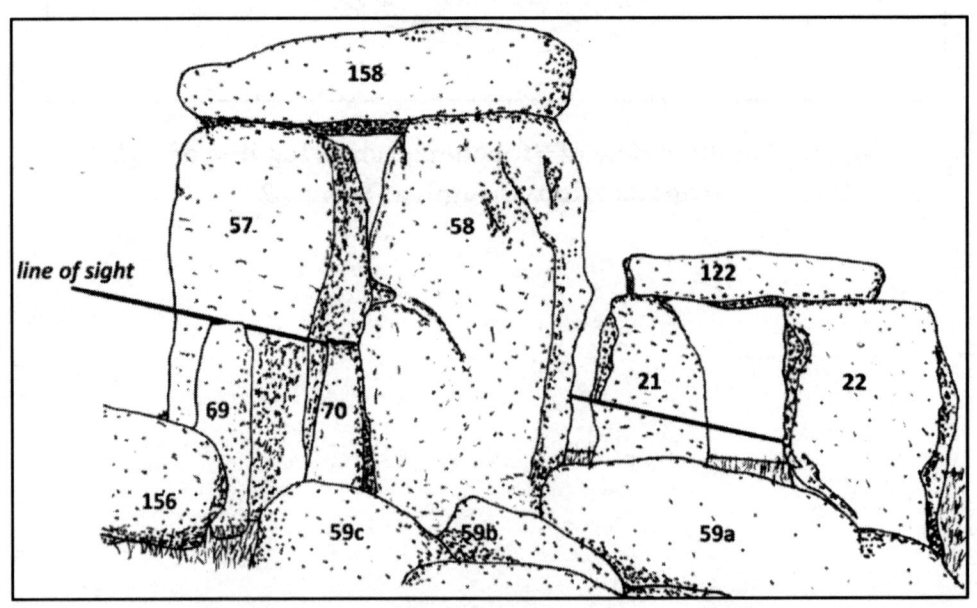

Figure 65c: Oblique view of same line of sight, looking northeast from inside the horseshoe of sarsens (based on North, J. 1997. p. 464, fig. 182))

6—Stonehenge as a Device for Measuring Space and time

Astronomical alignments resulting by emplacing Orion onto the sub-phase 3ii monument demonstrate clearly that the construction was intended to support observing cyclical events at specific times. With Orion centered at the middle of the monument, the Station Stone quadrilateral (and constellation therein) may be envisioned to rotate around the monument in a clockwise fashion. Betelgeuse and Bellatrix follow along the circle of sarsens, while Alnitak, Alnilam and Mintaka rotate around the center of the monument within the horseshoe of trilithons.

Each day the azimuth of the long axis of the quadrilateral changes by about 1° (360°/365.24 days = 0.99° per day) with respect to the polar axis. On the evening of August 10 (51.5 days after solstice) local zenith is oriented 139.33° away from the dip line of the celestial plane represented by the long axis of the quadrilateral. However, at summer solstice (assumed at sunrise) the polar axis and dip line are 90° from each other, the former oriented toward the sun, the latter along the dip line. In other words, between August 10 and the following summer solstice Orion rotates clockwise (sun-wise) about the center of Stonehenge from α 139.33° to α 90°.

The orientation of Earth's polar axis relative to positions of fixed stars changes constantly. This axial precession has a period of about 25,800 years. The two intersection points between the ecliptic and the celestial equator are called the equinoctial points. At summer equinox and winter equinox the sun appears at one of those two vernal and autumnal points of intersection. Precession of the equinoxes is the apparent movement of those points along the celestial equator at a rate of about 1° every 71.57 years over the 25,800 year period of precession. As precession continues, the sun appears to cross the equinoctial points where specific stars along the celestial equator are located.

There is a specific attribute of Orion's right arm that should be noted. The arm is perceived extending from the shoulder point (Betelgeuse) to the outside of elbow (Xi Orionis) and inside of elbow (Nu Orionis) and then farther on to outside of wrist (Chi 2 Orionis) and inside of wrist (Chi 1 Orionis). A line extending from the midpoint between Xi Orionis and Nu Orionis, to the midpoint between Chi 2 Orionis and Chi 1 Orionis, approximates the azimuth (± 0° 15') of the long axis of the Station Stone quadrilateral. Therefore when the quadrilateral is rotated about the center of Stonehenge, the azimuths of long axis and forearm of Orion are essentially the same as the azimuth of the Avenue and sunrise at summer solstice. The symbolism at that moment is of Orion lifting the sun into the sky. It is evident now that Orion can be thought to rotate about the plane of earth's surface, the quadrilateral aligned with any astronomical event during solstices, equinoxes, quarter days, or other times of interest.

Sunrise occurred in the constellation Cancer during summer solstice morning in 2500 BCE. On summer solstice morning June 20, 2012 CE the sun rises at α 50° 38', near the star TYC1863-1500-1 in the extreme west area of Taurus. At that time the sun is slightly less than half degree azimuth and six degrees below altitude of the galactic anti-center. The sun has an apparent diameter of about 0.5° and approaches its closest point within that width to galactic-anticenter. At the same time, Orion will be below the east horizon, not appearing in full until Saiph's heliacal rising on August 2. However, if we could see below the horizon at sunrise on summer solstice Orion would appear with right arm raised, pointing directly toward the sun, as if bringing forth the sun into the sky (Figure 66). In this capacity we see why Orion (and many deities the comstellation represents, including Lugh) is called the 'Bringer of Light'.

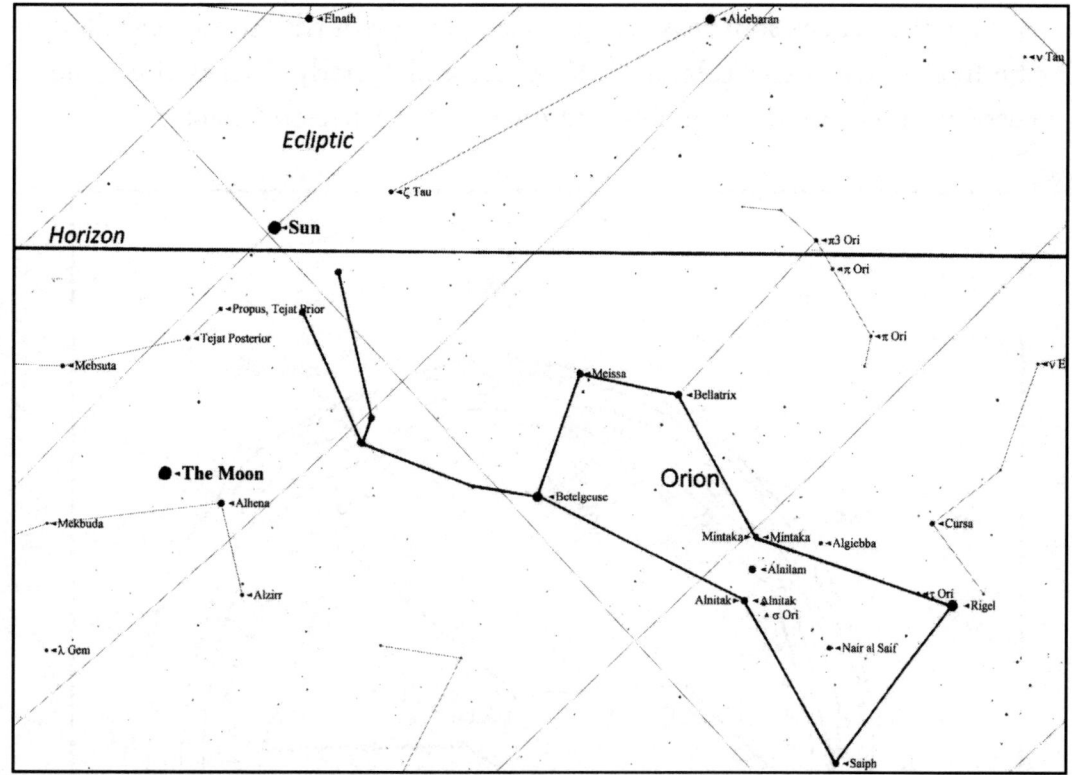

Figure 66: Sunrise on summer solstice June 21, 2014. Orion, although still below the morning horizon, is holding the sun up near its closest point to the galactic anti-center.

7—Orion and the DWS Complex

Another aspect of the translocated Orion that connects the monument with other important features of the local landscape concerns the right arm reaching out toward the sun and the galactic anti-center. Orion can be rotated so that Betelgeuse is oriented toward the same azimuth as sunrise on summer solstice (α 49.37°) ca. 2500 BCE.[25] This is depicted in Figure 67. The scale of Orion is then adjusted such that his right arm extends from Betelgeuse northeast to where the Avenue turns east.[24] The latter location may be perceived as the center point of Orion's elbow (Figure 68). The mid-line azimuth of the forearm, collinear with the Avenue, continues eastward for about one half mile (800 m). The Avenue then turns southeast and the east portion of the Avenue parallels the line between the galactic anti-center and Alnath. This is the same correlation between Orion and the Avenue described in Chapter 6.

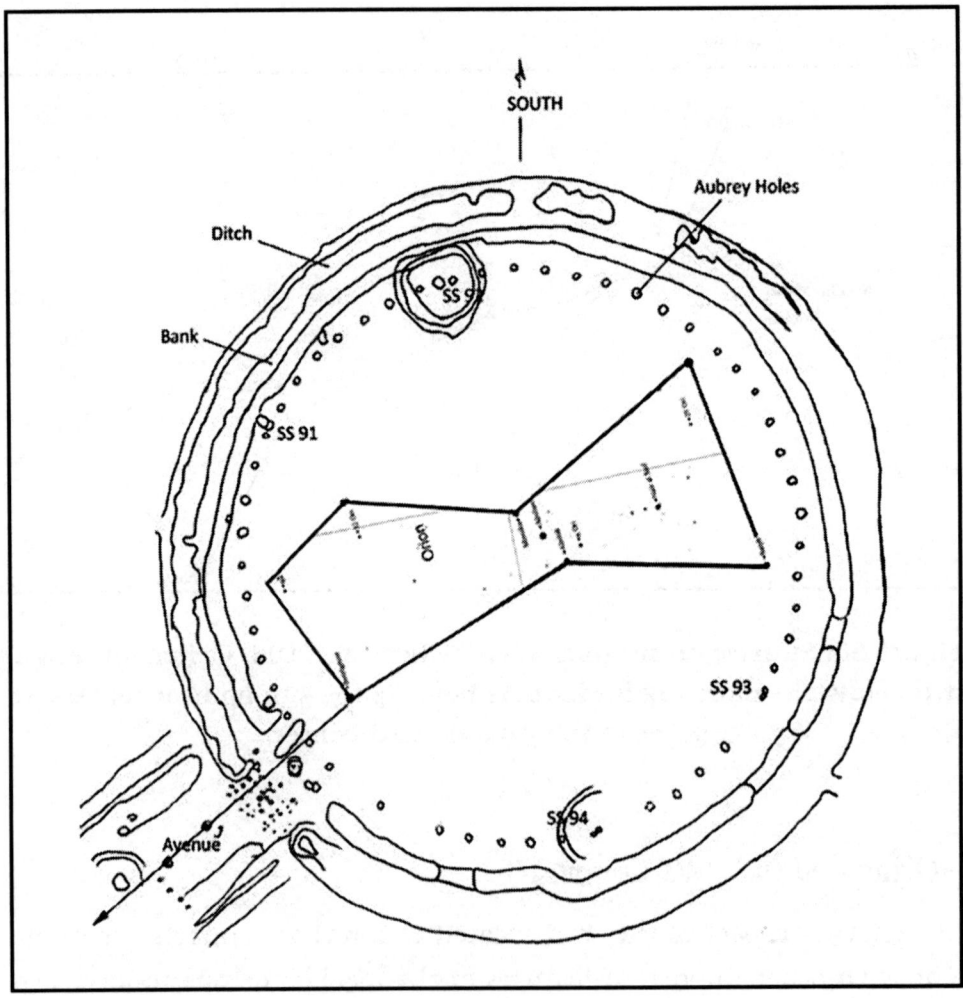

Figure 67: Orion oversized and oriented with Betelgeuse aligned with the Avenue.

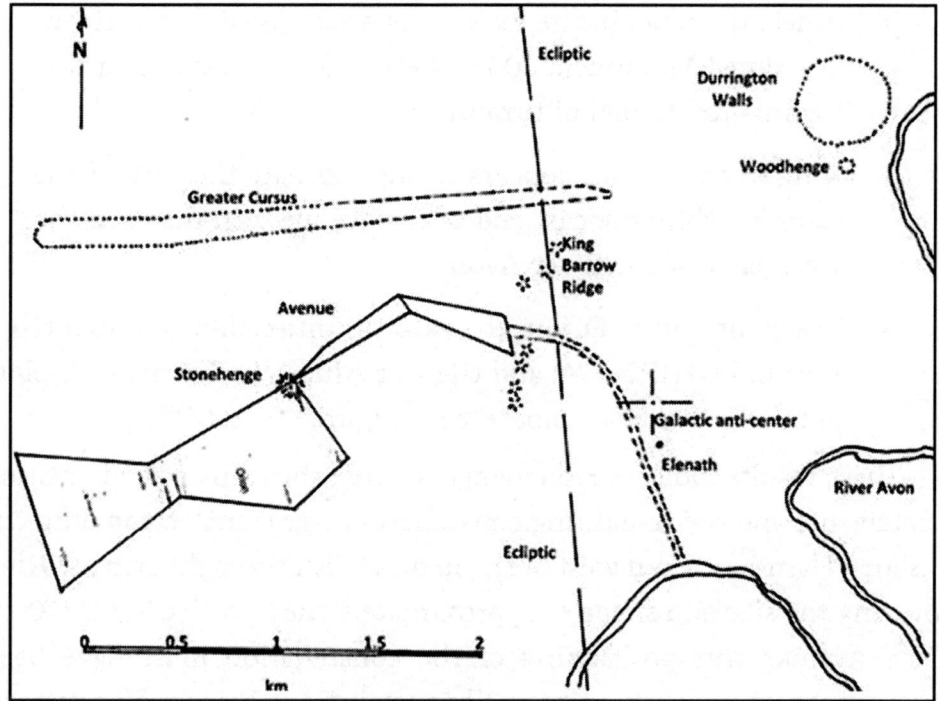

Figure 68: Orion oriented with the right arm reaching up (east) toward the ecliptic and Galactic anti-center

In addition,

- The Greater Cursus is oriented along azimuth of the galactic plane north of Orion's right arm. The cursus could be interpreted as Orion's stave, spear or long hammer.

- Sirius plots at H40, the large round 'bell' barrow located immediately south of the west end of the Greater Cursus. That location may be envisioned equivalent to Station Stone 94 (translocated Sirius along the Aubrey circle).

- Scheduled Monument 10314, a Bronze Age Bell Barrow north of Normanton Gorse . . . A primary skeleton, grooved dagger, drinking cup and other artefacts were recovered from the barrow over 200 years ago. Rigel plots onto the round barrow located 0.6 mi (0.95 km) southwest of Stonehenge, south of the A303.

- Aldebaran plots in the vicinity of an undated disc barrow, Scheduled Monument 10471, located at the east end of the Normanton Group of tumuli.

- King Barrow Ridge appears to approximate the path of the ecliptic, while the east end of the avenue terminates at the west bank of the River Avon.

- The right arm of Orion, the galactic anti-center (represented here in by HIP26574) and the star Alnath in Taurus each plot onto the Avenue (compare with Figure 49 and 50).

These results indicate Stonehenge became the translocated position of Betelgeuse and the remaining constellation was translocated onto the Salisbury Plain south and west of the henge. With the right arm of Orion providing the size and shape of approximately the first 4500 ft (1370 m) of the Avenue, this positioning of the constellation must have been contemporaneous with sub-phase 3ii construction. This agrees with the schedule of sub-phase 3ii construction period for the Avenue proposed by Parker Pearson *et al* (2007).[27] Figure 69 depicts the size and orientation of Orion as described, situated within an hypothetical oversized Station rectangle as reference.

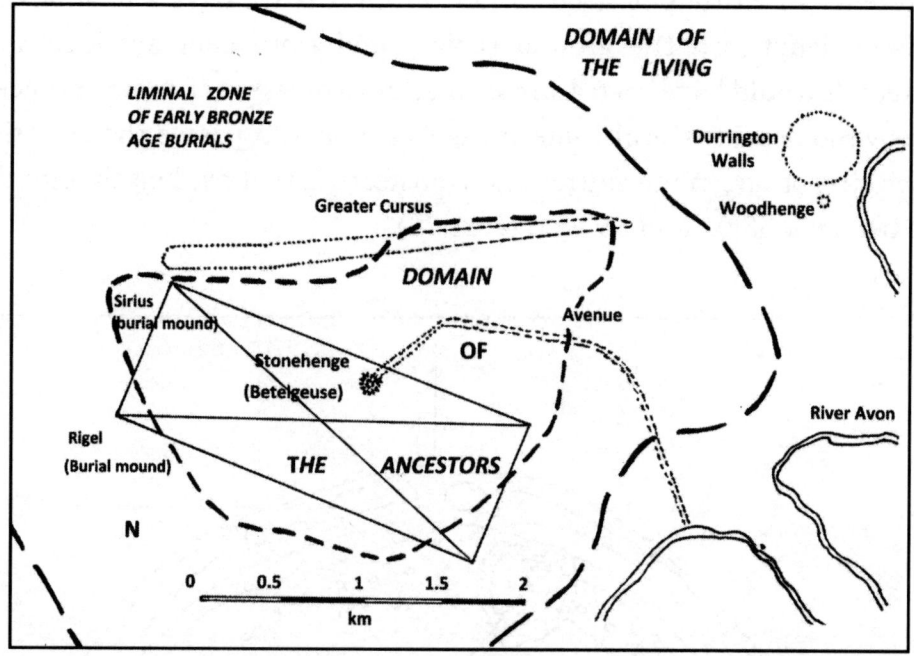

Figure 69: The Station Stone quadrilateral re-sized with SS 93 (Rigel) and SS 94 (Sirius) located at large burial mounds and Betelgeuse centered at Stonehenge. The quadrilateral approximates the south portion of the 'Domain of the Ancestors' based on Parker Pearson and Ramilisonina (1998).

The area of the rectangle accords generally with the south portion of the 'Domain of the Ancestors' defined by Parker Pearson and Ramilisonina (1998) within which few Bronze Age burial sites are located. However, it is notable that a burial mound is located at the center of the rectangle, about 1000 feet (300 m) southwest of the monument.

8—A method for tracking precession

It may be significant that translocation of Orion onto Stonehenge results in Rigel plotting along the line between Stone 92 and Stone 93, outside the sarsen circle. Importantly, it is the distance between SS 93 and the point where Rigel was translocated onto that line that represents an altitude of about 9° 58'. From this we have a relationship between length on the ground surface and equivalent arc length in degrees. It would have been a simple matter to measure the rate of precession by monitoring the altitude of Rigel as soon as it passed the west side of the ring of sarsen megaliths, and transferring that arc length onto the line between SS 92 and SS 93 (Figure 70).

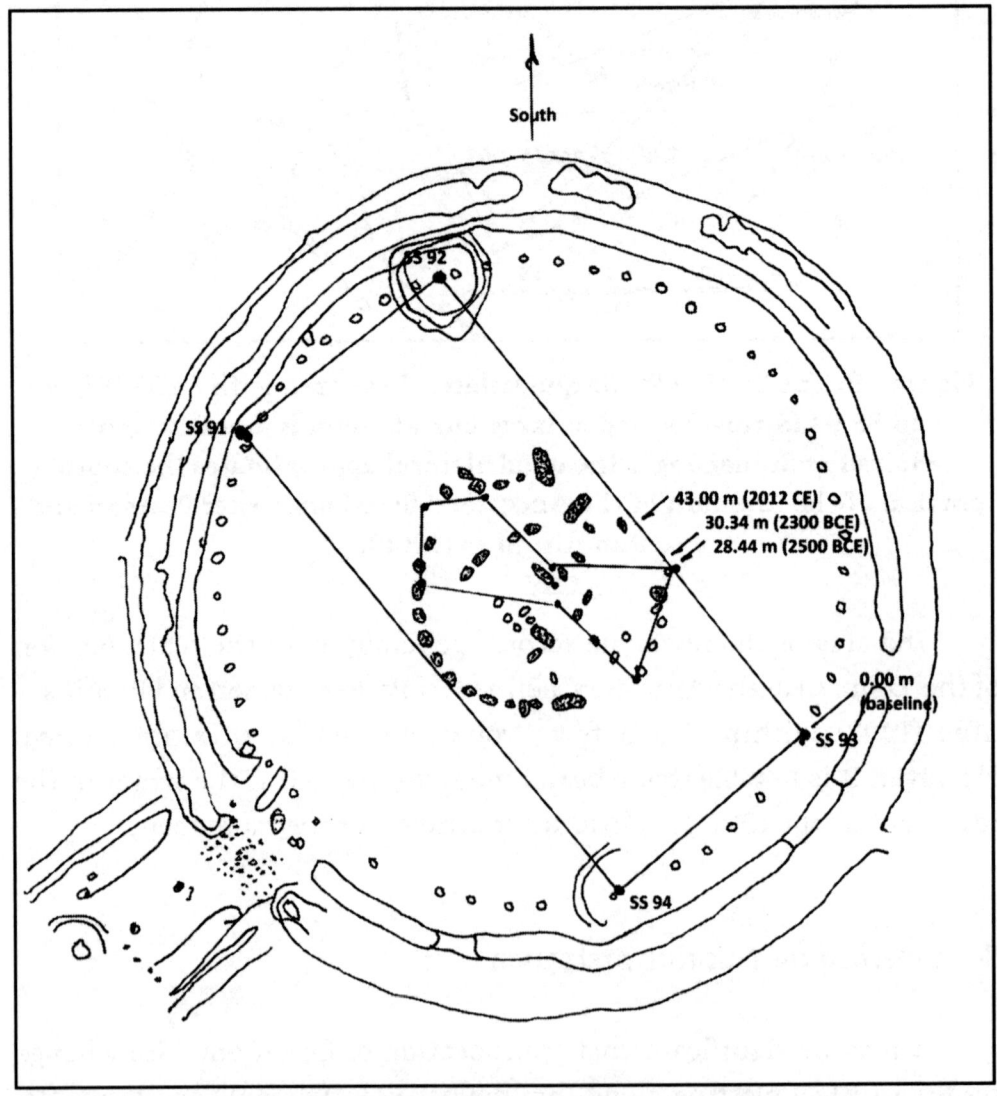

Figure 70: Measuring the rate of precession by plotting Rigel's altitude between SS 92 and SS 93. Distances shown measured from baseline (SS 93) for years 2500 BC, 2300 BC and 2012 AD.

The rate of precession could be measured by tracking the apparent temporal motion of the star. Stars other than Rigel could have been studied in similar fashion, although megaliths in the central portion of the monument obstruct direct measurement of altitude (and azimuth) if measurements were made from the northwest quadrant of the site, for example between SS 93 and SS 94. This indicates the importance of Rigel's position along the line between SS 92 and SS 93. At the same time, with the sightline from SS 94 to SS 91 equivalent to alignment SS 93 to SS 92, two concurrent measurements of Rigel's azimuth and altitude could have been made. It is possible that measuring the cycle of precession as a union of space and time was part of an ancient yet vital late summer ritual.

Discussion

There are cultural traditions which may explain a sacred ritual-based transfer of Orion from sky to Stonehenge. The connection may be associated with a Late Neolithic festival and ritual similar to the Iron Age Celtic Lughnasadh. In ancient Irish mythology Lugh is a hero and a High King. His name derives from the pan-Celtic Lugus from which we have the Irish Lugh *Lámhfhada* (Lugh of the Long Arm, or Long Hand; *Ildánach*: master of many crafts; *Lonnbeimnech*: 'fierce striker'), and the Welsh *Lleu Llaw Gyffes* (Lleu of the Skillful Hand, or Bright One with the Strong Hand). Lugh is also related to Latin *lux*:light. The Irish word *násadh* means feast or celebration, and so Lughnasadh is the feast of Lugh, or celebration of the light (energy, power) of life and good harvest. Lugh is aptly named the Bright One with a Strong Hand when we see him represented by Orion lifting the Sun into the Sky (Figure 65) in the same manner as he did 4500 years ago.

Lughnasadh originated as a harvest festival celebrated between mid-July and mid-August (Galic: *Lúnasa*, the month of August), equivalent to the English Lammas. It is a traditional Gaelic holiday celebrated on August 1 north of the equator. Cultures south of the equator hold similar celebrations on February 1. There are 184 days (six months) between those dates, within one and a half days of dividing the year into halves. The azimuths of the dip slope of the equatorial plane on those two dates are approximately 180° of each other, making August 1 in the northern hemisphere equivalent to February 1 in the southern hemisphere, at least symbolically.

The Celtic festival of Imbolc (Old Irish: *i mbolg*, 'in the belly') celebrated new life near the beginning of February, the festival name indicating pregnancy, particularly with regard to ewes and birthing of lambs at that time of the year. Significance of the date during the Neolithic is evident at Newgrange dating to 3200 BC, and other mound sites in Ireland. It is notable that on February 1, 2500 BC, Orion would have been seen approaching the meridian (due south) at Stonehenge at sunset. The azimuth of the dip of the equatorial plane is 139.3° on February 9. On February 15 Orion would have straddled the meridian at sunset.

Results of the analysis presented above indicates that the beginning of a prototypal two week Lughnasadh celebration ca. 2500 BC coincided with the first appearance (heliacal rising) of Orion, ending with the joining of Orion with Earth at Stonehenge during mid-August. For the people of Salisbury Plain, of course, this intercourse ensuring new life in the following year was between Lugh—the hero of the day, the new King on High (Sky King)—and the Earth Goddess. Artefacts found in pits at Stonehenge and DWS complex as a whole are indicative of Lughnasadh-type festivities including tribal assemblies, drinking and feasting, wakes for the dead, interment of cremated remains, anointment of a new king of fertility and prosperity, and thanks for the bounty about to be harvested. Bulls and at times humans were considered appropriate sacrifices for the good of the people. The old king—the Corn god—was sacrificed (harvested) on his festival day, becoming the new psychopomp, potentially represented by Orion. By the end of the celebration Lugh began his reign as the new King of fertility.

With little evidence to support detailed description of events, we may imagine that the festivities generally included eating, drinking, games, visiting with the larger community, and preparations for ritual release of the dead from Earth to the Otherworld. The Celtic day began at sunset, and this may explain the orientation of the Station Stone quadrilateral toward azimuth 139.3°, when the dip of the equatorial plane achieved that azimuth at dusk on August 10, 2500 BCE. With appearance of the symbolic king (Lugh as Orion) the people may have begun anticipating consummation of life by the new king and Earth inside the goddess's enclosure—her womb—the center of Stonehenge.

It is important to understand that mythology and cosmology associated with the Sky god and Earth goddess are in fact gender neutral. In many ancient cultural traditions Orion is the stellar representation of both god and goddess of peace and fertility, as well as the god and goddess of war and destruction. The Hindu deity Shiva is androgynous and represented by Orion, an excellent example of this understanding of duality in the world. And while Lugh is the Sky god and King of fertility, he is also *Lámhfhada* and *Ildánach and Lonnbeimnech*, the fierce striker with a long arm, a mighty warrior. Isis, the consort of Osiris in mythology of ancient Egypt, is the womb of the world. The center of her womb is the intersection of the galactic plane and ecliptic, like the Lakotan Hocoka at the center of the red racetrack, womb of the universe. The constellation of Orion is perceived to be gender neutral, juxtaposed with life on Earth as the product of the fertility of both female and male. The Sky deity is both male and female. The Earth deity is that same entity made manifest.

Of the many associations Lugh has with fertility and protection of the people, one of them was doorways. The four Station Stones are sacred symbolism: Lugh appearing in the summer night sky, captured at the door to the Otherworld where the sacrificed king travels upon his death and from which the new king—Lugh, the stepson—approaches Earth. The size of Lugh (Orion) at Stonehenge was determined by the doorway—perhaps by the diameter of the Aubrey circle, SS 92 to SS 94—while orientation of the Station Stone quadrilateral identified the date when Lugh and the Earth Goddess would join.

The doorway was rotated from the upper hemisphere represented by the cosmic dome, onto the lower hemisphere represented by Earth, placed onto Stonehenge at the midpoint (interface, equator) between the physical and metaphysical, life and death, sacred and profane. Then, on one much anticipated sunrise in mid-August, Sirius made its heliacal rising, allowing full view of the celestial doorway between Sirius and Aldebaran, signaling the rise of the new king as protector of life. Viewing Grooved Ware culture as one devoted to a sacred lifeway, the purpose of sub-phase 3ii design of Stonehenge appears intended to interact with metaphysical forces binding humans, Earth, cosmos, and Creator with each other.

Conclusion

Stonehenge sub-phase 3ii was constructed for far more than a means to observe solar and lunar risings and settings, events at azimuths that would have been known by the 26th century BCE. The Long Man of Wilmington and nearby long barrows setting sightlines for observing Orion 'walking' across the southern horizon, are evidence of not only a recognition of astronomical events from the perspective of Earth, but purposeful modification of the landscape to enhance observations and create an artistic rendition of Orion upon the landscape across time and space.

The four symbols at Skara Brae, representing stars located across the Milky Way, demonstrate that Orion was important to GW cosmography by the time megaliths were introduced to Stonehenge. It is not surprising then that Orion was introduced to Stonehenge as a vital symbol relating contemporary understandings of life and death, natural fertility, cosmography and geometry, architecture, and human interaction with the cycles of space and time.

The bilateral symmetry of Stonehenge (including the Station Stone quadrilateral) indicates the monument may have served in some capacity during festive celebrations held in August and February. In early February and early August the azimuth of the Station Stone quadrilateral's long side is equivalent to the angle between the dip slope of Earth's equatorial plane and the line between Earth and Sun. On those dates the four

Stations define a specific region of the celestial dome—a rectangular area defined by the stars Sirius and Aldebaran. Orion, within that area of space, was conceptually translocated to the ground surface defined by the Station Stones. With Orion emplaced and centered at Stonehenge, locations and alignments of various other features of the cultural landscape about the henge appear related to the constellation's geometrical configuration.

Transfer of Orion onto Earth's surface may represent spatial and temporal aspects of nature during an ancient prototypal celebration similar to the Celtic festival of Lughnasadh. Emplacing Orion upon the landscape at a particular point in time, evident by the orientation of the four Stations, created a potential means for measuring the rate of precession. Soon after bluestone and sarcen megaliths (including the Station Stones) were installed inside the henge, the Avenue was constructed between Stonehenge and the River Avon. The Avenue represents Lugh's long arm along which ceremonial transport of the dead could proceed from the river to the monument for sacred rituals related to death of the body and release of the spirit to follow the spirit path back to the origin of life in the cosmos.[28]

Additional research may help explain the progression of development in which Orion was first emplaced upon the monument, later to be perceived occupying much of the area about the DWS complex, and limiting the area allowed for Bronze Age burials on Salisbury Plain.

CREATING THE CURSUS

Appendix A

The Greater Cursus is situated in the central area of the Stonehenge Landscape alignment network (Figure A1). Paying attention to the alignments we find the following.

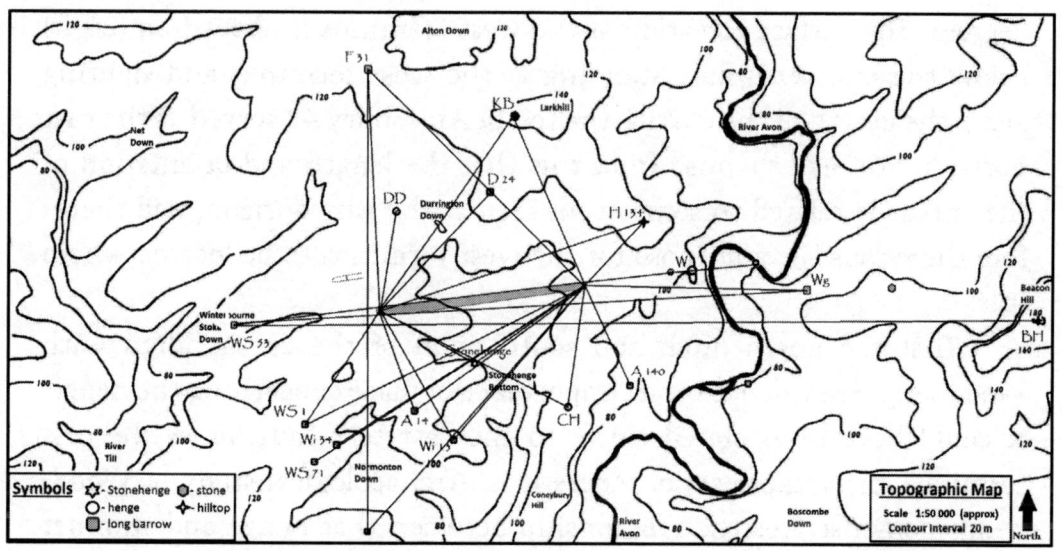

Figure A1: Greater Cursus and associated alignments

- The west portion of the south ditch is an accurate west-east baseline (azimuth 90°) from the southwest corner of the cursus to the point of intersection (PI) in the south

ditch where the ditch's azimuth changes to 84°. The alignment extends west to Winterbourne Stoke 53 and east to
Watergate.

- The remaining length of the south ditch is defined by alignment between the PI in the ditch and two posts that were
situated along the summer solstice sunrise at Woodhenge.

- The north ditch is defined by the alignment from Winterbourne Stoke 53 to the two posts situated along the summer
solstice sunrise at Woodhenge.

Now we see why the Greater Cursus has a rather streamlined yet
awkward shape. It conforms to alignments between WS53 and Watergate, WS53 and Woodhenge, and the east-west baseline. The reason for
the PI in the south ditch line remains unanswered at this point of the
analysis, as does the purpose of the 2.74 km length of the cursus, and
purpose for the cursus oriented along an azimuth of about 84 to 85
degrees. The surface elevation at the west terminus is about 6 m (20 ft)
below the east terminus. Standing at the west terminus and sighting
along the length of the cursus, the top of Amesbury 42 served as the east
horizon. We may surmise from this that the length and orientation of
the cursus is related to some event seen at the east horizon, and therefore there must be a purpose for the west terminus to be located where
it is.

That the north ditch and south ditch of the cursus align with
Woodhenge is evidence of the importance of place concerning the henge.
It could have been placed closer to the east terminus, or at the east
terminus, or farther east of where it is. Archaeological study of Woodhenge demonstrates the relationship between that henge and summer
solstice. Such information is readily available elsewhere and not presented
herein. The reason for Woodhenge's circular shape, like the majority of
ancient and indigenous sacred circular structures, is discussed in detail
elsewhere.[1]

Appendix B
LONG BARROW 15 (UNKNOWN DURRINGTON DOWN)

Curiously there is no mid-Neolithic monument of known significance on Durrington Down, north of the west end of the Greater Cursus, even though the local relief is quite gentle and a large part of the west portion of the Stonehenge Landscape is visible from that location. Figure 18 in the main text is provided below as Figure B1 to assist the reader when needing to refer to the figure while reading the appendices.

There is a wealth of evidence for barrows, other structures, ditches and ground disturbance on Durrington Down. Locations of former round barrows, pond barrows and other features are documented in the area (Figure B2 and Figure B3). Many more are known to have been located in the area but were destroyed as a result of agricultural activities including ploughing of fields which leveled the ground surface over many years. Durrington Down was likely occupied in some way or form from the mid-Neolithic through the Iron Age. In fact a number of former barrows and other structures are evident in crop marks in the area north of the west portion of the Greater Cursus and south of the Packway road leading west from Larkhill.

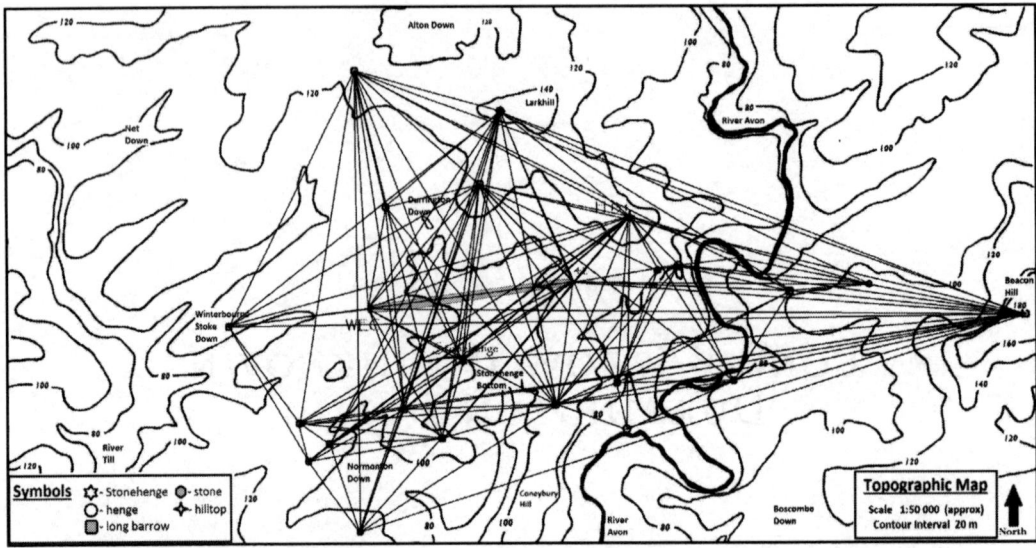

Figure B1: This is also Figure 18 in the main text. Durrington Down is located southwest of Larkhill. UDD is immediately west of where the down is labeled on the map. A structure located on the broad, shallow slope of Durrington Down would have the potential to offer naked eye alignment with nine other nodes of the network. UDD is along alignment between KB (top of Larkhill) and west-east baseline control point WS53 located on Winterbourne Stoke Down (farthest west point of the alignment network). It is also along alignment between north-south baseline control point F31 to the north and W13 to the south. It is the only node within the network situated at the intersection of two alignments associated with two baseline control point.

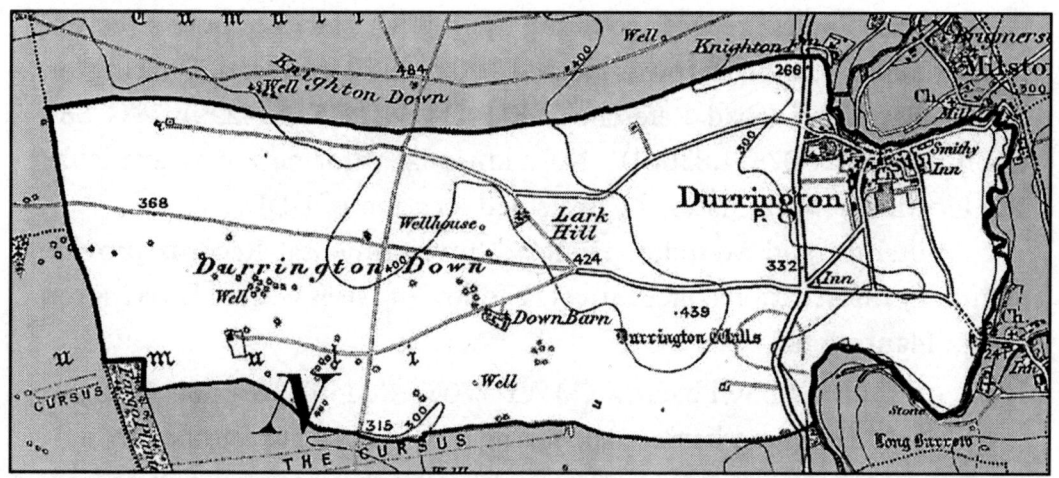

Figure B2: Locations of various archaeological sites mapped at Durrington Down and surrounding area. Note concentration of barrows located in the west portion of Durrington Down. Estimated plot of UDD is vicinity of first 'D' in Durrington Down. Greater Cursus shown in lower left.[1]

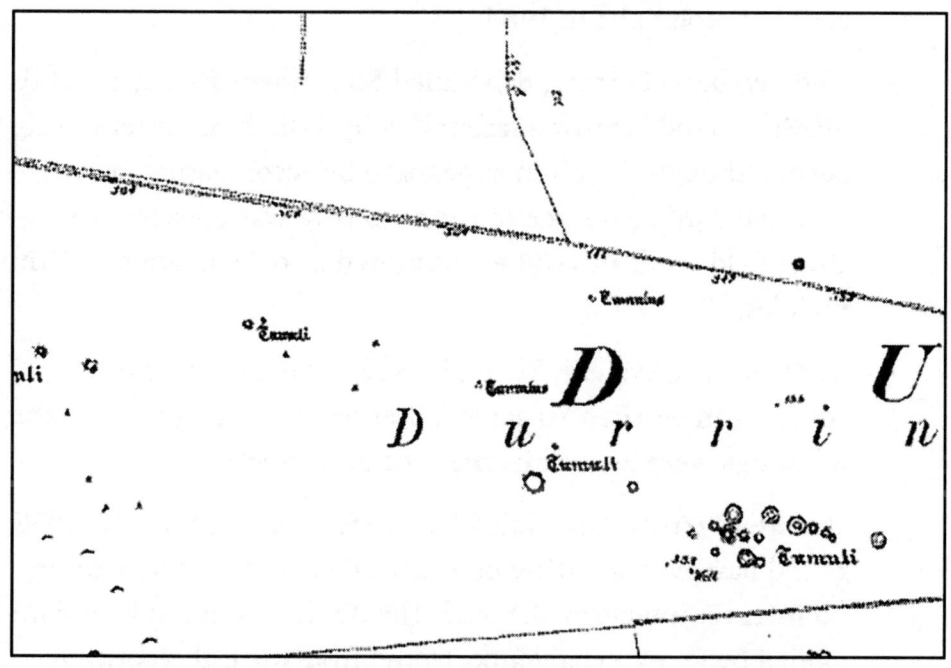

Figure B3: Map depicting Tumuli on west portion of Durrington Down ca. 1887.[2] Estimated location of UDD is vicinity of large 'D' (bold print).[2]

Archaeological records retained by English Heritage note a feature interpreted as a bowl barrow is located 200 m (660 ft) west of Durrington Down Plantation (Grid Reference SE114114 (411415, 144299); WG S84 Coordinates 51.1973,-1.83661).[3] No additional information is available. The location approximates the projected location of UDD.

Wiltshire and Swindon Historic Environmental Records provide summary information concerning the following sites west of Durrington Down Plantation:[4]

- Undated bowl barrow (MWI12705—SU14SW624); SU 1158 4422; round barrow appearing as a mound surrounded by a ditch, no intervening berm although the ditch appears to be accompanied by an external bank. The site was first recorded in 1957; in 1970 there was no trace of the site on the ground. The area is under cultivation.

- Undated enclosure; SU 1135 4445; rectangular area bounded by a ditch, bank, wall, palisade or other barrier; noted on aerial photographs in 1984.

- Undated bowl barrow; Scheduled Monument 10395; SU 1141 4429; a round barrow surrounded by a ditch, no intervening berm although the ditch appears to be accompanied by an external bank. No trace of the structure was apparent in 1970; field work in 1984 encountered a concentration of flint nodules.

- Undated field system; SU 1135 4432; a system of fields covering more than 70 acres; observed on aerial photographs; buildings were located in the area during WWII.

- Undated barrow; Scheduled Monument 10279; SU 1110 4438; round barrow consisting of a mound surrounded by a ditch, no intervening berm although the ditch appears to be accompanied by an external bank. Noted in historical records as destroyed with no visible indication in 1970 but shown extant on an OS map dated 1924.

- Undated bowl barrow; Scheduled Monument 10279; SU 1108 4438; round barrow consisting of a mound surrounded by a ditch, no intervening berm although the ditch appears to be accompanied by an external bank. It was excavated prior to the 20th century; Hoare noted it had been disturbed; by 1970 the mound was 1 m (3.3 ft) high and 16 m (52 ft) in diameter, the west portion destroyed by road construction. In 1984 the mound was described as rendered square due to ploughing.

- Undated bowl barrow; MWI12707—SU14SW626; Scheduled Monument 10234; SU 1149 4417; round barrow consisting of a mound surrounded by a ditch, no intervening berm although the ditch appears to be accompanied by an external bank. It was excavated prior to the 20th century; Hoare noted it had been disturbed; in 1970 it was recorded as 0.5 m (1.6 ft) high and 23 m (75 ft) in diameter; by 1984 it was visible as only a slight rise in the crop.

- Area of modern military trenching; MWI12592—SU14SW528; SU 1126 4419; system of trenches noted in 1995; excavated by troops for practice purposes.

Several low mounds are apparent in the large field south of the Packway and west of Durrington Down Plantation, in the field where the above referenced sites are situated, and where UDD may have been located. The referenced sites have also been mapped as ring barrows, which may indicate that UDD could be an unrecognized henge similar to Coneybury Henge which had originally been misidentified as a barrow. It is also possible that UDD was a less developed site resulting in little indication of its presence, or former presence. Numerous undated artefacts have been collected during unintrusive archaeological field-walking surveys of the area. The area has undergone long term ploughing that has smoothed the ground surface. That activity would have promoted soil erosion and reduced topography. This causes the apparent lowlying mounds to be curious topographical features. Aside of affecting soils the ploughing would also impact distribution of archaeological artefacts on and within perhaps a foot or two of the current ground surface.

There are instances of archaeological artefacts encountered on the Stonehenge Landscape that have been incorrectly dated. This includes a Neolithic barrow incorrectly dated to the Bronze Age, and three Bronze Age barrows overlying a long barrow that was not previously recognized.

For these reasons there remains the potential for encountering evidence of Neolithic site UDD on Durrington Down in the area indicated above. Additional archaeological investigation would help to further evaluate the potential for a previously unrecognized Neolithic structure to have been located in that area.

Appendix C
LONG BARROW, HENGE, CURSUS AND HIGH POINT ALIGNMENTS

There are 94 line of sight alignments between two or more locations depicted in Figure B1. The 94 alignments include only those between two sites that can be seen from one to the other by naked eye. A clear line of sight could be made from one end of each alignment to the other when the Stonehenge Landscape was grassland ca. 3500 BC.

There is readily apparent bi-lateral symmetry in the network of nodes and links apparent in Figure B1, with the axis of symmetry oriented east-west along the length of the Greater Cursus and beyond. This would be a surprising result if significant elements from the Neolithic—both natural and manmade—were located randomly across the landscape. The finding is notable as the analysis continues.

As might be expected the majority of alignments occur between points located in the central portion of the landscape. That area is between Larkhill to the north and Normanton Down to the South, and from the west terminus of the Greater Cursus to the west and the River Avon to the east. We know triangulation could be used to locate each of the Neolithic long barrows, henges and cursus. Now we can reduce the number of alignments of concern to triangulations between the Greater Cursus and each long barrow or henge located in the central area of the landscape. Figure C1 shows triangulations situated in the central portion of the landscape.

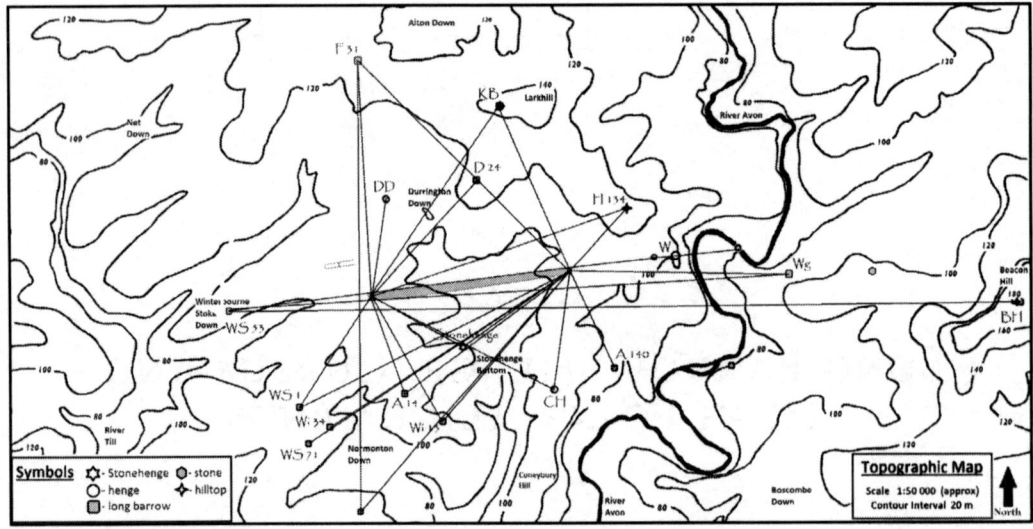

Figure C1: Triangulations formed between Neolithic features, cursus and hilltops located in the central region of the landscape. North-South and East-West baselines are shown.

When preparing to a build an engineered structure, a surveyor will place control points not only in the area where the structure will be built, but beyond that area as well. The peripheral control points are set so they can be used to locate additional points in the construction area, and to re-locate points that might be disturbed or destroyed as construction work proceeds. Control points often form baselines oriented in directions important to the project.

At the Stonehenge Landscape three baselines are apparent. They are shown in Figure C1. A due north-south baseline extends between long barrows F31 and WS71. The second baseline is oriented due east-west between WS53 and the Bulford Stone (BS). The third baseline extends from WS53 to the top of Beacon Hill (BH). It is amazing to see the care taken to ensure monuments were placed precisely in accordance with the plan in mind, evident by construction of the baselines extending well beyond the central portion of the landscape.

Comparison of Figures B1 and C1 indicates that each of the Neolithic elements and hilltops could be surveyed by triangulation using other points within the central area. While the baselines were important to construction of the Stonehenge Landscape, they are not essential with regard to reverse engineering to discover the grand plan. We know more than one triangulation could be used to locate each of the Neolithic long barrows, henges and cursus. We can reduce the number of alignments of concern to those between the Greater Cursus and each long barrow or henge located in the central area of the landscape. This is shown in Figure C2.

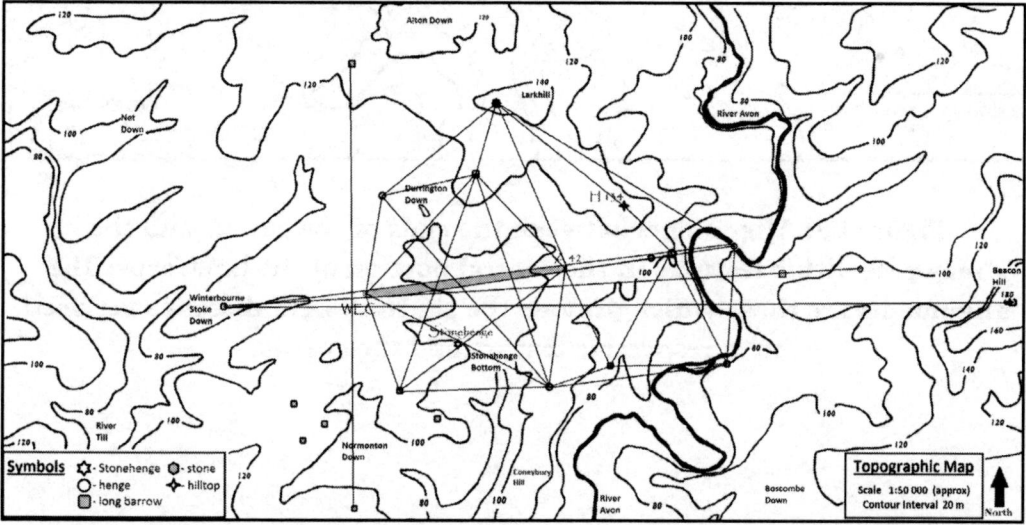

Figure C2: Line of sight alignments to ends of the Greater Cursus from locations in the central portion of the landscape. Note that a web of alignments is available for triangulating each location from several others. The three baselines are shown as well.

The number of alignments may be reduced further to only those between the ends of the Greater Cursus and the major sites in the central area of the landscape including A14, Coneybury Henge, KB, UDD and Stonehenge. In addition the alignment between WS53 and LS is retained as it serves as a primary alignment from one end of the cursus to the other, and also includes WS53, CS, WH and LS. Once again bi-lateral symmetry is apparent north and south of that line. This is shown in Figure C3.

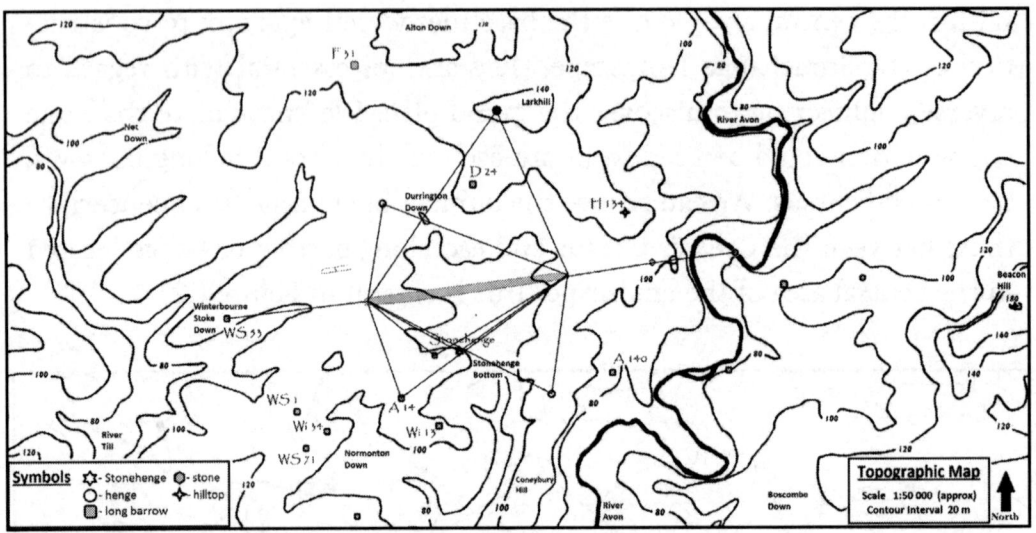

Figure C3: Alignments between the ends of the cursus and the major Neolithic features in the central portion of the landscape. The alignments are those which provide the shortest sight distance between then respective feature and the cursus.

Appendix D
TRIANGULATION BETWEEN LONG BARROWS AND TERMINI OF THE GREATER CURSUS

We can see locations of the long barrows, henges, hilltops and cursus in Figure B1. Of what further value is triangulation once the cursus and barrows are in place? The answer is each alignment between barrow and end of cursus can itself be used as baseline. Any two of those alignments can be extended such that they demarcate a point common to both alignments. (Two lines that are not parallel intersect at only one point.) What beside the cursus and individual barrows was being located on Stonehenge's sacred landscape?

We assume that the purpose for aligning the major axis of long barrows to one end or the other of the Greater Cursus was to create additional control points. Those locations provided builders of this sacred landscape ca. 3500 BC a way of setting additional points using triangulation. In fact, given the extensive network of alignments, the location of each long barrow was probably set using triangulation once the baseline for the cursus was set. Our hypothesis is that the additional points are locations of important features of the landscape that together explain the purpose of the long barrow-cursus alignments. If the additional points are of no importance then the assumption of long barrow-cursus alignments being used as triangulation controls will be in question.

The ends (termini) of the Greater Cursus have a direct or almost direct line of sight to Meaden's nine long barrows located within about two kilometers. The major axis of each long borrow is oriented toward the cursus (Figure 17b, reproduced below at figure D1).

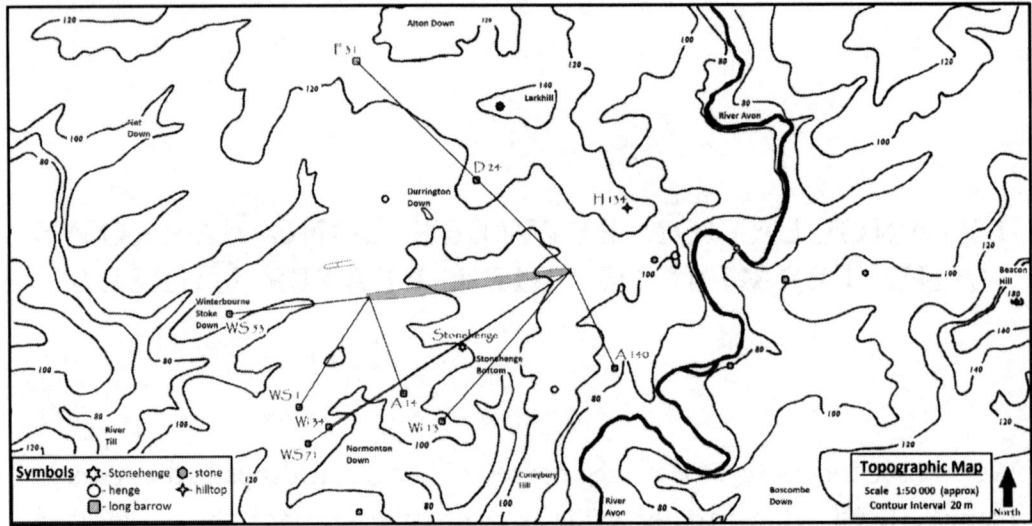

Figure D1: Alignments between Meaden's nine long barrows and the Greater Cursus. Each alignment can be viewed in two directions—either from the long barrow through the end of the cursus, or from the end of the cursus through the long barrow.

Similarly a line in the opposite direction can be drawn from one or the other end of the cursus to the respective long borrow. Note that each alignment between long barrow and cursus has an easterly or westerly component, except one, that being the alignment between Amesbury 14 and the west end of the cursus. The alignment of the Amesbury 42 is due north-south.

Appendix E
LOCATING POINTS OF THE WINTER HEXAGON ONTO THE LANDSCAPE

Within the limits of accuracy in measuring the orientation of five of the long barrows, it is possible that only D24 and Wi13 were intended to mark the location of the east terminus of the Greater Cursus (representing the elliptic). One each of the other three long barrows (A14, WS71, A140) appear intended to either point toward, or represent, symbolic locations of the stars Rigel, Bellatrix and Alnath.

The hexagon constructed on the Stonehenge Landscape is shown in Figure 33a, reproduced here as Figure E1. The Greater Cursus represents the Milky Way between Sirius (WEC) and the ecliptic (A42). Results of archeological investigations show that the Greater Cursus was constructed sometime between 3600 and 3300 BC. Archaeologists suggest 3480 BC as a reasonable estimate for the date of construction. The actual length of time devoted to the cursus construction remains unknown.

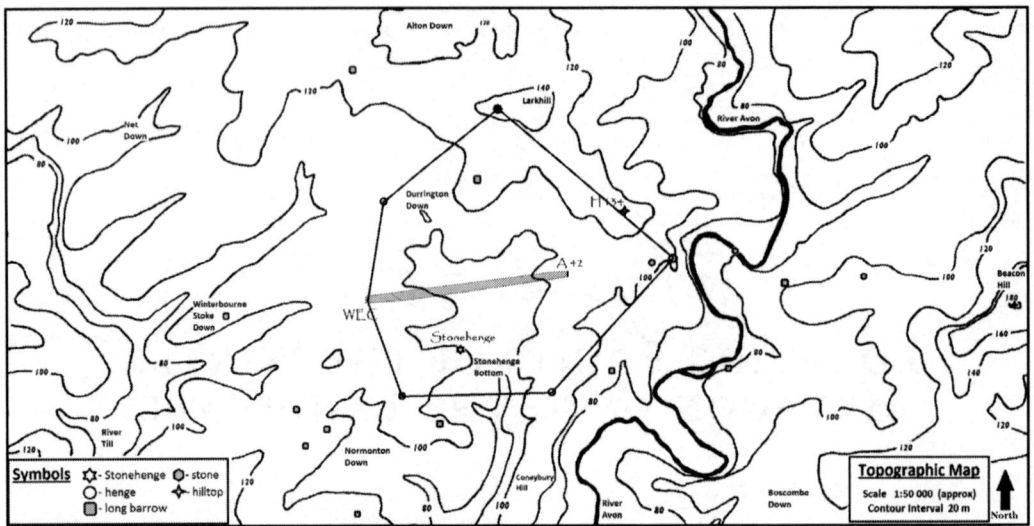

Figure E1: Stonehenge Landscape including the Greater Cursus and the six locations forming the hexagon

Long barrows in the area were probably built during or soon after the cursus was completed. They include long barrow 42 and long barrows with axes oriented toward the cursus (such as A14.) Henge construction was to follow hundreds of years later. Archaeological investigations have shown that the sites of Stonehenge, Coneybury Henge and Woodhenge were occupied long before the mid-Neolithic.

The Winter Hexagon constructed on the Stonehenge Landscape is shown in Figure E2. Each point of the hexagon is shown as a star labeled with the respective star it represents. Links between the Neolithic sites are not shown.

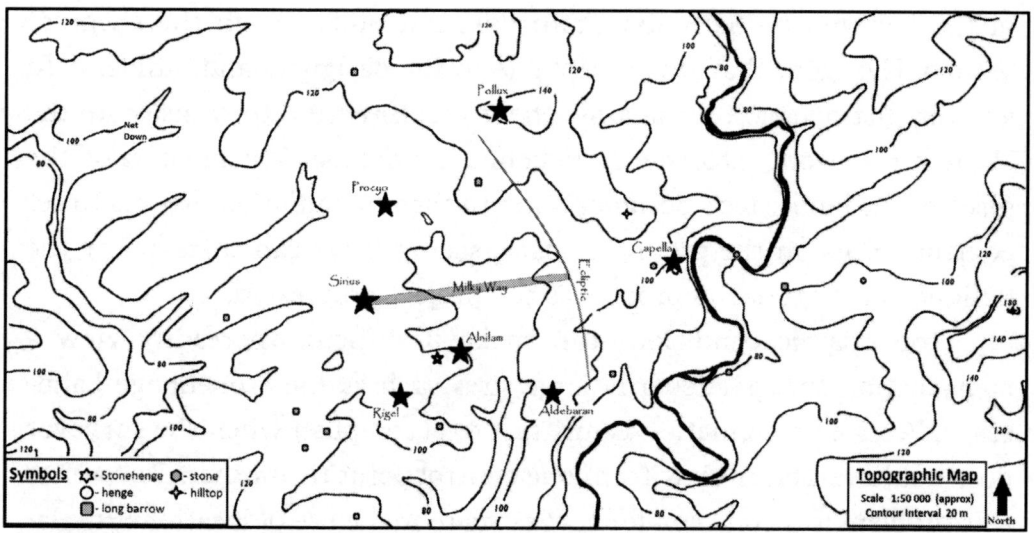

Figure E2: The hexagon emplaced upon the Stonehenge Landscape in about 3380 BC. It is a symbolic representation of the Winter Hexagon constellation. The hexagon is formed by WEC (Sirius), UDD (Procyon), KB (Pollux), WH (Capella), CH (Aldebaran) and A14 (Rigel). The Greater Cursus represents the Milky Way between Sirius (WEC) and the ecliptic (A42). Stonehenge is the symbolic location of Alnilam.

Alnilam, middle star of Orion's belt, plots precisely at the location of Stonehenge. A long barrow located about 330 m west of Stonehenge (small star) is where the Orion Nebula, brightest feature of Orion's sword, would plot upon the landscape. The star Alnath plots onto long barrow Amesbury 140 (shown as a small circle to the east (right) of Aldebaran (Coneybury Henge).

The lost megalith (LS) reported to have been formerly located in or adjacent to the River Avon east of Woodhenge until quite recently, is not available for study to determine its date of placement in or adjacent to the river. However its former location along the north ditch alignment of the Greater Cursus, might be indicative of a mid-Neolithic date for the stone's placement.

In summary, construction dates of the cursus, long barrows and henges generally conform to potential contemporary construction and use. However, at this point in the analysis it is apparent that the shape of the hexagon on Salisbury Plain does not quite match the shape of Winter Hexagon. Was this acceptable to the designers and builders? To answer that question we assume there was intention to translocate the Winter Hexagon onto the Stonehenge Landscape. We must take the place of the landscape's designer and use the triangulation process to set control points on the ground surface, seeing if we can then follow the designer's thoughts and process as the project progressed.

Topographic conditions can make it difficult to readily view a construction site, particularly large sites such as the Stonehenge Land-scape. Precise triangulation is difficult to accomplish when the surveyor does not have a clear view from one control point to another. To counter this problem it is common for surveyors to make use of locations at rela-tively high elevations to improve direct viewing as much of the site as possible. Hilltops typically serve that purpose.

Almost the entire Stonehenge Landscape can be seen from the top of Beacon Hill. However that vantage point is 4-to 9 kilometers from the area defined by the translocated hexagon, too far for use as an effi-cient and effective control point for the surveyors needs. The next highest hilltop is Larkhill. Of course, KB is located there and the long barrow appears to represent the star Pollux. Therefore we have good reason to believe KB was a valuable control point in more than one way for the project.

Unfortunately areas such as the central portion of the Greater Cursus, Amesbury 42, Woodhenge, and LS cannot be seen from KB. The designer must have realized additional control points on the hill would be needed. This explains the reason for siting Durrington 24 where lower south facing slopes of Larkhill can be observed, and using H134 for control east of Larkhill. Figure E3 illustrates the ease of setting points D24 and H134 from KB. This may have been one of the first triangula-tions made for the project.

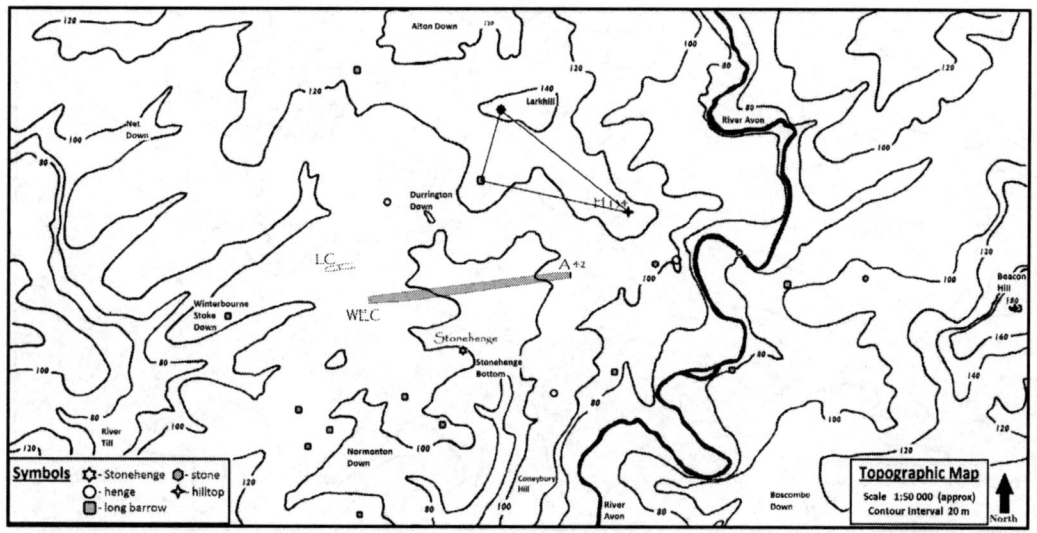

Figure E3: Potential first triangulation between KB, H134 and D24. These are three north-centrally located high points overlooking the Stonehenge sacred landscape.

With D24 and H134 as control points, additional triangulations can be accomplished to set the ends of the Greater Cursus. It is also possible, perhaps probable, that the size and location of the cursus was decided prior to setting other control points. Figure E4 depicts triangulations for the ends of the cursus using D24 and H134 as control.

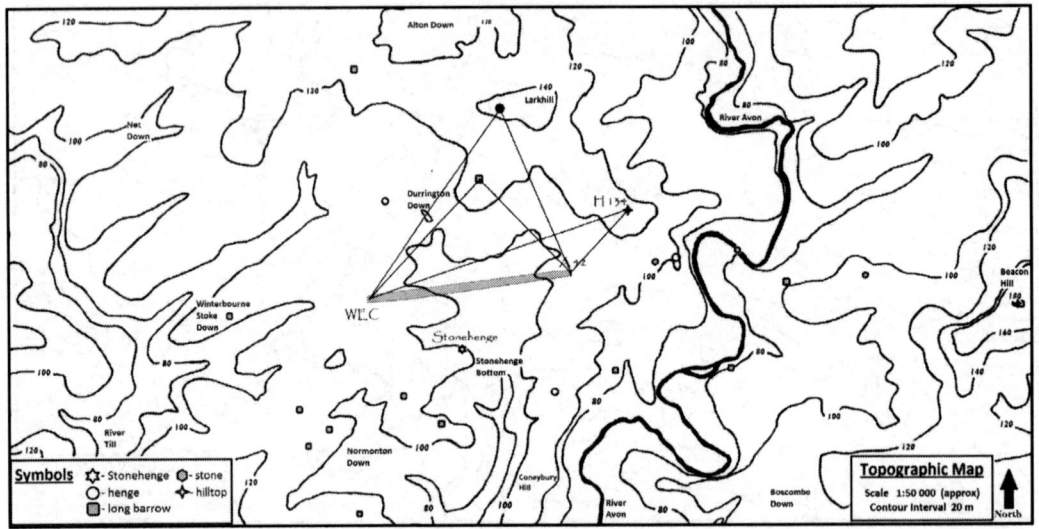

Figure E4: Triangulations between KB, H134, D24 and the ends of the Greater Cursus.

Another site at a relatively high elevation is Coneybury Henge, situated tactically along a ridgeline although not on a hilltop. CH had potential use as control for locations either side of Coneybury Hill, in the east and west portions of the landscape. Figure E5 shows potential triangulation of the ends of the Greater Cursus using CH for control from the south side of the landscape.

Figure E5: Triangulations between centrally located high points D24, H134, CH and the ends of the cursus.

With views of Stonehenge Landscape provided by four high points, two of which will serve as symbolic star locations, additional control points would be beneficial when the many other sites are surveyed for construction of monuments. A set of perpendicular baselines are effective for this purpose, and it is evident that those alignments were placed across the landscape. A north-south baseline begins in the north at Figheldean 31 and extends south to long barrow Wilsford 30 at Normanton Down; it passes just west of the west end of the Greater Cursus.

A west-east baseline begins at WS53 and extends west through the southwest corner of the greater Cursus, the PI in the cursus south ditch, long barrow Wg, and the Bulford Stone. The entire Stonehenge Landscape is located within the quadrangle defined by those two baselines. With two perpendicular baselines and four control points at upper elevations, triangulation can be applied for placing the remainder of the Winter Hexagon-related features. This is illustrated in Figure E6.

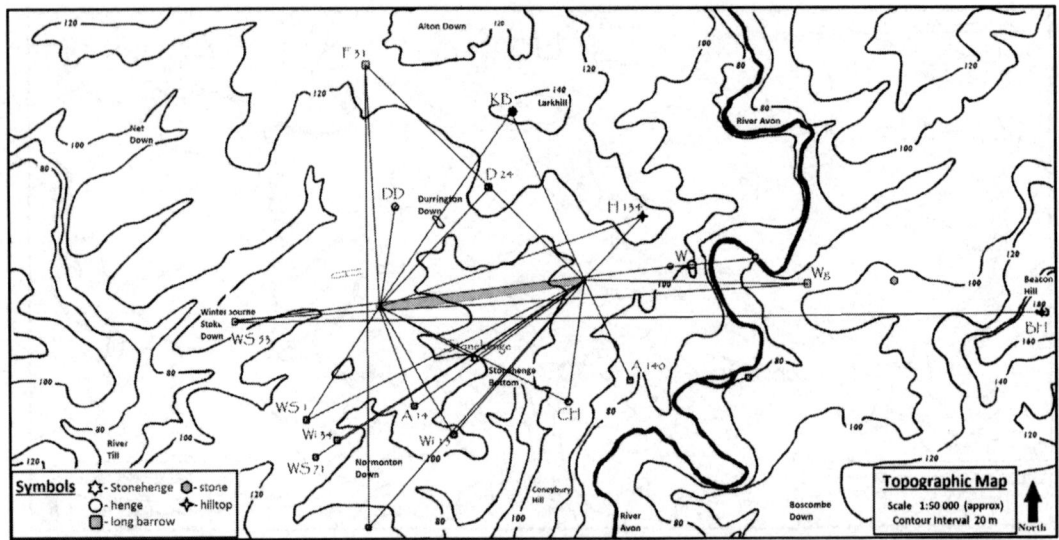

Figure E6: Lines of sight between features referenced in Figure 15 and Figure 16, and additional sites thus forming a North-South baseline and the baseline between W53 and W, including the north ditch of the cursus.

An important alignment extends east-west at the azimuth of the north ditch of the Greater Cursus. It begins at WS53, follows the north ditch, then to the Cuckoo Stone (CS) and Woodhenge before terminating at LS. The line divides the hexagon into halves, with symbolic Sirius and Capella (WEC, LS) on the alignment, symbolic Pollux and Procyon (KB, UDD) to the north, and symbolic Rigel and Aldebaran (A14, CH) to the south. In this way it can be considered a third baseline.

Figure E7 shows alignments between control points along the third baseline and A14, CH, KB and UDD. A point is marked as a diamond between WS53 and WEC. Another diamond is shown south of KB and a third diamond north of CH. If the apparent distance between Procyon and Rigel was accurately scaled to set the corresponding locations of UDD and A14, and that same scale was used to plot the remaining symbolic star locations for the hexagon, then Capella would plot precisely at Woodhenge, and the three remaining stars would plot where the three diamonds are shown in Figure E7. Dashed lines show the shape and size of an accurately plotted Winter Hexagon onto the landscape.

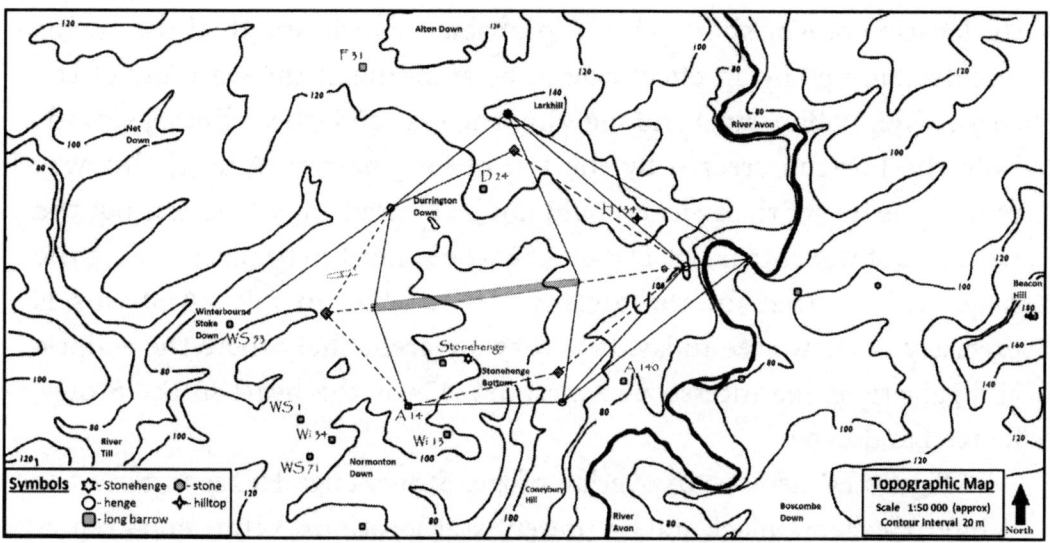

Figure E7: Alignments between WS53 and LS including the cursus, symbolic Winter Hexagon, and Winter Hexagon produced by accurate positioning of Sirius, Procyon, Pollux, Capella, Aldebaran and Rigel onto the landscape (dashed lines).

From this diagram it appears that symbolic Sirius would need to be moved east to locate it at WEC. This is not so. The location, orientation and length of the Greater Cursus are what the design for the rest of the landscape is based on. The length of the cursus is the symbolic length from Sirius to the ecliptic. Therefore the diamond west of the cursus WEC was never intended to be the location of Sirius. Sirius *was* WEC and would remain at WEC.

This should not be seen as an error in translocating Sirius onto the Stonehenge Landscape. Based on archaeological analyses it is very evident that the Greater Cursus was surveyed and possibly constructed prior to locating sites for the long barrows. Thus the scale used for setting locations of the symbolic hexagon would need to be the same one used for setting the length from Sirius to the ecliptic, represented by the length of the cursus. But there is one more factor to consider.

Translocation of the Winter Hexagon was dependent on the length and orientation of the cursus, and the cursus length was dependent on the location of Amesbury 42. It is probable that the length of the cursus was determined by an effect caused by standing at the west end of the cursus (symbolic Sirius) and viewing the east end (the ecliptic), specifically the horizon created by the top of long barrow A42. If this was indeed the intent then Sirius could not be located anywhere else but the west end of the cursus. UDD and A14 would need to be placed using the same scale as that for the distance from WEC to EEC. And this is precisely what we see today. It is very apparent that where the ecliptic and galactic plane intersect—Amesbury 42—is the heart of the Stonehenge Landscape.

Figure E8 depicts an overlay of the Stonehenge Hexagon onto the Winter Hexagon. Black stars represent star locations. White stars represent symbolic locations of the stars surveyed onto Salisbury Plain. The illustration applies the same scale for the distance from Sirius to the ecliptic, and from Rigel to Procyon. For both hexagons Sirius is shown at its relative location based on the length of the cursus. Amesbury 42 is the lynch pin for the entire structure. From A42's location, Sirius must locate at the west terminus of the cursus, and UDD and A14 must plot as shown if the project was to be successful as an accurate translocation of the stars to Earth.

The overlay shows placing star locations in the west half of the symbolic Winter Hexagon onto the ground was an amazing feat surveying. Triangulations from the cursus to A14 (Rigel) and UDD (Procyon) are almost perfect. Procyon and Rigel were placed almost exactly where they should.

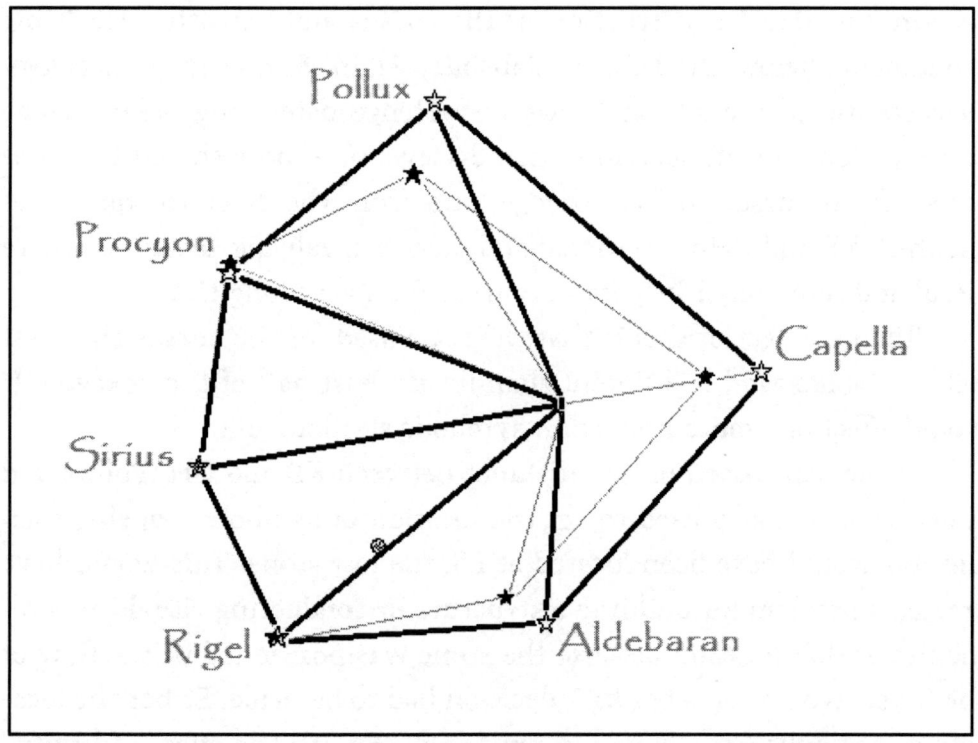

Figure E8: Symbolic Winter Hexagon with triangulation lines, and hexagon plotted accurately (dashed lines) using cursus scale for distance between Sirius and ecliptic.

Unfortunately surveying for the east half of the hexagon—Pollux, Capella and Aldebaran—did not fare as well. The designer encountered a problem because of a change in scale. The distance between KB and CH is greater than it should be, as shown in Figure E7 and E8. Depicted in Figure E8, Pollux and Aldebaran should be placed as indicated by the respective diamond rather than at KB and CH. The decision was made to keep symbolic Pollux and Aldebaran at the control locations KB and CH. From the standpoint of engineering this can be perceived as an error in construction. However, from the standpoint of symbolism—sacred symbolism being the purpose of the entire effort—Pollux and Aldebaran were located precisely where they needed to be. This is because KB is at the apex of Larkhill, the highest point on the landscape and the location from which surveying would begin. The cultural importance of Larkhill certainly predated construction of the cursus and the other Neolithic monuments below the hill, on Salisbury Plain. Similarly, archaeology suggests use of the site at Coneybury Henge dates long before henge construction, and its location offered views of almost the entire landscape—from cursus to Woodhenge, and from the river to the top of Larkhill. KB and CH were sacred and practical, valuable locations where ritual and ceremony likely had occurred for a very long time.

The net effect of this is that the scale used for the cursus and west half of the hexagon is different than for the east half of the hexagon. It would affect one more important symbolic star location.

If the scale based on the distance between KB and CH (Pollux and Aldebaran) was also used to set the location of symbolic Capella, then the star would have been located at LS, the lost stone. This would have created a problem for building a structure or conducting rituals or ceremonies at that location because the stone was positioned in the flow of the River Avon or on a bank. A decision had to be made. Either the location of symbolic Capella would remain at LS with the effect of limited use of the location for sacred purpose, or a different site would need to be chosen where the needs the people would be better served.

Evidence suggests the decision was to locate symbolic Capella to another location. The simplest solution was to remain somewhere along the WS53-LS alignment and shift the location to the first suitable location west of the river. Locating Capella on the west side of the river would be important because all other portions of the hexagon are also west of the river. This would ensure ease of movement to and from the various monuments and likely improve efficiency and effectiveness of rituals and ceremonies related to the Stonehenge Landscape. Also, there is no perceived disconnect between cosmic Capella and the rest of the Winter Hexagon. The symbolic hexagon needed to be recognized as one unified structure.

With the intent being to create a symbolic Winter Hexagon on Earth it is reasonable to keep the unity of the structure and symbolism intact. The site chosen for symbolic Capella is Woodhenge. Beyond concern for where LS was unfortunately located, there was a more important reason for symbolic Capella located at the site of Woodhenge.

Woodhenge is where Capella would plot if the Winter Hexagon had been translocated accurately using the same scale as that of the Greater Cursus for the distance between Sirius and the ecliptic. Figure E9 shows consideration for relocating Capella from LS to WH. It is probable that the decision made for symbolic Capella's location as an alternative to LS, if the decision had to be made at all, was to apply the scale that was originally intended for the entire hexagon. This would result in translocation of Capella to the site of Woodhenge.

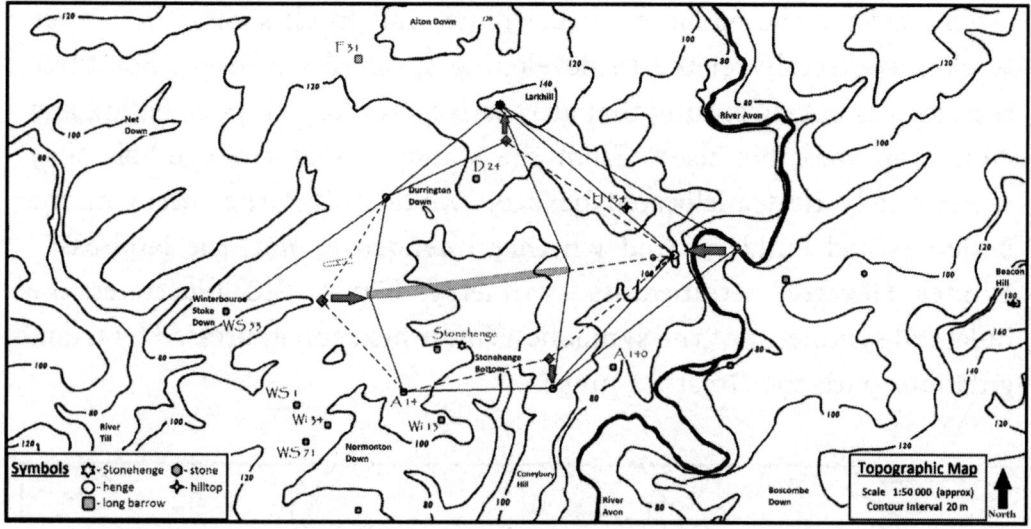

Figure E9: Difference in location of Sirius, Pollux, Capella and Aldebaran from accurate survey points (represented by diamonds) to where they are symbolized by locations of WEC, KB, WH and CH and their respective Neolithic structures. While each arrow may be perceived as an indicator of a relocation of the respective symbolic star, the relocations never needed to happen.

This potential relocation of symbolic Capella should not be seen as an error in surveying or construction. Symbolic Capella is where it should have been, applying the same scale as that used for the cursus. KB and CH are farther apart than they should be with respect to locations of the other symbolic stars. They are the only points that do not conform to the intention to build the hexagon in accordance with the scale resulting from the length of the Greater Cursus. Geometric accuracy of KB and CH, as symbols of Pollux and Aldebaran, was not as important as the cultural value of place—the top of Larkhill and the location of Coneybury Henge.

Hilltops were viewed by many ancient and indigenous cultures as sacred sites. Monument locations including Stonehenge, Woodhenge, and Coneybury Henge provide evidence of use dating back to the Mesolithic, and may have been seen as important, sacred sites that should remain integral parts of the mid-Neolithic landscape. High points were often used for the purpose of surveying, and in this case the survey work was directly related to developing a sacred landscape. For these reasons it is not surprising that alternative sites for symbolic Pollux and Aldebaran were not used. From the standpoint of the symbols they represented, the translocated hexagon would fulfill the intent of the designers and builders. And whether intended or not, the land-based Winter Hexagon retained its symmetry. Figure E10 illustrates the bi-lateral symmetry of the symbolic Winter hexagon expressed by triangulations with the Greater Cursus.

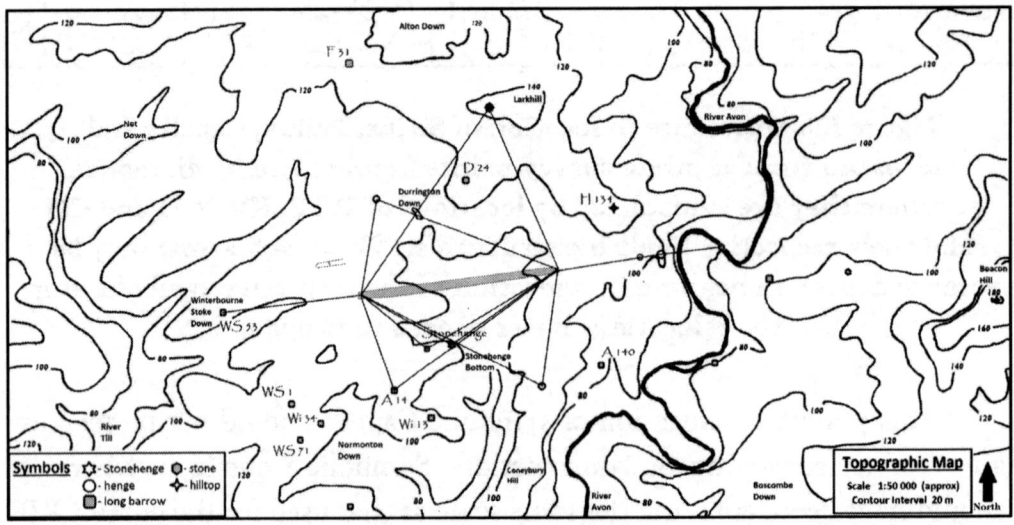

Figure E10: Approximate symmetry about the WS53 to LS alignment (including the cursus) illustrated by triangulations for UDD, KB, CH and A14.

Removing the topographic map from the figures helps highlight the similarities and differences between the cosmic Winter Hexagon and the configuration built on the ground. Figure E11 is an accurately scaled illustration of the Winter Hexagon and symbolic hexagon. Figure E12 includes the location of the intersecting galactic plane and ecliptic. Figure E13 includes the Greater Cursus.

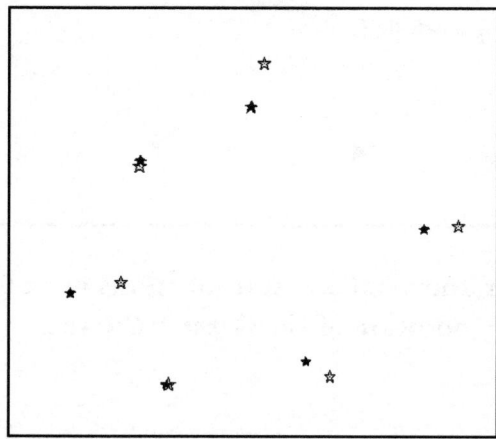

Figure E11: Scaled locations of (clockwise from left) Sirius, Procyon, Pollux, Capella, Aldebaran and Rigel. Black stars form the n asterism. White stars represent locations of the respective symbolic stars surveyed onto the landscape.

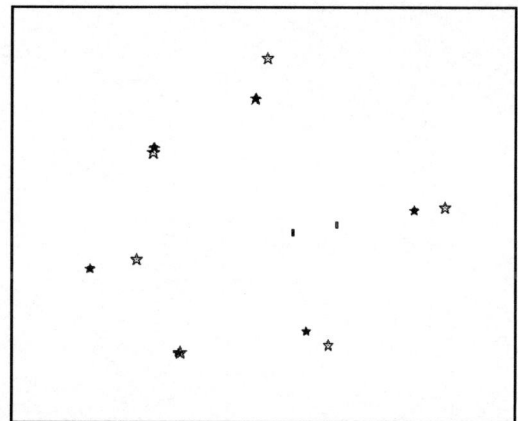

Figure E12: Star and symbolic star locations as in Figure E12, with addition of respective location of the intersection of the galactic plane and ecliptic. By drawing lines between star locations we form the six edges of the Winter Hexagon.

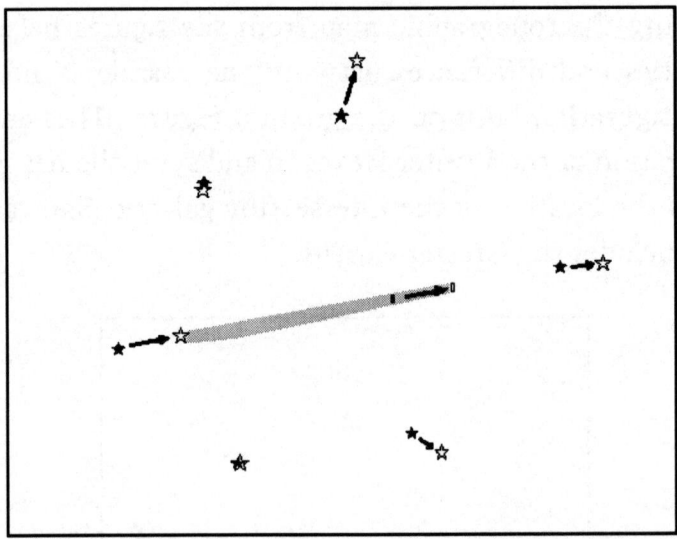

Figure E13: : Star and symbolic star locations as in Figure E13, with addition of the Greater Cursus.

Appendix F
LOCATING THE TERMINI OF THE GREATER CURSUS

Long barrow Amesbury 42 is located at the east end of the Greater Cursus and with its primary axis oriented north-south, approximately perpendicular to the 5.1 degree azimuth of the cursus north ditch line. The top of the long barrow was level and at least 4 feet above the surrounding ground surface. A42 symbolically represents the ecliptic at its crossing of the galactic plane between Sirius and Capella. The east end of the cursus and location of the adjoining log barrow remained in place during placement and possible adjustment of other elements of the grand design.

Similarly the west terminus of the Greater Cursus remained in place, meaning its purpose was to serve as the symbolic location of Sirius. Capella is represented symbolically at Woodhenge, located along the alignment of the cursus such that when a person stands at the west end of the cursus (Sirius) and looks east along the length of the cursus, Woodhenge (Capella) is along the extrapolated alignment between the person and Amesbury 42.

Our assumption now is that the purpose of the Greater Cursus was for it to represent the Milky Way between Sirius and the intersection of the galactic plane with the ecliptic, with Capella father east and in line with the cursus. For evidence supporting the assumption our task is to determine if and when a person standing at the west end of the cursus could have seen this astronomical event. That analysis is presented in Appendix G.

Appendix G
TIME FRAME OF THE SIRIUS-ECLIPTIC-CAPELLA ALIGNMENT WITH THE GREATER CURSUS

A line drawn between Sirius and Capella intersects the ecliptic. Imagine someone standing at the west end of the cursus and looking toward Amesbury 42 during the mid-Neolithic. Could that person have seen the cursus intersect the ecliptic at the horizon, with Capella above the horizon and along the alignment? If so, what was the time frame during which that event occurred?

Figure G1 is a graph showing when the ecliptic on the eastern horizon was located along the azimuth of the Greater Cursus, and the azimuth of Capella at the same moment. The graph covers the period from 4000 to 3000 BC. Data was recorded for evenings of 20 September, a time of the year when the sky was dark enough for the astronomical events to be seen with naked eye. The ground surface rises about 20 feet from the west end to the east end of the cursus, with an equivalent average gradient of about 0.00022 foot per foot, equivalent to an arc of 7.5 minutes. Thus the sightline is nearly flat, with the horizon moderately close 2.75 km (1.71 mi) to the viewer.

Each end of the cursus has a width of about 100 meters. Standing at the north end of the west terminus, Amesbury 42 would have been seen between about 84.9 to 86.9 degrees azimuth. From the center, the long barrow would be 83.9 to 85.9 degrees azimuth, and from the southwest corner 82.9 to 84.9 degrees azimuth. Therefore, looking from the west end of the cursus the horizon at Amesbury 42 ranges from 82.9 to

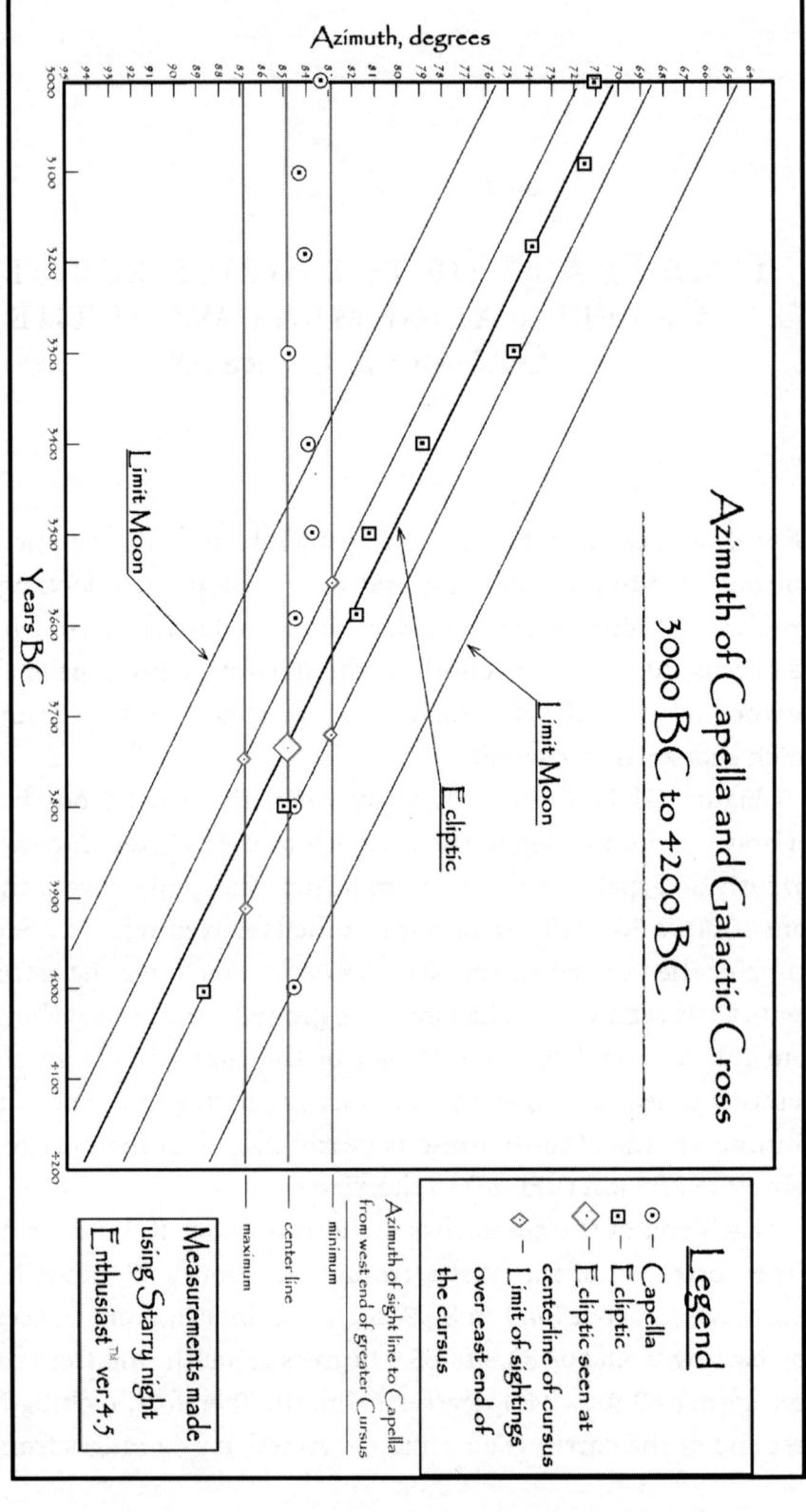

Figure G1: Graph of timeframe for potential sighting from symbolic Sirius (west end of the cursus) of the intersection (galactic crossing) of the galactic plane and ecliptic over the east end of the Greater Cursus.

86.9 degrees azimuth. Figure G1 shows the azimuth of the ecliptic at the horizon when Capella could be seen between 82.9 and 86.9 degrees azimuth from the perspective of the west end of the cursus. If daylight was not an issue Capella could have been seen above the long barrow once every 24 hours. It remains so to this day.

At one extreme, if the ecliptic is defined as the line traced by the center of the sun, then Capella was potentially viewable above Amesbury 42 when the ecliptic was at the horizon (82.9 to 86.9 degrees azimuth) between about 3835 and 3640 BC. However, if we define the ecliptic as the width of the Moon's travels between about 5 degrees above and 5 degrees below the trace of the center point of the sun, then Capella was potentially viewable above Amesbury 42 when the ecliptic was at the horizon between about 4100 and 3365 BC.

Archaeological analyses document that the cursus constructed between 3600 and 3300 BC. Assuming the 10 degree band width for the ecliptic the graphical data suggests the cursus would satisfy its intended purpose within that timeframe. The data also indicates that the archaeologically derived estimated date about 3480 BC for cursus construction means the size and orientation of the cursus would allow it to serve its purpose in a very strict sense for about 115 years. If the symbolism allowed less strict interpretation of the cursus providing an alignment of Milky Way—ecliptic—Capella, then the cursus might have had a useful life of perhaps 250 years for its originally intended purpose, between about 3500 and 3250 BC. By the end of that period the ecliptic (liberally defined as 5 degrees below the trace of the Sun's center) would be about 2 degrees north of the cursus when it rose above the horizon, and Capella would be south of Amesbury 42 by the time the ecliptic was above the long barrow.

It is of interest that cursus monuments appear to have first developed in northern Scotland during the early Neolithic timeframe of 3800 to 3650 BC.[1] That period coincides very well with Figure 30 in which the ecliptic is strictly defined as the trace of the center of the Sun such that Capella would have been viewable above Amesbury 42 with the ecliptic at the horizon, the timeframe being 3835 and 3640 BC.

Notes and References

Introduction

1 Use of singular, plural and possessive words for cursus structures is not uniform. Plural forms have included *cursus* or *cursuses*. Derived from Latin, it seems appropriate to refer to two or more of the monuments as *cursi*, similar to such singular: plural words as cactus:cacti. The singular and plural form used herein is *cursus*. The possessive form applied for both singular and plural forms is *cursus'*.

2 The summer solstice solar alignment of Stonehenge was demonstrated by astronomical calculations by Sir J Norman Lockyer during the early 20th century. Numerous other alignments of stones with Sun and Moon have been suggested since then.

3 Professor Geoffrey Wainwright OBE, FSA, president of the Society of Antiquaries of London, and Professor Timothy Darvill, OBE of Bournemouth University. http://www.smithsonianmag.com/history/new-light-on-stonehenge-11706891/ Accessed 29 Jan 2014.

4 Mike Parker Pearson, archaeology professor at the University of Sheffield in England and head of the Stonehenge Riverside Archaeological Project https://web.archive.org/web/20080601081424/http://ap.google.com/article/ALeqM5iqofgTOoY9jVxd8Vir3t2lq-yfowD90VGRV80 Accessed 29 Jan 2014.

5 "Stonehenge boy 'was from the Med'". BBC News. 28 September 2010. Accessed 29 Jan 2014.

6 Cleal, R. M. J., Walker, K. E. and Montague, R., 1995, *Stonehenge in its landscape: Twentieth century excavations* English Heritage Archaeological Report 10

Note: English Heritage is a non-profit organization advising England's government with regard to the historic environment and charged with maintaining Stonehenge and its landscape.

7   Maev Kennedy (23 September 2008). "The magic of Stonehenge: new dig finds clues to power of bluestones".*Guardian* (UK). Accessed 29 Jan 2014

8   Parker Pearson, Mike. 2012, *Stonehenge: Exploring the Greatest Stone Age Mystery* London:Simon & Schuster, p.328

9   Ibid.

10 ibid., p. 23.

11 John G. Robb, The 'ritual landscape' concept in archaeology: a heritage construction. Landscape Research Volume 23, Issue 2, 1998

12 Curton, Rafael P. and Berón, Mónica A. *Percepción, Identidad y Sentido en la Construcción Social y Ritual del Paisaje*: las Sierras de Lihue Calel, La Pampa, Argentina. 2011. www.revistas.uchile.cl/index.php/RCA/article/download/18168/19025. Accessed 22 Jan 2014.

13 OED, Compact Edition, p.267. http://en.wikipedia.org/wiki/God Accessed 14 Jan 2014.

14 Meaden, Terence., 1992. Stonehenge: The Secret of the Solstice. London: Souvenir Press, p. 79.

Chapter 1

1   Lambeck, Kurt. *Glacial rebound and sea-level change in the British Isles.* Research School of Earth Sciences, The Australian National University, Canberra ACT 2601, Australia

2   Patterson, W, "Coastal Catastrophe" (paleoclimate research document), University of Saskatchewan http://en.wikipedia.org/wiki/Tsunamis_affecting_the_British_Isles Accessed 8 Jan 2014.

3   Smith, Christopher. *The Population of Mesolithic Britain*, Mesolithic Miscellany, Vol. 13, Number 1, 1992. http://archaeologydataservice.ac.uk/archives/archiveDownload?t=arch-468-1/dissemination/pdf/mm_v13n1.pdf Accessed 1 Jan 2014

4   Çiler Çilingiroğlu. *The concept of "Neolithic package" considering its meaning and applicability.* Documenta Praehistorica XXXII 2005. https://www.academia.edu/964591/The_concept_of_Neolithic_Package_Considering_its_meaning_and_applicability Accessed 22 Jan 2014.

5   Thomas, Julian. *Current debates on the Mesolithic-Neolithic transition in Britain and Ireland,* UDK903'13(410+417)"631/624", Documenta Prehistorica XXXI http://arheologija.ff.uni-lj.si/documenta/pdf31/31thomas.pdf, Accessed on 1 Jan 2014.

6   Collard, M; Edinborough, K; Shennan, S; Thomas, MG; (2010) Radiocarbon evidence indicates that migrants introduced farming to Britain. J ARCHAEOL SCI , 37 (4) 866–870.

7   Smith, Christopher. 1992.

8   Thomas, Julian. Ibid.

9   Ibid.

Chapter 3

1 Cajete G. 2000. Native Science: natural Laws of inrerdependence. Santa Fe (NM): Clear Light. p..

2 Brown JE. 1989 [1970]. The Sacred Pipe: Black Elks Account of the Seven sacred Rites of the Oglala Sioux. Norman (OK): Univeristy of Oklahoma Press. p.89.

3 Ibid. p.108.

4 Cajete G. 2000. p.48.

5 Ibid. p.

6 De Loof A. 2008. 17 Nov. Definition of Lofe: At Last "What is Life?" can be answered, simply and logically. SciTopics.

   http://www.scitopivs.com/Definition_of_Life_At_Last_What_is_Life_can_be_answered_simply_and_logically.html Accessed 2 Mar 2011.

7 Ibid.

8 Burley P. 2012. The Sacred Sphere: exploring sacred concepts and cosmic consciousness through universal symbolism. Edina (MN): Beavers Pond Press. p.6.

9 Ibid.

10 Deloria V. 1973. God is Red. New York: Dell Publishing. P.200.

11 Cajete, 2000. P14.

12 Ibid. p2.

13 Ibd. P.2-3, 13.

14 Burley (2012) addresses this point in detail.

15 Rolleston T. 1990. Celtic Myths and Legends. Dover Publications: Mineola (NY). p.89.

Chapter 4

1 Mircea E. 1991. Images and Symbols: Studies in Religious Symbolism. Princeton (NJ): Princeton University Press. p.24-25.

2 Loveday R. The Greater Stonehenge Cursus: The long view. Proceeding of the Prehistoric Society 78 2011,p.341-350.

3 Ibid.

4 Ibid.

5 Ibid. Subreferences

Barclay. A & , A. 1999. Cursus monuments and the radiocarbon problem. In A. Barclay & J. Harding (eds), Pathways and Ceremonies. The Cursus Monuments of Britain and Ireland, p.11-29, Oxford: Neolithic Studies Group Seminar Paper 4.

Loveday, R. 2006a. Inscribed Across the Landscape: the Cursus Enigma. Stroud: Tempus.

Thomas J, Marshall P, Parker Pearson M, Pollard J, Richards C, Tilley C & Welham K. 2009. The date of the Greater Stonehenge Cursus. Antiquity 83 p.40-53.

6 Burley, P, 2012.

7 Meaden T. 1997. Stonehenge: The secret of the solstice. London: Souvenir Press. pp.52-73.

8 ibid. p.79.

9 Thomas J *et al.* 2009. pp.40-53.

10 Ibid.

11 Meaden T. 1997. p.80.

12 Azimuths listed in Table 1 for long barrows 1-9 are based on Meaden T. 1997. p.80.

13 "Early Prehistoric Monuments – Henges, English Heritage http://www.eng-h.gov.uk/mpp/mcd/sub/henges1.htm Accessed 30 Dec 2013.

14 Whittle, A. 2005 *The Neolithic Period* in *The Archaeology of Britain*, Hunter, I. and Ralston, J. (eds.), Routledge, London

15 Malone, C. 2001 *Neolithic Britain and Ireland*, Tempus, Stroud.

16 Burl, A. 1969 'Henges: internal features and regional groups', *Archaeological Journal*, 126, pp. 1–28.

17 Cunliffe, B. 2001. *Facing the Ocean: the Atlantic and its Periphery 8000 BC–AD 1500*, Oxford University Press, Oxford.

18 Burley P. 2012 p.255-256.

Chapter 5

1 Hong-Sen Y & Marco C. 2009, *International Symposium on History of Machines and Mechanisms: Proceedings of HMM 2008*, Springer, p. 107.

2 http://www.birmingham.ac.uk/news/latest/2011/11/25Nov-Discoveries-provide-evidence-of-a-celestial-procession-at-Stonehenge.aspx Accessed 2 Dec 2013

3 Ibid.

4 Ibid.

Chapter 8

1 Meaden, T. 2012. Achaeology of Mother Earth Sites and Sactuaries through the Ages: Rethinking rymbols and images, art and artefacts from history and prehistory. Oxford: Archaeopress, British Archaeological. Reports. BAR International Series 2389.

2 Hawkins, G S, and White, J B. 1965. Stonehenge Decoded. New York: Knopf Doubleday.

3 Hawkins G.1965. Stonehenge Decoded. New York: Doubleday. 1965.

4 Burley P, 2012.

5 Cleal, R., Walker, K. and Montague, R. Stonehenge In Its Landscape, Twentieth-Century Excavations. London: English Heritage. 1995.

6 Cunliffe, B. and Renfrew, C., eds. Science and Stonehenge. London: The British Academy. 1997.

7 Parker Pearson M. 2012. P.23.

8   Parker-Pearson, M. and Cleal, R.
    and Marshall, P. and Needham,
    S. and Pollard, J. and Richards, C.
    and Ruggles, C. and Sheridan, A.
    and Thomas, J. and Tilley, C. and
    Welham, K. and Chamberlain, A. and
    Chenery, C. and Evans, J. and Knsel,
    C. and Linford, N. and Martin, L.
    and Montgomery, J. and Payne, A.
    and Richards, M. P. (2007) 'The age of
    Stonehenge.', Antiquity., 81 (313). pp.
    617-639.

9   North, J. Stonehenge: Neolithic
    Man and the Cosmos. London:
    HarperCollinsPublishers, 1997.

10 Knight, K and Lomas R. Uriel's
    Machine. Gloucester, MA:Fair Winds
    Press. 2001. P.166.

11 Victor Douville, LS Rank A, History
    & Culture Coordinator, Department
    of Lakota Studies, Sinte Gleska

    University, Mission, South Dakota.
    Personal communication.

12 Douville, V. 2011. Pesla: Hocoka:The
    Center. http://www.slideshare.net/
    barobba/pesla Accessed 19 April

    2013.

13 Ibid.

14 Ibid.

15 North, J. 1997. p. 574.

16 Burley, P. 2012.

17 Burl, A. Stonehenge: A Complete
    History and Archaeology of the
    World's Most Enigmatic Stone Circle.
    New York: Carroll & Graf, 2007. p.
    40.

18 Ibid. p. 220-221.

19 Ibid. p. 207-207.

20 Atkinson, R. Stonehenge: Archaeology
    and Interpretation. Harmondsworth:
    Penguin. 1979.

21 Hawley, W. 1926. p. 2. Cleal et al.
    1995. p. 149, table 69. Burl, A. 2007.
    p. 178.

22 Burl, A. 2007.

23 North, J. 1997.

24 Ibid. p. 570.

25 Avenue alignment based on Parker
    Pearson, M. and Ramilisonina. 1998.
    'Stonehenge for the Ancestors: the

    Stones Pass on the Message.'
    Antiquity. 72: 308-26. Also see Parker
    Pearson et al. 2006. p. 230.

26 Parker Pearson et al, 2007.

27 Parker Pearson, M and Ramilisonia.
    2007.

28 This book does not address 'bog
    bodies' that have been found in
    Britain and date from at least the
    mid-Neolithic to the Iron Age.
    However recent theories for social,
    political, ritual and ceremonial
    reasons for disposing of bodies in
    bogs may be related to cultural
    traditions founded on this duality of
    spirit returning to the stars whilst
    the body is returned to Earth.

Appendix A

1 Burley, P. 2012.

Appendix B

1 **Andrews' and Dury's Map of Wiltshire, 1810.**
http://history.wiltshire.gov.uk/gallery/map/
durrington_map004.jpg Date accessed: 26 January
2014.

2 'England - Wiltshire: 054', *Ordnance Survey 1:10,560
- Epoch 1* (1887). URL: http://www.british-history.
ac.uk/mapsheet.aspx?compid=55143&sheetid=9
212&ox=0&oy=0&zm=1&czm=10&x=242&y=222
Copyright (c) and database right Crown Copyright
and Landmark Information Group Ltd (all rights
reserved 2014). Date accessed: 26 January 2014.

3 http://www.ancientmonuments.info/en10395-bowl-
barrow-200m-west-of-durrington-down-p Date
accessed: 26 January 2014.

4 http://www.wiltshire.gov.uk/
artsheritageandlibraries/museumhistoryheritage/
wiltshireandswindonhistoricenvironmentrecord.
htm. Date accessed: 26 January 2014.

Appendix G

1 Cook, M, Ellis, C and Sheridan, J A 2010
'Excavations at Upper Largie quarry, Argyll and
Bute, Scotland: new light on the prehistoric ritual
landscape of the Kilmartin Glen', *Proceedings of the
Prehistoric Society* 76, 165–212

Bibliography

Atkinson, R. Stonehenge: Archaeology and Interpretation. Harmondsworth: Penguin. 1979

Barclay. A & , A. 1999. Cursus monuments and the radiocarbon problem. In A. Barclay & J. Harding (eds), Pathways and Ceremonies. The Cursus Monuments of Britain and Ireland, p.11-29, Oxford: Neolithic Studies Group Seminar Paper 4

Brown JE. 1989 [1970]. The Sacred Pipe: Black Elks Account of the Seven sacred Rites of the Oglala Sioux. Norman (OK): Univeristy of Oklahoma Press

Burl, A. 1969 'Henges: internal features and regional groups', Archaeological Journal, 126

Burl, A. Stonehenge: A Complete History and Archaeology of the World's Most Enigmatic Stone Circle. New York: Carroll & Graf, 2007

Burley P. 2012. The Sacred Sphere: exploring sacred concepts and cosmic consciousness through universal symbolism. Edina (MN): Beavers Pond Press

Cajete G. 2000. Native Science: natural Laws of inrerdependence. Santa Fe (NM): Clear Light

Çiler Çilingirog̈lu. The concept of "Neolithic package" considering its meaning and applicability. Documenta Praehistorica XXXII 2005

Cleal, R., Walker, K. and Montague, R. 1995. Stonehenge In Its Landscape, Twentieth-Century Excavations. English Heritage Archaeological Report 10, London: English Heritage

Cook, M, Ellis, C and Sheridan, J A 2010 'Excavations at Upper Largie quarry, Argyll and Bute, Scotland: new light on the prehistoric ritual landscape of the Kilmartin Glen', Proceedings of the Prehistoric Society 76

Cunliffe, B. and Renfrew, C., eds. Science and Stonehenge. London: The British Academy. 1997

Cunliffe, B. 2001. *Facing the Ocean: the Atlantic and its Periphery 8000 BC–AD 1500*, Oxford University Press, Oxford

Curton, Rafael P. and Berónii, Mónica A. *Percepción, Identidad y Sentido en la Construcción Social y Ritual del Paisaje*: las Sierras de Lihue Calel, La Pampa, Argentina. 2011

De Loof A. 2008. 17 Nov. Definition of Lofe: At Last "What is Life?" can be ansewered, simply and logically. SciTopics

Deloria V. 1973. God is Red. New York: Dell Publishing

Douville V. 2011. Pesla: Hocoka:The Center. History & Culture Coordinator, Department of Lakota Studies, Sinte Gleska University, Mission, South Dakota

English Heritage. "Early Prehistoric Monulents – Henges".London. 2008

Hawkins, G S, and White, J B. 1965. Stonehenge Decoded. New York: Knopf Doubleday

Hawkins, G. and White, J. Stonehenge Decoded. London: Souvenir. 1966

Hawley, W. 1926. 'Report on the excavations at Stonehenge during 1925 and 1926.' Arch. J. 6:149-7.

Hong-Sen Y & Marco C. 2009, *International Symposium on History of Machines and Mechanisms: Proceedings of HMM 2008*, Springer

John G. Robb, The 'ritual landscape' concept in archaeology: a heritage construction. Landscape Research Volume 23, Issue 2, 1998

Lambeck, Kurt. *Glacial rebound and sea-level change in the British Isles.* Research School of Earth Sciences, The Australian National University, Canberra ACT 2601, Australia

Loveday, R. 2006a. Inscribed Across the Landscape: the Cursus Enigma. Stroud: Tempus.

Loveday R. The Greater Stonehenge Cursus: The long view. Proceeding of the Prehistoric Society 78 2011

Malone, C. 2001 *Neolithic Britain and Ireland*, Tempus, Stroud.

Meaden, T, 1992 (1997). Stonehenge: The Secret of the Solstice. London: Souvenir Press

Meaden, T. 2012. Achaeology of Mother Earth Sites and Sactuaries through the Ages: Rethinking rymbols and images, art and artefacts from history and prehistory. Oxford: Archaeopress, British Archaeological. Reports. BAR International Series 2389.

Mircea E. 1991. Images and Symbols: Studies in Religious Symbolism. Princeton (NJ): Princeton University Press

Newall, R. 1929. 'Stonehenge.' Antiquity 3

Newall, R. Stonehenge, Wiltshire. London: HMSO. 1953.

North, J. Stonehenge: Neolithic Man and the Cosmos. London: HarperCollinsPublishers, 1997

Parker Pearson, M. and Ramilisonina. 1998. 'Stonehenge for the Ancestors: the Stones Pass on the Message.' Antiquity. 72

Parker Pearson, M., Pollard, J., Richards, C., Thomas, J., Tilley, C., Welham, K. and Alberella, U. 2006. "Materializing Stonehenge: The Stonehenge Riverside Project and New Discoveries," Journal of Material Culture 11

Parker Pearson, M., Cleal, M., Marshall, P., Needham, S., M., Pollard, J., Richards, C., Ruggles, C., Sheridan, A., Thomas, J., Tilley, C., Welham, K., Chamberlain, A., Chernery, C., Evans, J., Knüsel, C., Linford, N., Martin, L., Montgomery, J., Payne, A., and Richards, M. 2007. "The age of Stonehenge." Antiquity. 81:617-639.

Parker Pearson, Mike. 2012, *Stonehenge: Exploring the Greatest Stone Age Mystery* London:Simon & Schuster

Patterson, W, "Coastal Catastrophe" (paleoclimate research document), University of Saskatchewan

Rolleston T. 1990. Celtic Myths and Legends. Dover Publications: Mineola, NY

Royal Commission on the Ancient and Historical Monuments of Scotland. 'Skara Brae. Archaeological Notes.' 2011

Ruggles, C. 1997. 'Astronomy and Stonehenge.' in eds. Cunliffe, B. and Renfrew, C. 1997

Smith, Christopher. *The Population of Mesolithic Britain*, Mesolithic Miscellany, Vol. 13, Number 1, 1992

Thomas, Julian. *Current debates on the Mesolithic-Neolithic transition in Britain and Ireland*, UDK903'13(410+417)"631/624", Documenta Prehistorica XXXI

Thomas J, Marshall P, Parker Pearson M, Pollard J, Richards C, Tilley C & Welham K. 2009. The date of the Greater Stonehenge Cursus. Antiquity 83

Whittle, A. 2005 *The Neolithic Period* in *The Archaeology of Britain*, Hunter, I. and Ralston, J. (eds.), Routledge, London

Index